AVATAR

AVATAR

Lord from Heaven

Rajesh Jain

PARTRIDGE

To order additional copies of this book, contact
orders@patridgepublishing.com
www.patridgepublishing.com

CONTENTS

Preface

How the Universe come into being, who and how is been controlled and what is role of GOD in its creation, Sustenance and Dissolution, What is role of consciousness in matter and biological world, How the GOD connect with masses through provision of its AVATAR in its Divine plan, How this divine plan is revealed to mankind through prediction by Nostradamus and birth of Man from East ?

For the EAST concept of AVATAR is quite old but to west this idea is strange and naive.

When I entered in Benaras hindu university in 1990, January month, I was not aware that GOD and his aliens wants to Contact me for the coming changes they wants to introduce for the mankind on earth. How that GOD can Incarnate in human form and gives him powers not only to dominate in world but also provide knowledge and wisdom of GOD & Its Universe, that God is infinite in its potential, How he can Incarnate in human form, even he is born as human no power can comes its way.

I am very grateful to my many friends and colleagues for their important suggestions, and sharing their thoughts about GOD, religion, Consciousness, soul, brain-Mind dualism, Monism.

Significant contribution has come from Chris king through his chapter on Central enigma of Consciousness,on biological and emergent role of consciousness through fractal nature of consciousness and subject-object complementary interaction of consciousness and matter.

I am grateful to Arif Khan editor of www.tombofjesus.com, Morse Elliot from www.morssglobalfinance.com, tom gubler from www.prem-rawat-bio.org, Primi editor from www.prem-rawat-maharaji.info, Patrick Mulcahy on Metaphysics of Pi, chris Clugston on American Nonsustainability. I am extremely greatful to Katherine Webster who is the first women Journalist who has researched on Indian Guru Swami ram of india through her detail article "Case against swami ram published in Yoga International.

I am also thankful to my Project coordinator Ms Karoline for sharing her thoughts for my Project on Diabetes supported by world Diabetes Foundation, Denmark.

For the deep support, love and understanding, under frequently difficult circumstances, I am profoundly indebted to my Dearest wife Rachna, whom I will always be grateful.

Finally my elder son Nishchal and younger Pushkar for continous encouragement and good cheer.

AVATAR

From the beginning of time, humanity has longed for the day when Justice, Peace, Equality and Compassion envelop the world. The scriptures and holy books of various religions in the past have spoken of a future World Leader who will bring the accomplishment of the god's will on this planet Earth. He will take birth as a human and will establish righteousness, peace and compassion of God, and he will bring about the final defeat of evil, and establish the Kingdom of Heaven on earth. He will be chosen, commissioned and empowered by God to align and attune earth with the cosmic Energy and its sacred laws, he will unite religion with science. Various religions call him by various names: Jews long for the promised Messiah; for Christians, the Messiah is Jesus of Nazareth, who has already come and ascended to heaven but will reappear (perhaps in a new guise) at his Second Coming. Muslims also waits for the second advent of Jesus, who will come as a future Imam Mahdi. Buddhist sutras prophesy the coming of the Maitreya Buddha; Vaishnavite Hindu scriptures prophesy the future descent of an avatar named Kalki; Zoroastrian scriptures prophesy the coming of the Saoshyant; and some Confucian texts speak of a future True Man who will finally bring peace to the world by perfectly instituting the Way of Confucius. Various prophecy of the coming of this future World Leader are compiled below as per the scriptures.

1. *Jews are looking for 'Meshiack,' their messiah.*
2. *Christians are looking for Jesus Christ to return as second coming to bring kingdom of God on earth.*
3. *Muslims are looking for the 'Imam Mahdi to come on earth to restore Peace and Justice'*
4. *Buddhists are looking for the Fifth Buddha, as 'Maitreya'. (Means friend of mankind.)*
5. *Hindus are looking for its last Tenth Avatar, 'Kalki'*

There is much awaited need that one single man will actually fulfil all these religions expectations!

Chapter 1

Coming of Messiah as Per Jews/ Jesus Christ Second Coming from East

'Father will send in my name the man of Aquarius, He will be the man of both head and heart, he will bring peace to earth' . . . Undocumented Saying of Jesus Christ.

He will appear in ASIA and will grow above all other power in East . . . X. LXXV. Nostradamus

. . . Unto them that look for Him shall he appear the second time (Heb. 9: 28)

Surely I am coming soon. Amen. Come, Lord Jesus! Christianity. (Rev. 22:20)

'For just as lightning comes from the east, and shineth unto the west, so shall also the coming of the Son of Man be'. In (Matt. 24–27)
Second Coming will be from East

'And behold, the Glory of the God of Israel came from the way of the east . . .' (Ezek. 43: 2)
Again Prophecy clearly says second coming will be from East

'The Lord, your God will raise up for you a prophet like me . . . You must listen to him'.
(Deut. 18: 15)

'The Glory of the Lord came into the house by the way of the Gate facing towards the east'. (Ezek. 43–4)
He will be from East.

'Do not think that I came to bring peace on earth. I did not come to bring peace but a sword'. (Matt. 10: 34)
War of his second coming

That when He cometh and knocketh, they may open unto Him immediately (Luke 12: 36)

If ye love Me, keep My commandment, and I will pray the Father, and He shall give you another Comforter, that He may be with you for ever . . . (John 14: 15–16)

But when the comforter comes, whom I shall send to you from the Father, even the spirit of truth, who proceeds from the Father, He will bear witness of me . . . (John 15: 26)

I have yet many things to say unto you, but you cannot bear them now. However when He, the Spirit of Truth, is come, He will guide you into all truth for He will not speak on His own, but whatever He hears . . . (John 16: 7–13)

For to us a child is born, to us a son is given, and the government shall be upon his shoulder, and his name shall be called 'Wonderful Counsellor, Mighty God, Everlasting Father, Prince of Peace.'

Of the increase of his government and of peace there will be no end, upon the throne of David, and over his kingdom, to establish it, and to uphold it with justice and with righteousness, from this time forth and for ever more. The zeal of the Lord of hosts will do this. (Isa. 9: 6–7)

'I saw in the night visions, and behold, with the clouds of heaven there came one like a son of man. He came to the Ancient of Days and was presented before him. And to be given dominion and glory and kingdom that all peoples, nations, and languages should serve him. His dominion is an everlasting dominion, which shall not pass away. And his kingdom one that shall not be destroyed.' (Dan. 7: 13–14)

For the Son of Man is going to come in the Glory of His Father with His angels; and He shall reward every man according to his works. (Matt. 16–27)

'Not everyone who says to me, "Lord, Lord," shall enter the kingdom of heaven, but he who does the will of my father who is in heaven'. (Matt. 7: 21)

So the last shall be first, and the first last, for many are called but few chosen. (Matt. 20: 16)

Verily, Verily I say unto you, The Son can do nothing of himself, but what he seethe the Father do. (John 5: 19)

Seek I '. . . and ye shall find!' Matthew

For many are called, but few are chosen. (Matt. 22: 14)

He shall be the victorious Benefactor by name and World-Renovator by name. He is Benefactor because he will benefit the entire world; he is World-Renovator because he will establish the physical living existence indestructible. He will oppose the evil of the progeny of the biped and withstand the enmity produced by the faithful. Zend Avesta (Favardin Yast 13: 129)

And behold! He comes with ten thousand Holy Ones, to execute judgment upon them, and to destroy the impious, and to contend with all flesh, concerning everything that the sinners and the impious have done and wrought against Him (Enoch 1: 9)

Immediately after the tribulation of those days the sun will be darkened, and the moon will not give its light, and the stars will fall from heaven, and the powers of heaven will be shaken; then will appear the sign of the Son of man in heaven, and then all the tribes of the earth will mourn, and they will see the Son of man coming on the clouds of heaven with power and great glory; and he will send out his angels with a loud trumpet call, and they will gather his elect from the four winds, from one end of heaven to the other (Matt. 24: 29–31)

. . . When the Son of God comes in His glory, and all the angels with Him, then He will be seated on the throne of His glory, and all nations will be gathered before Him. (Matt. 25: 31–32)

And I saw heaven opened, and behold a white horse;
And he that sat upon him was called Faithful and True,

And in righteousness he doth judge and make war.
His eyes were as a flame of fire, and on his head were many
crowns;
And he had a name written, that no man knew, but he himself.
And he was clothed with vesture dipped in blood:
And his name is called the Word of God.
And the armies which were in heaven followed him upon white
horses,
Clothed in fine linen, white and clean.
And out of his mouth goeth a sharp sword,
That with it he should smite the nations:
And he shall rule them with a rod of iron:
And he treadeth the winepress of the fierceness and wrath of
Almight God.
And he hath on his vesture and on his thigh a name written,
King of Kings and Lord of Lords' (Rev. 19: 11–16)

Take thee also unto thee wheat, and barley, and beans, and
lentils, and millet, and fitches, and put them in One vessel,
and make Bread . . . (Ezek. 4: 9)

Remember not the former things, neither consider the things of
old, behold, I do a new thing, now it shall spring forth . . . shall
ye not know it? . . . (Isa. 43: 18).

Verily I say unto you, the hour is coming, and now is, when
the dead shall hear the voice of the son of God, and they that
hear shall live . . . Marvel not at this, for the hour is coming,
in which all they that are in the graves, shall hear his voice.
And they shall come forth; they that have done good unto the
resurrection of Life, and they that have done evil, unto the
resurrection of death . . . (John 5: 25–29)

The wise shall understand . . . (Dan. 12: 10)

The secret of the Lord is with them that fear Him, He will shew them His covenant . . . (Ps. 25: 14)

'He will turn the hearts of the fathers to the children, and the hearts of the children to their fathers, lest I come and strike the earth with a curse'. (Mal'akhi (Mal. 3: 22–24)

Why, seeing times are not hidden from the Almighty, do they that know Him not see His days? . . . (Job 24: 1)

When the stars of heaven and the constellations there of shall not give their light: the sun shall be darkened in his going forth, and the moon shall not cause her light to shine (Isa. 13: 10)

'And you shall hear of wars and rumors of wars . . . For nation shall rise against nation, and kingdom against kingdom'. (Mat. 24: 7)

Surely the Lord will do nothing but He revealeth His secrets to His servants the prophets. The Lion hath roared, who will not fear? The Lord hath spoken, who can but prophecy? . . . (Amos 3: 7)

Measure thou the time diligently . . . Then shalt thou understand that it is the very time wherein the Highest will begin to visit the world which He made. Therefore, when there shall be seen earthquakes and uproars of people in the world, then shalt thou well understand that the Most High spake of these things from the days that were before thee . . . The times of the Highest have plain beginnings in wonders and powerful works, and endings in effects and signs . . . (2 Estrus 9: 2–6)

He answered them, When it is evening (where the Sun sets in the West) you say, it will be fair weather for the sky is red, and in the morning (where the Sun rises in the East), it will be stormy for the sky is red and lowering (descending) . . . Hypocrites, ye know how to interpret the face of heaven but ye cannot discern the sign of the times . . . (Matt. 16: 1–3).

When the spirit of Truth shall come . . . (John 16: 1–21)

Blessed and holy is he that hath part in the First Resurrection: on such the Second death (the death of the body itself) hath no power, but they shall be priests of God and of Christ, and shall reign with him a thousand years . . . (Rev. 20: 6).

And take the helmet of Salvation, And the sword of the spirit, which is the word of God . . . (Eph. 6: 10–17)

Muhammad himself said: 'Happiness is for the one who will attend the Qa'im of my Ahl'ul-Bayt and will follow him before his rise. This person will love his (Qa'im's) lovers and hate his enemies, and will accept the leadership of the A'immah from before his advent. These ones are my friends, and are the most sincere members of my Ummah whom I honor very much'.

'When the appointed hour is come, there shall suddenly appear that which will cause the limbs of mankind to quake. Then and only then will the Divine Standard be unfurled, and the Nightingale of Paradise warble its melody'. – Baha'u'llah

Over the centuries, a number of different visionaries and prophets have foretold the arrival of the 'Great Monarch', otherwise known as a world-leader and statesman who will unite the world after a conflict between Nations. Here is below quotes from different religious personalities and modern day saints about Coming of Worldwide Messiah from fifth century onward.

Jeane Dixon (mid-twentieth Century), 'He will bring together all mankind'. 'There was nothing kingly about his coming . . . no kings or shepherds to do homage to this newborn baby'.

St. John-Mary Vianney, Curâ of Ars (nineteenth century), 'He will re-establish a peace and prosperity without precedent'.

'I had a vision of . . . (the Great Monarch) Henry. I saw him at night kneeling alone at the foot of the main altar in a great and beautiful church . . . and I saw the Blessed Virgin coming down all alone . . . Mary came up to Henry, and she extended her right hand towards him . . . She urged him not to falter'.

. . . Catholic mystic Anne Catherine Emmerich, 1820

Sister Marianne (d 1804) '. . . whom people will seek, that before did not esteem him'.

Sister Marianne (d 1804) 'All injustices will be repaired, civil laws will be formed in harmony with the laws of God'.

Fr. Laurence Ricci, S. J. (d 1775) 'At gathering(s) of men noted for piety and wisdom, he will . . . introduce new rules'.

Monk of Werl (1701) 'This man will restore true peace to the nations'.

Rudolph Gekner (d.1675) 'He shall subdue . . . the Mohammedan(s)'.

Bartholomew Holzhauser (d 1658) 'There will be many wise and just men . . . and peace will be established over the whole earth'.

Johannes Amadeus de Syloa (d 1482), 'All nations (will) unite under the Great Ruler and peace and prosperity will follow'.

Monk Hilarion (d 1476) 'God will send the Eagle who will bring much happiness and good'.

St Francis of Paola (1470) 'He shall reform (the world) . . . with the help of . . . the best men upon earth in holiness, in arms, in science, and in every virtue'.

St. Bridget (fourteenth century) 'The Eagle (will conquer) . . . the Mohammedan(s)'.

St. Bridget (fourteenth century), '. . . and the earth shall enjoy peace'.

St. Hildegarde 'Peace will return'.

Werdin d'Otrante (thirteenth century), 'The Great Monarch will come to restore peace'.

Zoroaster in The Zend Avesta (Favardin Yast 13: 129) 'He shall be the Victorious Benefactor by name, and World Renovator by name'.

'An incomparable leader of men. He will establish his law, glorious in its spirit and in the letter . . . His disciples will number many thousands while mine number many hundreds' . . . Gautam Buddha

Imam Ali ibn Abu Talib's Nahj'ul Balagha, Khutba 141, 187 'He, in the beginning, will be a poor stranger unknown and uncared for . . . With such a start he will establish an empire . . . in this world'.

Variously, Moslems call him Dajjal, meaning 'impostor'. Dajjal will travel the entire world no part of the world left which he will not dominate.

St. Remy (sixth century AD), '(He) shall reign over the entire ancient Roman Empire'.

Jesus: For the coming of the Son of Man will be just like the days of Noah. For as in those days which were before the flood they were eating and drinking, they were marrying and giving in marriage, until the day that Noah entered the ark, and they did not understand until the flood came and took them all away; so shall the coming of the Son of Man be (Matt. 24: 37–39).*No man knoweth the son but the Father; neither knoweth any man the Father save the Son, and he to whomsoever the Son will reveal him. (Matt. 11: 27)*

For whosoever will save his life shall lose it: and whosoever will lose his life for my sake shall find it. (Matt 16: 25)

I and my Father are one. (John 11: 30)

That which is born of the flesh is flesh; and that which is born of the spirit is spirit. (John 3: 6)

The life is more than meat, and the body is more than raiment. (Luke 12: 23)

For what shall it profit a man, if he shall gain the whole world, and lose his own soul? Or what shall a man give in exchange for his soul? (Mark 8: 36–37)

Love your enemies, bless them that curse you, do good to them that hate you, and pray for them which despitefully use you, and persecute you. (Matt. 5: 44)

Thou shalt love the Lord thy God with all thy heart, and with all thy soul, and with all thy mind. Like unto it, Thou shalt love thy neighbor as thyself. (Matt. 22: 37–39)

He that loveth not knoweth not God; for God is love. (1 John 4: 8)

I do nothing of myself; but as my Father hath taught me, I speak these things. (John 8: 28)

Be ye doers of the Word, and not hearers only

Except a man be born again, he cannot see the Kingdom of God. (John 3: 3)

Except a man be born of water and of the spirit, he cannot enter the Kingdom of God. (John 3: 5)

The Kingdom of God cometh not with observation: Neither shall they say, Lo here! or, lo there! for behold, the Kingdom of God is within you. (Luke 17: 20–21)

Take thee also unto thee wheat, and barley, and beans, and lentils, and millet, and fitches, and put them in One vessel, and make Bread . . . (Ezek. 4: 9)

Revelation James Version Bible: Second Coming of Christ

1: 3 Blessed is the one who reads the words of this prophecy aloud, and blessed are those who hear and obey the things written in it, because the time is near!

1: 7 (Look! He is returning with the clouds, and every eye will see him, even those who pierced him, and all the tribes on the earth will mourn because of him. This will certainly come to pass! Amen.)

1: 8 'I am the Alpha and the Omega,' says the Lord God – the one who is, and who was, and who is still to come – the All-Powerful!

1: 12–20, I turned to see whose voice was speaking to me, and when I did so, I saw seven golden lamp stands, and in the midst of the lamp stands was one like a son of man. He was dressed in a robe extending down to his feet and he wore a wide golden belt around his chest. His head and hair were as white as wool, even as white as snow, and his eyes were like a fiery flame. His feet were like polished bronze refined in a furnace, and his voice was like the roar of many waters. He held seven stars in his right hand, and a sharp double-edged sword extended out of his mouth. His face shone like the sun shining at full strength . . . When I saw him I fell down at his feet as though I were dead, but he placed his right hand on me and said: 'Do not be afraid! I am the first and the last, and the one who lives! I was dead, but look, now I am alive – forever and ever – and I hold the keys of death and of Hades! Therefore write what you saw, what is, and what will be after these things. The mystery of the seven stars that you saw in my right hand and the seven golden lamp stands is this: The seven stars are the angels of the seven churches and the seven lamp stands are the seven churches'.

2: 25–29 However, hold on to what you have until I come. And to the one who conquers and who continues in my deeds until the end, I will give him authority over the nations – he will rule them with an iron rod and like clay jars he will break them to pieces, just as I have received the right to rule from my Father – and I will give him the morning star. The one who has an ear had better hear what the Spirit says to the churches.

3: 7–13 'To the angel of the church in Philadelphia write the following:' This is the solemn pronouncement of the Holy One, the True One, who holds the key of David, who opens doors no one can shut and shuts doors no one can open: 'I know your deeds. (Look! I have put in front of you an open door that no one can shut.) I know that you have little strength, but you have *obeyed my word and have not denied my name. Listen! I am going to make those people from the synagogue of Satan – who say they are Jews yet are not, but are lying – Look, I will make them come and bow down at your feet and acknowledge that I have loved you. Because you have kept my admonition to endure steadfastly, I will also keep you from the hour of testing that is about to come on the whole world to test those who live on the earth. I am coming soon. Hold on to what you have so that no one can take away your crown. The one who conquers, I will make a pillar in the temple of my God, and he will never depart from it. I will write on him the name of my God and the name of the city of my God (the new Jerusalem that comes down out of heaven from my God), and my new name as well. The one who has an ear had better hear what the Spirit says to the churches'.*

3: 19–22 All those I love, I rebuke and discipline. So be earnest and repent! Listen! I am standing at the door and knocking! If anyone hears my voice and opens the door I will come into his home and share a meal with him, and he with me. I will grant the one who conquers permission to sit with me on my throne, just as I too conquered and sat down with my Father on his throne. The one who has an ear had better hear what the Spirit says to the churches.

The Amazing Scene in Heaven

4: 1–11, After these things I looked, and there was a door standing open in heaven! And the first voice I had heard speaking to me like a trumpet said: 'Come up here so that I can show you what must happen after these things'. Immediately

I was in the Spirit, and a throne was standing in heaven with someone seated on it! And the one seated on it was like jasper and carnelian in appearance, and a rainbow looking like it was made of emerald encircled the throne. In a circle around the throne were twenty-four other thrones, and seated on those thrones were twenty-four elders. They were dressed in white clothing and had golden crowns on their heads. From the throne came out flashes of lightning and roaring and crashes of thunder. Seven flaming torches, which are the seven spirits of God, were burning in front of the throne and in front of the throne was something like a sea of glass, like crystal. In the middle of the throne and around the throne were four living creatures full of eyes in front and in back. 4: 7. The first living creature was like a lion, the second creature like an ox, the third creature had a face like a man's, and the fourth creature looked like an eagle flying. Each one of the four living creatures had six wings and was full of eyes all around and inside. They never rest day or night, saying: 'Holy Holy Holy is the Lord God, the All-Powerful, Who was and who is, and who is still to come!' And whenever the living creatures give glory, honor, and thanks to the one who sits on the throne, who lives forever and ever, the twenty-four elders throw themselves to the ground before the one who sits on the throne and worship the one who lives forever and ever, and they offer their crowns before his throne, saying: 'You are worthy, our Lord and God, to receive glory and honor and power, since you created all things, and because of your will they existed and were created!'

5: 13–14 Then I heard every creature – in heaven, on earth, under the earth, in the sea, and all that is in them – singing: 'To the one seated on the throne and to the Lamb be praise, honor,

Rajesh Jain

glory, and ruling power forever and ever!' And the four living creatures were saying 'Amen,' and the elders threw themselves to the ground and worshiped.

6: 1–2, I looked on when the Lamb opened one of the seven seals, and I heard one of the four living creatures saying with a thunderous voice, 'Come!' So I looked, and here came a white horse! The one who rode it had a bow, and he was given a crown, and as a conqueror he rode out to conquer.

11: 15–19 Then the seventh angel blew his trumpet, and there were loud voices in heaven saying: 'The kingdom of the world has become the kingdom of our Lord and of his Christ, and he will reign for ever and ever'.

Then the twenty-four elders who are seated on their thrones before God threw themselves down with their faces to the ground and worshiped God with these words: 'We give you thanks, Lord God, the All-Powerful, the one who is and who was, because you have taken your great power and begun to reign. The nations were enraged, but your wrath has come, and the time has come for the dead to be judged, and the time has come to give to your servants, the prophets, their reward, as well as to the saints and to those who revere your name, both small and great, and the time has come to destroy those who destroy the earth'. Then the temple of God in heaven was opened and the ark of his covenant was visible within his temple. And there were flashes of lightning, roaring, crashes of thunder, an earthquake, and a great hailstorm.

The Woman, the Child, and the Dragon

12: 1–6 Then a great sign appeared in heaven: a woman clothed with the sun, and with the moon under her feet, and on her head was a crown of twelve stars. She was pregnant and was screaming in labor pains, struggling to give birth. Then another sign appeared in heaven: a huge red dragon that had seven heads and ten horns, and on its heads were seven diadem crowns. Now the dragon's tail swept away a third of the stars in heaven and hurled them to the earth. Then the dragon stood before the woman who was about to give birth, so that he might devour her child as soon as it was born. So the woman gave birth to a son, a male child, who is going to rule over all the nations with an iron rod. Her child was suddenly caught up to God and to his throne, and she fled into the wilderness where a place had been prepared for her by God, so she could be taken care of for 1,260 days.

Babylon is Destroyed

18: 1–10, After these things, I saw another angel, who possessed great authority, coming down out of heaven, and the earth was lit up by his radiance. He shouted with a powerful voice: 'Fallen, fallen, is Babylon the great! She has become a lair for demons, a haunt for every unclean spirit, a haunt for every unclean bird, a haunt for every unclean and detested beast. For all the nations have fallen from the wine of her immoral passion, and the kings of the earth have committed sexual immorality with her, and the merchants of the earth have gotten rich from the power of her sensual behavior'. Then I heard another voice from heaven saying, 'Come out of her, my people, so you will not take part in her sins and so you will not receive her plagues, because her sins have piled up all the way to heaven and God has remembered her crimes. Repay her the same way she repaid others; pay her back double corresponding to her deeds. In the cup she mixed, mix double the amount for her. As much as she exalted herself and lived in sensual luxury, to this extent give her torment and grief because she said to herself, 'I rule as queen and am no widow; I will never experience grief!' For this reason, she will experience her plagues in a single day: disease, mourning, and famine, and she will be burned down with fire, because the Lord God who judges her is powerful!'

Then the kings of the earth who committed immoral acts with her and lived in sensual luxury with her will weep and wail for her when they see the smoke from the fire that burns her up. They will stand a long way off because they are afraid of her torment, and will say, 'Woe, woe, O great city, Babylon the powerful city! For in a single hour your doom has come!'

'19: 1–2 After these things I heard what sounded like the loud voice of a vast throng in heaven, saying,' Hallelujah! Salvation and glory and power belong to our God, because his judgments are true and just. For he has judged the great prostitute who corrupted the earth with her sexual immorality, and has avenged the blood of his servants poured out by her own hands!

The Son of God Goes to War

19: 11–16 Then I saw heaven opened and here came a white horse! The one riding it was called 'Faithful' and 'True,' and with justice he judges and goes to war. His eyes are like a fiery flame and there are many diadem crowns on his head. He has a name written that no one knows except himself. He is dressed in clothing dipped in blood, and he is called the Word of God. The armies that are in heaven, dressed in white, clean, fine linen, were following him on white horses. 19: 15. From his mouth extends a sharp sword, so that with it he can strike the nations. He will rule them with an iron rod, and he stomps the winepress of the furious wrath of God, the All-Powerful. He has a name written on his clothing and on his thigh: 'King of kings and Lord of lords'.

19: 19–21, Then I saw the beast and the kings of the earth and their armies assembled to do battle with the one who rode the horse and with his army. Now the beast was seized, and along with him the false prophet who had performed the signs on his behalf – signs by which he deceived those who had received the mark of the beast and those who worshiped his image. Both of them were thrown alive into the lake of fire burning with sulfur. The others were killed by the sword that extended from the mouth of the one who rode the horse, and all the birds gorged themselves with their flesh.

The Thousand Year Reign

20: 1–3 Then I saw an angel descending from heaven, holding in his hand the key to the abyss and a huge chain. He seized the dragon – the ancient serpent, which is the devil and Satan – and tied him up for a thousand years. The angel then threw him into the abyss and locked and sealed it so that he could not deceive the nations until the one thousand years were finished. (After these things he must be released for a brief period of time.)

20: 4–6 Then I saw thrones and seated on them were those who had been given authority to judge. I also saw the souls of those who had been beheaded because of the testimony about Jesus and because of the word of God. These had not worshiped the beast or his image and had refused to receive his mark on their forehead or hand. They came to life and reigned with Christ for a thousand years. (The rest of the dead did not come to life until the thousand years were finished.) This is the first resurrection. Blessed and holy is the one who takes part in the first resurrection. The second death has no power over them, but they will be priests of God and of Christ, and they will reign with him for a thousand years.

20: 11–15, Then I saw a large white throne and the one who was seated on it; the earth and the heaven fled from his presence, and no place was found for them. And I saw the dead, the great and the small, standing before the throne. Then books were opened, and another book was opened – the book of life. So the dead were judged by what was written in the books, according to their deeds. The sea gave up the dead that were in it, and Death and Hades gave up the dead that were in them, and each one was judged according to his deeds. Then Death and Hades were thrown into the lake of fire. This is the second death – the lake of fire. If anyone's name was not found written in the book of life, that person was thrown into the lake of fire.

21: 6–8 'I am the Alpha and the Omega, the beginning and the end. To the one who is thirsty I will give water free of charge from the spring of the water of life. The one who conquers will inherit these things, and I will be his God and he will be my son. But to the cowards, unbelievers, detestable persons, murderers, the sexually immoral, and those who practice magic spells, idol worshipers, and all those who lie, their place will be in the lake that burns with fire and sulfur. That is the second death'.

22: 12–13 (Look! I am coming soon, and my reward is with me to pay each one according to what he has done! I am the Alpha and the Omega, the first and the last, the beginning and the end!)

Jesus lived in India

(Bhavishya Purana: Pratisarga Parva, Chaturyuga Khanda Dvitiyadhyayah, nineteenth Chapter, Texts 17 to 31)

Texts 17–21

vikramaditya-pautrasca pitr-rajyam grhitavan
jitva sakanduradharsams cina-taittiridesajan
bahlikankamarupasca romajankhurajanchhatan
tesam kosan-grhitva ca danda-yogyanakarayat
sthapita tena maryada mleccharyanam prthak-prthak
sindhusthanam iti jneyam rastramaryasya cottamam
mlecchasthanam param sindhoh krtam tena mahatmana
ekada tu sakadiso himatungam samayayau

'Ruling over the Aryans was a king called Salivahana, the grandson of Vikramaditya, who occupied the throne of his father. He defeated the Shakas who were very difficult to subdue, the Cinas, the people from Tittiri and Bahikaus who could assume any form at will. He also defeated the people from Rome and the descendants of Khuru, who were deceitful and wicked. He punished them severely and took their wealth. Salivahana thus established the boundaries dividing the separate countries of the Mlecchas and the Aryans. In this way, Sindusthan came to be known as the greatest country. That personality appointed the abode of the Mlecchas beyond the Sindhu River and to the west'.

Text 22

ekadaa tu shakadhisho himatungari samaayayau hunadeshasya madhye vai giristhan purusam shubhanodadarsha balaram raajaa

Once upon a time, the subduer of the Sakas went towards Himatunga and in the middle of the Huna country (Hunadesh – the area near Manasa Sarovara or Kailash mountain in Western Tibet), the powerful king saw an auspicious man who was living on a mountain. The man's complexion was golden and his clothes were white.

Text 23

ko bharam iti tam praaha su hovacha mudanvitah
iishaa purtagm maam viddhi kumaarigarbha sambhavam

'The king asked, "Who are you sir?" "You should know that I am Isha Putra, the Son of God". he replied blissfully, and "am born of a virgin"'.

Text 24

mleccha dharmasya vaktaram satyavata paraayanam
iti srutva nrpa praaha dharmah ko bhavato matah

"'I am the expounder of the religion of the Mlecchas and I strictly adhere to the Absolute Truth." Hearing this the king enquired, "What are religious principles according to your opinion?"'

Texts 25–26

shruto vaaca mahaaraaja praapte satyasya samkshaye
nirmaaryaade mlechadeshe masiiho ham samagatah
iishaamasii ca dasyuunaa praadurbhuutaa bhayankarii
taamaham mlecchataah praapya masiihatva mupaagatah

Hearing this questions of Salivahara, Isha putra said, 'O king, when the destruction of the truth occurred, I, Masiha the prophet, came to this country of degraded people where there are no rules and regulations. Finding that fearful irreligious condition of the barbarians spreading from Mleccha-Desha, I have taken to prophethood'.

Texts 27–29

mlecchasa sthaapito dharmo mayaa tacchrnu bhuupate
maanasam nirmalam krtva malam dehe subhaasbham

naiganam apamasthaya japeta nirmalam param
nyayena satyavacasaa manasyai kena manavah

dhyayena pujayedisham suurya-mandala-samsthitam
acaloyam prabhuh sakshat-athaa suuryacalah sada

'Please hear Oh king which religious principles I have established among the mlecchas. The living entity is subject to good and bad contaminations. The mind should be purified by taking recourse of proper conduct and performance of Japa. By chanting the holy names, one attains the highest purity. Just as the immovable sun attracts, from all directions, the elements of all living beings, the Lord of the solar region, who is fixed and all-attractive, attracts the hearts of all living creatures. Thus by following rules, speaking truthful words, by mental harmony and by meditation, Oh descendant of Manu, one should worship that immovable Lord'.

Text 30

isha muurtirt-dradi praptaa nityashuddha sivamkari
ishamasihah iti ca mama nama pratishthitam

'Having placed the eternally pure and auspicious form of the Supreme Lord in my heart, O protector of the earth planet, I preached these principles through the Mlecchas' own faith and thus my name became "isha-masiha" (Jesus the Messiah)'.

Text 31

iti shrutra sa bhuupale natraa tam mlecchapujaam
sthaapayaamaasa tam tutra mlecchasthaane hi daarune

'After hearing these words and paying obeisances to that person who is worshipped by the wicked, the king humbly requested him to stay there in the dreadful land of Mlecchas'.

Notovitch claimed that the chief lama at Hemis told him of the existence of the work, which was read to him, through an interpreter, the somewhat detached verses of the Tibetan version of the 'Life of Issa', which was said to have been translated from the Pali. Notovitch says that he himself afterward grouped the verses 'in accordance with the requirements of the narrative'. As published by Notovitch, the work consists of 244 short paragraphs, arranged in fourteen chapters. The otherwise undocumented name 'Issa' resembles the Arabic name Isa used in the Koran to refer to Jesus and the Sanskrit 'īśa', the Lord.

The 'Life of Issa' begins with an account of Israel in Egypt, its deliverance by Moses, its neglect of religion, and its conquest by the Romans. Then follows an account of the Incarnation. At the age of thirteen, the divine youth, rather than take a wife, leaves his home to wander with a caravan of merchants to India (Sindh), to study the laws of the great Buddhas. Issa is welcomed by the Jains but leaves them to spend time among the Buddhists and spends six years among them, learning Pali and mastering their religious texts. Issa spent six years studying and teaching at Jaganath, Rajagriha, and other holy cities. At twenty-nine, Issa returns to his own country and begins to preach. He visits Jerusalem, where Pilate is apprehensive about him. The Jewish leaders, however, are also apprehensive about his teachings, yet he continues his work for three years. He is finally arrested and put to death for blasphemy, for claiming to be the son of God. His followers are persecuted, but his disciples carry his message to the world.

Life of Jesus Christ in East

The St Issa scroll is mentioned repeatedly by 'Jesus in India' scholars and was groundbreaking in starting to piece together the life of Jesus.

Recent attempts to obtain the scroll and gain more information about it have failed.

The Discovery

During the latter part of the 1870s, Notovitch decided to embark on an 'extended journey through the Orient'.

In 1887, Notovitch visited the famous Golden Temple at Amritsar India, eventually moving on to Ladak. He went to Kargil where he began a horseback trek on his way to Leh, the capital of Ladak. At a place called Mulbek, near the Wakha River, he decided to visit two monasteries, one of which was Buddhist, located above a hill. There he met a Lama, and the two conversed about religion. At one point in the conversation, the monk stated:

We also respect the one whom you recognize as Son of the one God. The spirit of Buddha was indeed incarnate in the sacred person of Issa [Jesus], who without aid of fire or sword, spread knowledge of our great and true religion throughout the world. Issa is a great prophet, one of the first after twenty-two Buddhas. His name and acts are recorded in our writings.

Notovitch then left the area, but while riding his horse near Hemis Monastery, Notovitch suffered a terrible fall from his horse and broke his right leg, and he was forced to remain under the care of the Buddhist monks at Hemis until his leg healed. During this time, he had the scrolls read to him and his translators translated it for him. Notovitch took notes, and this formed the core content for his book.

The Name Issa

Kersten states that the name 'Isa', or 'Issa', derives from the Syrian, Yeshu (Jesus), 'being altered to conform to Musa (=Moses)'. It is very interesting that Jesus is referred to as 'Issa' in Buddhist documents, as 'Isa' in the scripture of Islam, the Quran, and as 'Isa' in the Hindu scripture, the Bhavishya Mahapurana.

That the religious documents of these three religions mention Jesus as 'Isa' suggests that this was actually a name by which he was known in the East. Buddhism and Hinduism predate Islam.

Name of Visitor	Year	Reported
Nicholas Notovitch	1887	Saw document
Henrietta Merrick	1921	Visited and later wrote in her book, *In the World's Attic*, 'In Leh is the legend of Jesus who is called Issa, and the Monastery at Himis holds precious documents fifteen hundred years old which tell of the days that he passed in Leh where he was joyously received and where he preached'.
Swami Trigunatitananda	1895	Visited and confirmed that Notovitch had spent time there – this is cited in *Swami Trigunatita: His Life and Works* by Marie L Burke
Swami Abhedenanda	1922	Saw document
Nicholas Roerich and son	1925	Saw document
Mrs Gasque	1939	Saw document: Shown by Lama Nawong Zangpo
E. Caspari	1939	Saw document by Lama Nawong Zangpo
Edward Noack and Wife	1970s	A monk there told him: 'There are manuscripts in our library that describe the journey of Jesus to the East'.
Dr R. Ravicz	1973	Oral reference: informed by Tibetan friend
U. Eichstadt	1974	Saw document

Notovitch – Was He Really There?

There are those that say Notovitch never visited Hemis and that the St Issa scrolls do not exist, yet the following diary entry is a powerful vindication of the account of Notovitch:

'When I visited the Lamasery [Monastery] at Hemis, and together with the Lama Ishe Tundup and Mr Stobden interviewed the "Manager" (The young head Lama being in Tibet studying), the other Lamas who also were present belonging to the Monastery immediately said that their older monks did remember an Englishmen being injured and brought to their Monastery and that some MSS [manuscripts] were shown to him'.

This account was given in the 'PS' section of a diary entry for the 'Moravian Mission', who had in the rest of the entry tried to discredit and write of the St Issa scroll.

This translated diary entry is now well-known and documented in several books on Jesus in India.

In addition, Dr Fida Hassnain during his own enquiries in to the scrolls spoke to people at the monastery who talked about both Notovitch's visit and the scrolls. So was he really there? The answer appears to be a resounding **Yes.**

Diary Entry Clue

We have obtained from Dr Fida Hassnain a copy of the English translation of portions of the German Mission Diary.

The photo of the pages of the diary was made in 1958 by the journalist Mrs Amlabai Ketkar. Mrs Ketkar brought the photograph from the Moravian Mission house in Leh/Ladakh, got it translated into English and furnished copies, along with her comments, to Mr Aziz Kashmiri.

Others Hemis visits

Islam: Coming of Imam Mehdi to Bring World Order

'And we gave Moses the Book, and after Him sent succeeding Messengers: and we gave Jesus . . . the clear signs . . . and whensoever there came to you a Messenger with that your souls had not desire for, did you become arrogant, and some cry lies to, and some slay'.
Qur'an, Surih of the Heifer: 2:87

'The Imam Mehdi who will create a world state will make the ruling nations pay for their crimes against society. He will bring succor to humanity. He will take out the hidden wealth from the breast of the earth and will distribute it equitably amongst the needy deserving. He will teach you simple living and high thinking. He will make you understand that virtue is a state of character which is always a mean between the two extremes, and which is based upon equity and justice. He will

revive the teaching of the Holy Qur'an and the traditions of the Holy Prophet after the world has ignored them as dead letters. He will control over these resources of science and supreme knowledge. His control over these resources will be complete. He will know how supreme they are and how carefully they will have to be used. His mind will be free from desires of bringing harm and injury to humanity. Such knowledge to him will be like the property, which was wrongly possessed by others and for which he was waiting for the permission to repossess and use. He, in the beginning, will be like a poor stranger unknown, and Islam then will be in the hopeless and helpless plight of an exhausted camel that has laid down its head and is wagging its tail. With such a start he will establish an empire of God in this world. He will be the final demonstration and power of God's merciful wish to acquaint man with the right ways of life'.
Islam (Shi'i Tradition), Khutba 141:187

'And (Jesus) shall be a sign of The Hour (of Judgment); therefore have no doubt about it, but follow Me: this is a straight way'.
Qur'an, Surih of the Ornaments of Gold 43.61

The Apostle of Allah said, "Were there remaining but one day of the duration of all time, God would send forth a man from the people of my house, who will fill the earth with equity as it has been filled with oppression".
Islam; Hadith of Abu Dawud

When the heavens burst asunder, and obey it's Lord and it must. And when the earth is stretched (out) and casts forth what is in it and becomes empty (of its mysteries), and obeys its Lord and it must. O man! Surely you must strive (to attain) to your Lord, a hard striving until you meet Him. Then as to him who is given his book in his Right Hand, He shall be reckoned with an easy reckoning . . . (Sura 84:1–8).

'When the Qa'im emerges, he will come with a new Commission, a new Book, a new conduct and a new Judgment, which will be strenuous for the Arabs. His work is nothing but to fight, and no one will be spared. He will not be afraid of any blame in the execution of his duty'. Imam Ja'far As-Sadiq

Imam Sadiq relates: 'When our Qa'im arises he will call people anew to Islam, guiding them to the old thing from which people have turned away. He will be called Mahdi because he will guide people to the thing from which they have been separated. He will be called Qa'im because he will be commanded to establish the truth'.

How do you deny Allah and you were dead and He gave you life? Again He will cause you to die and again bring you to life, then you shall be brought back to Him . . . (Sura 2:28).

May Allah help us all to recognize him when he rises, Muhammad himself said: 'Happiness is for the one who will attend the Qa'im of my Ahl'ul-Bayt and will follow him before his rise. This person will love his (Qa'im's) lovers and hate his enemies, and will accept the leadership of the A'immah from before his advent. These ones are my friends and are the most sincere members of my Ummah whom I honor very much'. Bihar-ul-Anwar, vol. 52, p. 129

'If our Shi'a would be firm on their promises whole heartedly, our meeting would not be delayed'. – Imam Al-Mahdi.

Islam has been a Sword in the Hand of Allah, an instrument of judgment. Islam is ultimately a judgment upon itself. Islam is the way of Peace for those who know the ways of Peace.

Muhammad himself said: 'Happiness is for the one who will attend the Qa'im of my Ahl'ul-Bayt and will follow him before his rise. This person will love his (Qa'im's) lovers and hate his enemies, and will accept the leadership of the A'immah from before his advent. These ones are my friends, and are the most sincere members of my Ummah whom I honor very much'.
Bihar-ul-Anwar, vol. 52, p. 129

Buddhist: Advent of Maitreya Buddha

'I am not the first Buddha who came upon earth, nor shall I be the last. In due time, another Buddha will arise in the world, a Holy One . . . He will reveal to you the same eternal truths, which I have taught you . . . He will proclaim a religious life, wholly perfect and pure, such as I now proclaim'.

Sermon of the Great Passing

Digha Nikaya 26: 25

'In those days, brethren, there will arise in the world an Exalted One named Maitreya. He will be an Arihant, Fully Awakened, abounding in wisdom and goodness, happy, with knowledge of the worlds, unsurpassed as a guide to mortals willing to be led, a teacher for gods and men, and Exalted One, a Buddha, even as I am now . . . The Law, lovely in its origin, lovely in its progress, lovely in its consummation, will he proclaim, both in

the spirit and in the letter; the higher life will he make known, in all its fullness and in all its purity, even as I do now. He will be accompanied by a congregation of some thousands of brethren, even as I am now accompanied by a congregation of some hundreds of brethren'.
Digha Nikaya 3: 76, Chakkavatti Sihanada Suttanta

. . . the venerable Sariputta questioned the Lord about the future Conqueror, The Hero that shall follow you, The Buddha – of what sort will he be? I want to hear of him in full. Let the Visioned One describe him. When he heard the elder's speech, the Lord spoke thus, 'I will tell you, Sariputta; listen to my speech. In this auspicious eon, three leaders there have been: Kakusandha, Konagaamana and the leader Kassapa too. I am now the perfect Buddha; and there will be Maitreya too before this same auspicious eon runs to the end of its years'.
Anagata-Vamsa

'Listen attentively with one heart. A man whose spirit shines brightly, a man whose mind is completely unified, a man whose virtue excels everyone – such a man will truly appear in this world. When he preaches precious laws, all the people will totally be satisfied, as the thirsty drink sweet drops of rain from heaven. And each and every one will attain the path of liberation from struggles'.
Sutra of the Great Accomplishment of the Maitreya

And Ananda, holding back his tears, said to the Buddha: 'Who will teach us when you are gone?' And the Blessed One answered: 'I am not the first Buddha who has come upon the Earth, nor shall I be the last. In the right time, another Buddha will arise in the world, a Holy One, a Supremely Enlightened

One, endowed with wisdom in conduct, auspicious, Knowing the Truth, an incomparable leader of men, a Master of Spirit and mortals. He will reveal to you these Eternal Truths. He will preach his Dharma, Glorious in its Origin, Glorious in the Middle, and Glorious in its end, in the Spirit as well as the letter. He will proclaim a life of Dharma, wholly Perfect and Pure, even as I now Proclaim said Ananda 'How shall we know him?' And the Buddha said: 'He will be known as Maitreya which means, the friend'.

. . . Mahaparinirvana Sutra V, Verses 1–14:

'At that period, brethren, there will arise in the world an Exalted One named Maitreya, Fully Awakened, abounding in wisdom and goodness, happy, with knowledge of the worlds, unsurpassed as a guide to mortals willing to be led, a teacher for gods and men, an Exalted One, a Buddha, even as I am now. He, by himself, will thoroughly know and see, as it were face to face, this universe, with Its worlds of the spirits, Its Brahmas and Its Maras, and Its world of recluses and Brahmins, of princes and peoples, even as I now, by myself, thoroughly know and see them.'

'26, Digha Nikaya'

Hinduism: Coming of Saviour to Restore the Balance.

Time and Period of Coming of Kalki Avatar

We referred Sanskrit Shlokas from Kalki Purana.

Dwadshabd sahsren devanamcha chatur yugam
Chatwari treeni dwai chekam sahsra ganitam matam

As per the above Shloka from Purana which states that four yugas, Satya, Treta, Dwapara and Kal Yuga consists of 12,000 years. Their sequence will be in ratios of 1 : 2 : 3 : 4, respectively, because mathematical law governs that when numbers are written in words in Sanskrit, it should be read from reverse, therefore ages of satya, treta, dwapara and kal yuga should be in ratios of 1 : 2 : 3 : 4, i.e 1,000 years of satya age, 2,000 years of treta, 3,000 years of dwapara and 4,000 years of kal yuga.

Joining period between yugas was taken also in the ratios of 1 : 2 : 3 : 4, 100, 200, 300 and 400 years before and after. If we take into account the joining period, satya, treta, dwapara and kal yuga respective duration comes to 1,200, 2,400, 3,600 and 4,800 years, respectively.

Therefore we can summarise that 12,000 years of Ascending and 12,000 years of Descending Couple which the Earth takes around Fixed Star or Vishnu Nabhi (Cosmic Umbilicus) or Vernal Equinox.

Treeni laxani varshanam dwij manushya sankhyaya.
Sashthichev sahasrani, bhavityesh vai kalih.
Shatani tani divyanam sapt panch cha sankhyaya nisheshen bhavishati tu punah kritam. – Vishnu Purana

Here is again a shloka from *Vishnu* Purana, which narrates that actual age of Kal Yuga can be calculated by dividing 360,000 by 75, which is equal to 4,800 years, age of Kal Yuga, i.e 360° of circle covered by 0.075° each year will take 4,800 years to cover.

Vishnu was the avatar in Satya Age, and the authors of Vishnu Purana were aware that future mistake may crop up about the calculation of various ages and particularly about Kal Yuga as it is one of the darkest ages. This is the wonderful slokas (Quatrain) for calculating the Age of Kal Yuga which is 4,800 years and not 432,000 years as calculated in various puranas.

Earlier authors have miscalculated the age of satya, treta, dwapara and kali on the basis of Deva Yuga, which they calculated by multiplying Deva Yuga into Human Years by 360 in the ratio of 4 : 3 : 2 : 1, again not interpreting as per maths law in Sanskrit.

Therefore, we arrived at the conclusion that previous calculation of satya, treta, dwapara and kal yuga, i.e 4,800 × 360 = 1,728,000, 3,600 × 360 = 1,296,000, 2,400 × 360 = 864,000 and 1,200 × 360 = 432,000 is wrong and misleading and most of the literature available mentioned this as true.

Very few Learned Rishis and Saints know this truth.

Therefore, 12,000 years of one half of Electric Couple will have this distribution and same 12,000 years of half Ascending Couple, this makes 240,000 years of 360° completion of zodiac around Vernal Equinox.

Sl. No	Name of Yug	Joining Period (beginning)		Actual Period		Joining Period (in end)		Total Age
1	Sat Yug	100	+	1,000	+	100	=	1,200 years
2	Treta Yug	200	+	2,000	+	200	=	2,400 years
3	Dwapar Yug	300	+	3,000	+	300	=	3,600 years
4	Kali Yug	400	+	4,000	+	400	=	4,800 years

Even Sri Yukteswar in his book had wrongly interpreted four yuga duration and mentioned this present time in Dwapara Yuga and Kal Yuga has long passed away, again not the true interpretation. He has not followed Sanskrit mathematical law (reading numbers in reverse, one used in words in the shlokas); seers and saints have forgotten to use and apply this mathematical law.

God chooses among us the wise man and he speaks through his mind. This is the power of truth and even he sometimes does not choose the best among us.

We have evidence from the Bible also after the Holy War and second coming of Jesus Christ, 1,000 years of Golden Period (Satya Age) will start. He (Jesus) has referred to the Man of Aquarius who will bring peace to earth. Most of Christians think Jesus will return from heaven and he will come as a king to rule the nation. This is impossible because no Prophet or son of *God* has returned back but New Man, who is selected and commissioned from heaven always comes to Earth as an Avatar or Prophet. Even Jesus never said that he will return but he has mentioned more than once, which are called unknown sayings of Jesus Christ, few I will mentioned here;

Father will send Man of Aquarius in my name – Jesus Christ.

Do not think that I have come to bring Peace on earth but Sword – Jesus Christ.

This is what he has mentioned that father will give *Sword* to Man of Aquarius, who will then make war.

He will make Peace on Earth. He will have heart and head both – Jesus Christ.

Jesus and Christ were two different powers which came in two different times; Christ was born long before Jesus. New Testament Bible do not mentioned Christ and only says about Jesus, although Christ was born about the time of Noah's ark 4,500–5,000 years before. Christ in the West and Krishna in the East might have appeared nearly at same time in two parts of the Earth.

Most of Christians do not know this fact, but this is the truth. We call Jesus Christ not Jesus, Christ lived long before birth of Jesus. Jesus was a carpenter by profession and has come to live in Kashmir in India and lived there for many years. He met various yogis and learned men in Kashmir, still there is a shrine devoted to Jesus. This was the time period which has not been mentioned in the bible and often known as the lost years of Jesus. He travelled widely to different parts of the world and lived many years in Kashmir valley. There is still a tribe of Jews living in Kashmir; they are one among the lost tribes of Jews.

> *When the practices taught by the Vedas and the institutes of law shall nearly have ceased, and the close of the Kali Age shall be nigh, a portion of that divine being who exists of his own spiritual nature in the character of Brahma, and who is the beginning and the end, and who comprehends all things, shall descend upon the earth. He will be born as and in the family of an eminent Brahman of Sambhala, endowed with the eight superhuman faculties. By his irresistible might, he will destroy all the barbarians and thieves, and all whose minds are devoted to iniquity. He will then re-establish righteousness upon earth; the minds of those who live at the end of the Kali age shall be awakened and shall be as clear as crystal. The men who are thus charged by virtue of that peculiar time shall be the seeds of human beings and shall give birth to a race who shall follow the laws of the Krita Age, Golden age, the Age of Purity.*

> *(Vishnu Purana 4.24)*

Those who are known as twice-born (Brahmins) are devoid of the Vedas, narrow-minded and always engaged in the service of the Sudras (low-born castes); they are fond of carnal desires, seller of religion, seller of the Vedas, untouchable and seller of juices; they sell meat, are cruel, engaged in sexual gratification and gratification of their appetite, attached to others' wives, drunk and producer of cross-breeds; have a low lifespan, mix with lowly people and consider their brother-in-law as the only friend. They like constant confrontation and are fond of argument, discontent, fond of jewellery, hair and style. The wealthy are respected as high-born, and Brahmins are respected only if they are lenders; Men are merciful only when they are unable to harm others; express displeasure towards the poor; talk excessively to express erudition and carry out religious work to be famous; Monks are attached to homes in this Koli Age and the homeless are devoid of any morality; Men of this age deride their teachers, display false religious affinity but tricks the good people; Sudras in Koli are always engaged in taking over others' possessions; in Koli, marriage takes place simply because the man and the woman agree to do so; Men engages in friendship with the crooked and show magnanimity while returning favours; Men are considered pious only if they are wealthy and treat only faraway waters (lands) as places of pilgrimage; Men are considered Brahmins simply because they have the sacred thread around their body and as explorers, simply because they have a stick in their hand; the Earth becomes infertile, rivers hit the banks, wives take pleasure in speaking like prostitutes and their minds are not attracted towards their husbands; Brahmins become greedy for others' food, the low-born castes are not averse to becoming priests, wives mix freely even after they become widows; the clouds release rain irregularly, the land becomes infertile, the kings kill their subjects, the people are burdened with taxes; they survive by eating honey, meat, fruits and roots; in the first quarter of the Koli Age, people deride God; in the second quarter, people do not even pronounce God's name; in the third quarter, men become cross-breeds; in the fourth quarter, men become the same (uniform) breed; nothing called race exists anymore; they forget God and pious works become extinct.

Vishnu Purana, I (1), Verses 23–38

Yada Yada hi dharmasya glanir bhavati bharata
abhyutthanam adharmasya tadatmanam srijamy aham

Whenever and wherever there is a decline in religious practice,
O descendant of Bharata, and a predominant rise of irreligion –
at that time, I descend Myself.
In order to deliver the pious and to annihilate the miscreants, as
well as to re-establish the principles of religion, I advent Myself
millennium (Age) after millennium.
(Bagawattam 4:7–8)

Gobind Singh writes in the *Sri Dasam Granth*:
When there is incest, adultery, atheism, hatred of religion, no
more dharma, and sin everywhere, the impossible Iron Age has
come; in what way the world will be saved? For the helpless, the
Lord Himself will manifest as the Supreme Purusha. He will
be called the Kalki incarnation and will be glorious like a lion
coming down from heaven.

Kalki avatar is the last of the ten major incarnations of Lord
Vishnu, who will appear in the end of this Kali Yuga to protect
religious principles.

O Kesava, O Hari, who have assumed the form of
Kalki! You appear like a comet and carry a terrifying
sword for bringing about the annihilation of the
wicked barbarian men at the end of the Kali-yuga.

(Sri Dasavatara Stotra, tenth Sloka).

People who have claimed to be Kalki

- Members of the Bahá'í faith have interpreted the prophecies of end time as references to the arrival of their founder Bahá'u'lláh, which has helped growth of the Bahá'í faith in India.
- Members of the Ahmadiyya Muslim community believe their founder, Mirza Ghulam Ahmad, to be the Kalki Avatar.
- Jean-Charles Bourquin, French pianist and self-proclaimed foreseer who claims to prevent the world from an extraterrestrial invasion.

Dashavatara: (from left) Matsya, Kurma, Varaha, Narasimha, Vamana, Parashurama, Rama, Krishna, Buddha, Kalki.

Dr Ved Prakash Upaddhay claimed Islamic prophet Muhammad as Kalki in his book 'Kalki Avatar aur Muhammad sahab' showing some reliable similarities of contexts with the predictions about Kalki mentioned in the scriptures above.

- Satya Sai also claimed himself to be kalki avatara.
- Bhagwan kalki and Amma of South India at present also claim to be kalkis.

CHAPTER 2

CHRISTIAN, INDIAN CULT AND MASTERS

Nostradamus in his Quatrain is forecasting the Prophecy of Avatar, about how he will take his second birth.

Jewish scholars and various others sources indicate that mankind is approaching Great Millennium changes.

Seven Great changes has been mentioned as per the Jewish sources before world will collapse

The first is religious deception as Christians, Muslims and Hindus have moved away from their religious believes, Muslim fundamentalism has grown in the form of terrorist groups. Organisations supported by many Islamic nations have become active and have taken many countries in its grip.

Recently, more and more terrorist groups have joined hands together and after the Syria unrest, they have gained the control of several Iraq cities and announced their leaders as the World Islamic State. As a result of downfall of ruler Sadaam Hussain, imbalance in power of two sects of Muslims has arisen. Abu Bakr al-Baghdadi, who declared himself caliph in imitation of the companions of Mohammad and set up a caliphate in the Middle East and North Africa in the seventh century.

Deception and cult of false saints: Gurus common in India and the West. Many gurus in India have been charged with criminal offence like rape and cheating their devotees of huge sums of money; to name a few, Swami Rama of India was charged with raping of a foreign devotee. There are numerous abuses and scandals that have emerged over the past two decades. In the December 1990 edition of *Yoga Journal*, Journalist Katharine Webster wrote about a long history of sexual harassment, outright sexual assault, financial exploitation, psychological manipulation, and a host of coercive practices on the part of Swami Rama, the founder of the Himalayan Institute, Honesdale, New York, which continues to teach meditation, yoga, spirituality, and holistic health in the ayurvedic tradition (Webster's article is available online at *http://www.*katharinewebster.com/text/0003.pdf). In 1997, however, jurors passed a verdict that the Himalayan Institute in Honesdale, New York, should pay US$ 1.875 million in damages to a woman who was sexually assaulted on thirty separate occasions by Swami Rama. Webster's article reveals that this woman was only one of many assaulted by the Swami, although most cases were not litigated.

Again recently, Indian saint Asharam Bapu along with his son Narayan was arrested on the charges of rape and molestation; he has followers in millions around India and abroad.

These fake gurus charge huge amount of money from their devotees and claim to initiate their disciples by giving them darshan of Astral light body in astral world, where devotees hear sound and see light between their eyes, at the seat of third eye (Divine eye). They cannot lead their devotees beyond astral plane into casual world and thus cannot complete the journey of soul in order to close the door of rebirth, and soul is still subject to birth and death cycle.

The only true saints in the past are Patanjali, Jesus Christ, Prophet Christ, Prophet Mohammad, Lord Budha, Rama Avatar, Krishna Avatar, Ramana Maharishi, Nanak, Hajur Savan Singh Ji Maharaj, his disciple Sant Kirpal Singh ji Maharaj. (List is huge and impossible to mention all here.) India had been the land of great seers and saints and had long tradition of true saints at any time on earth.

Appointment of any saint on earth is done by Cosmic Government (Aliens) to bring back the lost sheep to the kingdom of God. A person may be saint and fully competent as soul but cannot act as Satguru or Saint on earth and heaven, it has to be appointed by *godly* power to do specific work for certain time.

Even *Avatars* of *God* like Rama, Vishnu were not self-appointed on earth. They had come to earth under a grand arrangement from *God's* power to bring peace and truth from time to time and from ages to ages.

Biography of False Gurus from East to West

Source: www.prem-rawat-bio.org and www.prem-rawat-maharaji.info
published by former followers of Prem Rawat has the following to say:

Prem Rawat is very rich. He left India in 1971 at the age of thirteen, with no money, no education, and was disowned by his mother three years later. He has never had a paying job, never run a business, and does not own the patents to any successful inventions (contrary to rumors amongst his followers). His money has come from donations from his followers, including inheritances, trust funds, and shares in some very successful businesses. The statements on Elan Vital and Prem Rawat Foundation web sites that he supports himself and his family by independent means, and that he is a successful private investor, are lies. All his money has come from the guru business.

The question is, if Rawat was a fraud, who continued playing the guru after he grew up because he realised he could make a lot of money, he would be behaving exactly like he does. So, if he is genuine, he is deliberately acting like a fraud in order to . . . what? . . . test his devotees? . . . ensure that only the true students will find him?

The fact is, if Rawat was sincere in trying to reach as many people as possible, he would remove all obstacles, especially the appearance that he is obsessed with – material possessions. He could also use his wealth to advertise his message, instead of constantly soliciting funds from his followers to pay for every propagation initiative.

In fact, even when Rawat conducts discourses, the emphasis is on ensuring that he, his family including his mistress are kept in levels of luxury usually reserved for heads of states, all at the expense of the premies.

Fundraising has always been an important activity in Divine Light Mission and Elan Vital. Although 'Knowledge' is free, there is a constant need for cash to maintain expensive properties around the world and the expensive lifestyle of Maharaji and his family. Expenses, which include a US$ 40 million private jet, two helicopters (a Bell 206L and a Bell 430 worth over US$ 4.5 million), a US$ 7 million yacht, a multi-million dollar home in Malibu, a large house and grounds in Surrey, England, land and a home at the Ivorys Rock Conference Centre in Australia, as well as a 'residence' at Fig Tree Pocket (Brisbane suburb) in Queensland, Australia, have been justified by saying they help spread Maharaji's teachings. The ownership of these assets has always been clouded in mystery, but some curious ex-premies have been doing some research.

> *You know some people don't like rich people. They have this idea or that idea of what it is to be rich. But they really don't know. It's not easy to be rich. It isn't. Once you've made your first million, you need another to protect it. Then you have two million, and you'll need another two million to protect those two million. Then you'll have four million and you'll need another four million to protect those four million, and then*

*you'll have eight million. Of course then you'll need
another eight million to protect those eight million and
then you'll have sixteen million . . . it isn't easy, it's not
what you think.*
Maharaji – Long Beach, December 1995

Prem Rawat's 'Teachings'

Prem Rawat and his followers have developed a jargon in
which many English words have a meaning that is different
to the norm, and in some cases, its meaning has even
changed considerably over the decades. He has never written
anything, all his teachings are through speeches, mainly
extemperaneous but very repetitive, that he makes from
thrones or stages. His teachings are based on those of his
father, a guru in a Sant Mat tradition, but his father died
when he was eight years old and he has been developing his
own teachings for over fifty years. He claims his knowledge
is concept-free, that it is an experience beyond words, that
is unable to be understood by the mind, only by the heart.
He regularly repeats 'concepts' as being products of 'the
Mind' and does not seem to realise that his teachings are
also concepts. Over the decades, his language has become
vaguer and his speeches devoid of data except for morality
fables from his own life.

Worship of a Divine Child

Prem Rawat was one of a number of Indian 'gurus' who during the 1960s and early 1970s extend their activities to Europe, the Americas and Australasia. What set Prem Rawat apart from Maharishi Mahesh Yogi, Sai Baba and Bhagwan Shri Rajneesh (Osho) is that Rawat was just a child when he inherited a ready-made religious vehicle – the Divine Light Mission and was anointed its Satguru.

Prem Rawat was born near Haridwar in northern India in 1957, the youngest of four brothers. His father, Hans Ram Singh Rawat, was a well-known guru who taught a system of four meditation techniques, which he called 'the Knowledge'. These four techniques were claimed to reveal 'divine light', 'divine music', 'the primordial vibration' and 'divine nectar', and were taught in a secret initiation ceremony.

On his father's death in 1966, and following possible discussions and disagreements amongst the Rawat family and Rawat's senior followers (mahatmas), the eight-year-old Prem was given his father's honorific title of Guru Maharaj Ji, and the spirit of the Incarnation of God on earth was believed to have entered him. Prem Rawat then pronounced himself *Lord of the Universe*.

Prem Rawat inherited a following from his father of reputedly one million devotees, who were known as premies, a term meaning 'giver of love' in Hindi. The overwhelming majority of Rawat's current devotees live in India but even there the numbers are a fraction of what they once were as his eldest brother, Satpal Maharaj, has the loyalty of the majority of his father's devotees as well as the ashrams, mahatmas and the assets. With all the power of Western money and technology, Rawat can still only attract a crowd – a quarter the size of what he was able to do as a homegrown Godboy. Prem Rawat is still known as Guru Maharaj Ji in India, where he continues to promote himself in distinctly religious terms.

At the age of twelve in 1970, Prem Rawat addressed one of the largest rallies ever held anywhere in the world, with contemporary sources claiming that over one million people attended the gathering in Delhi. In front of this vast crowd, Rawat proclaimed his personal divinity and stated that he had come to deliver India from its materialism and rule the world, the speech becoming known as Rawat's 'Peace Bomb'.

In mid 1971, Prem Rawat then aged only thirteen travelled to London, where he was accommodated by several English followers who had been taught the Knowledge techniques of meditation in India. While Rawat was in the United Kingdom, funds were raised to enable Rawat to fly to the United States, which he eventually did before returning home to India. In the Autumn of 1971, American initiates registered an organisation called Divine Light Mission Incorporated (DLM Inc.) as a non-profit Church, listing Guru Maharaj Ji as its chief minister. A separate Divine Light Mission was created in the United Kingdom in 1972 and subsequently other Divine Light Missions were created in Australia, South Africa and Canada, as well as in several

European and South American countries. Rawat's senior disciples, saffron-robed 'mahatmas', were sent to support the fledgling missions and a system of ashrams, houses where Rawat's devotees observed a monastic rule, was instigated.

At age fourteen, against his mother's wishes Prem Rawat left India, and in 1972 once again travelled westward where he attracted large numbers of aspiring followers (I mean we're not talking Karbala on Arba'een or the Pope in the Phillipines or the Khumb Mela here). At a single event in Montrose, Colorado, 2,000 people were initiated into the 'Knowledge' and in total in the years 1971 to 1974, between 50,000 and 60,000 people underwent the Knowledge initiation in the United States.

In mid 1973, Prem Rawat stated that his coming November gathering at the Houston Astrodome – Millennium 73 – would be *the most holy and significant event in human history.* In the end, Millennium 73 attracted only 15,000 of the planned 144,000 attendees. Despite the abysmal failure of Millennium 73, Rawat continued to attract some new followers thanks to energetic propagation by his already committed devotees. There was considerable media interest in the 'teenage guru' though much of it drew sceptical attention to the luxury that was being demanded by the young Rawat.

By 1974, Prem Rawat was living in a hill top property at Malibu Beach, California. This mansion was in the ownership of DLM Inc. although following the financial restructuring of 1975–6, it came to be owned by SEVA Corporation of America. In the same year, at the age of sixteen, Rawat married an airline stewardess from San Diego named Marolyn Johnson. Devotees of Rawat's have always claimed that as a result of this marriage, there was a second family schism. However, Rawat's mother and Indian mahatmas and DLM administrators were explicit that he was denounced, deposed and disinherited because of his 'despicable lifestyle', which include drunkenness, meat-eating, smoking of marihuana and night-clubbing. Rawat refused to answer these accusations when questioned by journalists, but they were later confirmed by a bevy of Rawat's close administrators and aides. The eldest brother, Bal Bhagwan Ji (now known as Satpal Maharaj), after being ceremonially crowned by his mother, was recognised by the majority of Indian premies as the 'true' Guru Maharaji and rightful inheritor of the mantle of the Rawat brothers' late father, Hans Rawat. All but a handful of Divya Sandesh Parishad administrators and mahatmas followed them, and Prem Rawat was left without access to his father's movement.

Although no published figures exist, at some point in the mid 1970s, the number of new followers ceased to grow and the numbers leaving the movement increased. This is undoubtedly why there are no published figures. As James Downton explained, the pool of ex-hippies looking for enlightenment had dried up and there was no longer a large number of people interested in becoming converted and committed to any Eastern New Religious Movement. The source of the disaffection in Divine Light Mission and later Élan Vital is straightforward. Prem Rawat like other 1970s New Religious Movement leaders promised far more than he could deliver and so most people intrigued by what he offered eventually become disillusioned. This is not unusual. In Rawat's case, though there were a series of scandals and poor decisions that exacerbated this trend.

In 1975–6, the relationship between Prem Rawat and the US DLM Inc. was radically altered with consequences for the Divine Light Mission movement worldwide. In response to an impending IRS audit of DLM Inc., considerable assets held by the DLM church were transferred to Rawat's personal possession. Rawat ceased to be named as having any legal interest in the U.S. Divine Light Mission and was no longer listed as its chief minister. The DLM administration in Denver attempted to change its public perception and to downplay the Eastern rituals and Rawat's public status and cut back his spending. A series of workshops begun in December 1975 amongst administrators and the ashram and general members which focused on questioning the individual premie's understanding. Once this began, many premies took stock of their involvement, their beliefs and their 'experience' and left the ashrams for a more normal life, and in many cases, the movement as well.

In 1977, Prem Rawat reasserted his role as Guru, Perfect Master and Divine Incarnation and energetically restated the central importance of devotion to him personally as the prime prerequisite for achieving spiritual progress or living a life that had any real meaning and purpose. As part of this restatement of devotion, the ashram system was reinvigorated after a period of decline. A new, though barely altered, set of rules for ashram living was imposed, though how closely it was complied with was still variable and all of Rawat's followers were subject to stronger encouragement to enter the ashram system and especially to embark on a life in which attending the many Divine Light Mission festivals which were mainly held across the United States and Europe was the chief driving force of their lives. Rawat began a series of regular festivals that first occurred on three week intervals in Portland Oregon, Denver Colorado and Miami Florida. For the next three or four years, committed premies' lives became chaotic and exhausting, and fledgling communities fell apart under the strain.

The DECA project, begun in 1979, was set up to provide Prem Rawat with a customised Boeing 707 for his personal use. As an adjunct to the ashram system, DECA was reliant on unpaid labour and donated funds; the business model that developed within DECA served as the basis for subsequent projects designed to provide personal benefit to Prem Rawat such as the major upgrading of his Malibu home into the Malibu Mahal.

In 1982, without prior warning, Prem Rawat announced that the Divine Light Mission ashrams must close, the abruptness of the announcement was matched by the rapidity of the closure programme which was complete by the end of 1983. This period was marked by a sense of crisis in the wider movement, a reflection of the ongoing difficulties Rawat was experiencing in his personal life. The DUO ashrams in India were treated separately and remain to this day as largely monastic in character under the name Raj Vidya Kender.

With the Divine Light Mission ashrams closed, there were various attempts to recast the Rawat movement as non-religious, and through the 1980s and 1990s, the name Elan Vital progressively replaced that of Divine Light Mission as the title of the various national organisations, with the movement as a whole taking on a corporate veneer. The presentation of Rawat's 'message' was revised dramatically, becoming almost entirely secular, and Rawat began restricting his claims of personal divinity to his appearances in India and to closed meetings for devotees only outside of India. Following this image change, Maharaji, the name under which Rawat was by then being promoted, commenced an annual cycle of world tours visiting major cities to speak at events attended by devotees and newly interested people. A series of ever more expensive jets were purchased for Rawat's sole use, the costs justified on the grounds that the planes were essential to support Rawat's international mission. Rawat had been obsessed with planes and cars since he was a child. The rationale for any organisation to have an executive jet is that the executives can work or rest while travelling without the discomfort and distractions of commercial flight, but Rawat flies the plane himself, thereby having no time for work, and arrives needing rest. The cost/benefit ratio of cost of a personal jet divided by number of new students is extraordinarily high, and as numbers of followers are decreasing, the cost of each new student is astronomical. The cost of gasoline for a flight from Malibu to London (figures from 2008) exceeds US\$ 30,000, i.e. thirty to fifty times the cost of a commercial flight. Maybe Rawat is frugal in other areas of his life.

New initiations into the 'Knowledge' continued through the 1980s and 1990s, although the number of new recruits failed to replace the tens of thousands of followers who abandoned Prem Rawat from 1973 onwards. Since the 1990s, the incoming new premies have about balanced the outgoing in the West. No matter how he tries, Rawat cannot come up with a process that will allow him to create 'true believers' that will stay loyal to him. He'd have to be charismatic and to have a 'Knowledge' that 'works' considerably better than the only one he has to achieve that goal. Following the failure of the Millennium '73 festival, Prem Rawat kept a very low public profile and it was not until the arrival of web sites created by critical followers that the names Guru Maharaj Ji and Divine Light Mission once again attracted media attention. Subsequently, Rawat's remaining supporters have provided him with an uncritical presence on the Internet and the corporate presentation of Rawat includes a plethora of web sites offering DVDs and printed materials and attempting to flood the Internet with Rawat propaganda making the truth about him difficult to google.

Denials of Belief

In the late 1990s, annual gatherings in Long Beach, California, attracted up to 8,000 followers from around the world, more recent events (2005) in Florida and California have been attended by less than 2,500. Since 1996, claims of sexual abuse and financial malfeasance have caused a steady stream of followers to part company with Rawat, such that by 2010, outside of India, he retains only a few thousand followers.

Prem Rawat still lives at Malibu. Assets worth over US$ 80 million, including a US$ 60 million GulfStream jet (leased), are available for Prem Rawat's personal use. These are held via a number of administrative companies, including the SEVA Corporation of America. Prem Rawat continues to announce that he can relieve people of their suffering by teaching them four meditation techniques. The name Elan Vital as the marque for organisations which support Prem Rawat is being replaced by names employing the corporate term *Words of Peace*.

Prem Rawat's speeches are recorded on DVDs and shown around the world at small public venues, as well as being made available to individuals, while increasing use was being made of satellite and cable television programming to give Rawat a larger audience. The Internet now seems to be the focus of Prem Rawat's outreach.

It has been a consistent contention of Prem Rawat and his followers that what Rawat teaches has nothing to do with 'belief' that it is wholly 'experiential'. Despite this claim of 'no belief', prior to initiation, anyone seeking to be taught the Knowledge meditation techniques must adopt many beliefs about Prem Rawat in order to negotiate the 'aspirant' process that Rawat calls 'The Keys'. The Keys are only part of a very comprehensive belief system which exists throughout the Prem Rawat movement, although outside of Prem Rawat's often contradictory speeches, it has no supporting liturgy, prescribed text or publicly acknowledged historical reference but has a large body of concepts that Rawat has repeatedly mentioned in his speeches.

To become a follower of Prem Rawat, it is necessary to hold two incontrovertible beliefs.

The first belief is that each individual has an 'inner world', which is a source of secret reward. Prem Rawat most frequently refers to this 'inner world' as *your heart,* by which he means not the emotional centre of a person but rather an ill-defined mystical reality.

The second belief is that Prem Rawat, uniquely, has the power to take the individual to that 'inner world' and that it is impossible for a person to find their *heart* unaided by Prem Rawat.

The message contained within these two core beliefs can be summarised as: The essence of your own humanity lies within yourself (the *heart*) but that you are blocked from touching that *heart* by the everyday chatter and uncontrolled thoughts and feelings that swirl about inside you. Prem Rawat refers to this chatter as *the mind* and the *doubt maker* and often infers a Manichean malignity to it.

To overcome this 'block' to your 'inner world', to be able to *find your heart,* Prem Rawat prescribes a long process called the Keys (Since 2004, watching seventy hours of videos of him talking, since 2014 less than eight hours). Quite a remarkable improvement in efficiency. There is then a meeting at which the secret techniques are revealed. From then on, there are daily one hour personal and private meditation sessions. He calls this system Knowledge, or Self-Knowledge, and frequent times of 'keeping in touch' either by listening to him speak in person at 'events' or videos of him speaking at these events is needed to keep the inspiration and gratitude flowing. All contact is through the Internet. No personal contact with others following these guidelines is required. The meditation is described under the Four Techniques.

Once an individual has adopted these basic beliefs and lifestyle, they may further adopt a series of consequent beliefs which can be characterised as Rawatism. Predominant amongst the beliefs of *Rawatism* is the doctrine of 'the master is always needed'. This belief follows from the *mind* problem where the follower finds that even the Rawat meditation is inadequate to the task of permanently stilling conscious thought and that only listening to the words of the master (Prem Rawat), provides the impetus to reach the *peace* of one's *heart*.

Although the religious practices that once supported the Rawat belief system have been excised from public presentation, most, if not all, of Prem Rawat's remaining followers continue to pursue a devotional attachment to Rawat in private, which he now calls *gratitude*. Organisations which promote Prem Rawat sell 'inspirational' photographs of Prem Rawat as well as recorded music which is 'devotional' in style. The use of pictures of Prem Rawat as 'altar pieces' and the playing of devotional style songs as a liturgy still is a current practice among Rawat's followers. In addition, many followers continue to rely on the 'history' of the transference of 'guruship' to Prem Rawat from his father as an explanation of Prem Rawat's special status.

Prem Rawat's followers maintain that they follow no belief system whatsoever, that theirs is a wholly empirical approach based on the truth of the experience of meditation and, although this is less frequently specified, the experience of Prem Rawat's presence and words. Thus, when asked what do you believe? a Rawat follower may well answer that they do not believe in Prem Rawat or his 'Knowledge' but rather that 'they Know'.

Material Reward

The acquisition of wealth, particularly items of demonstrable value is important to Prem Rawat. In the early days, Rawat's Western followers justified this acquisitive behaviour in two ways – firstly as a 'realised soul' Prem Rawat was above attachment to the 'baubles' of materialism, secondly that as the Lord of the Universe, it was only right that Prem Rawat should have the best of everything. The question of Prem Rawat's personal wealth is currently explained by his followers in terms that he is a 'successful private investor'. The actual sources of Rawat's wealth are threefold:

- Personal donations from a broad follower base in the years 1971–76.
- Personal gifts from wealthy followers, including transfers of substantial business interests.
- A consistent flow of maintenance support provided via the DLM, Elan Vital and latterly Words of Peace

Global organisations in respect of Prem Rawat's promotional activities.

From 1971 to the present, raising funds to support Prem Rawat's lifestyle appears to have been a primary objective of the organisations he created. Michael Donner, former National Co-ordinator of the U.S. Divine Light Mission Incorporated, told *Good Weekend*, an Australian magazine, in September 2002:

'There were special fund-raisers for the extravagant birthday gifts. People flying around collecting bags of cash – often over US$ 100,000 – for a new car or whatever. The use of the organisation to collect and solicit this money was no doubt not too legal'.

In the 1970s and 1980s, Rawat's followers deposited money and gifts such as tape recorders and cameras at the entrance to darshan lines, where Rawat's feet were ritually kissed. According to senior organisers from this era, these efforts frequently saw suitcases of cash transported out of the United States, Australia and other countries, for deposit in Prem Rawat's Swiss bank accounts. The amounts in these transfers were as high as US$ 300,000. And another former organiser has written:

'I was deeply involved in the formation of Elan Vital [Prem Rawat's organisation] in Australia and the Pacific and I was personally aware of the guiding principles behind the formation of EV which were essentially to create an arm's length vehicle for MJ's [Rawat's] work which would support him, his family, his tours, aircraft and anything else he might want and need but in such a way as to allow him maximum legal flexibility and protection . . . It was well known amongst the higher echelon of premies what EV was all about . . . You didn't have to be Einstein to work out that everything revolved around supporting MJ's lifestyle at whatever cost'.

Today's climate of stricter governance of non-profit organisations has meant that Prem Rawat's organisations should no longer raise funds to support Rawat's lifestyle. However, the lack of impartial and independent appointees in the administration of the organisations that support Rawat continues to raise apprehension about the potential for the misapplication of funds. In the late 1990s, the majority of the directors of the Australian Elan Vital Incorporated resigned as a result of concerns that Prem Rawat's beneficial ownership of the Amaroo development in Queensland would place the directors at legal risk.

Direct ownership of the high-value assets available for Prem Rawat's exclusive use is achieved via a number of companies controlled by boards of directors comprised of committed followers of Prem Rawat. In the United States, the primary holding vehicle has been SEVA Corporation of America – Corporation and its many subsidiaries are or have been the owners of Rawat's numerous residences, including Anacapa View, Malibu USA, and Swiss House, Reigate, Surrey, United Kingdom, as well as the mega yacht Serenity (Serenity was sold in 2004) plus several helicopters and executive aircrafts. The Gulfstream G550 executive jet – registration number N550PR, which is flown personally by Prem Rawat is 'dry leased' from a bank (the Wilmington Trust) and is operated by 'Prem Rawat and the Priyan Foundation'.

The legal structuring of Prem Rawat's financial interests was conducted by tax lawyer Robert Jacobs, whose was the only non 'premie' name to appear on SEVA documents. From 1975, the legal and financial relationship between Prem Rawat and Divine Light Mission was overseen by Michael Dettmers who split with Rawat in 1987. Subsequently, the name of media lawyer Alvaro Pascotto has appeared on the documents of corporate recipients of funds donated to support Rawat's activities.

Rawat has established a formal network of 'major donors', who fund his lifestyle via bank deposits, by making him (or companies he controls) a shareholder in their businesses. The 'major donors' are invited to special conferences with Rawat and also receive front row seats and premium accommodation at his larger events. At one stage in the late 1990s, the major donors numbered over 400 but the global membership of the major donors group has fallen significantly as a result of both disaffection from Rawat and personal financial loss in the 2008 economic down turn.

Prem Rawat has been gifted shares in a number of businesses and corporations owned by his followers, the two most notable are the U.S.-based Sterling Educational Media and the Deltek Corporation. Sterling Educational Media is the trading name of Amtext an academic book buying business which reportedly underwrote the building of Rawat's US$ 25 million mansion. The founder of the company, Charles Nathan is said to have gifted 100 per cent of the company shares to Rawat. Don Delaski an eccentric accountant and philanthropist who created the Deltek company also gifted shares to Rawat with totals worth US$10 to US$ 20 million dollars transferred to Rawat via a corporate vehicle named the Onae Trust. Onae Trust has the same service address as the SEVA Corporation of America.

Many of Prem Rawat's former premie aides and financial advisors have become disaffected from him; their testimony provides evidence of the assets that Rawat enjoys. These include:

- His home, a US$ 25 million mansion at 31334 Anacapa View Drive, Malibu Beach, California (which replaced an earlier one on the same site). The mansion was re-built (chiefly by premies) in the late 1990s. Rawat controls via the SEVA Corporation nine other land titles in Los Angeles, with total land values of more than US$ 2 million.
- His Australian mansion is on 5 acres at 236 Jesmond Road in the Brisbane suburb of Fig Tree Pocket.
- He also has mansions in Reigate, Surrey (UK), Mauritius and Delhi, and a luxury apartment in South America.
- In 2007, a Gulfstream G550, at US$ 60 million the world's most expensive executive jet. Rawat's G550 is 'dry leased' and requires expenditures exceeding US$ 300,000 a month in leasing and maintenance costs. In 2013, he upgraded to a G650, but in 2015, he downgraded from the G650 back to a G550.

- Numerous luxury vehicles (including a Jaguar with the Californian license plate ENTELECHY).
- A Stemme S10-VT aircraft
- A G103 Twin II glider
- A Bell 206L helicopter
- A 106-foot mega yacht, Serenity, valued at US$ 7 million, but sold in 2004 for something less that $US 4 million.

Prem Rawat has a preference for lavish accommodation. His backstage area at Ivory's Rock Conference Centre (Amaroo) is essentially a two-storey luxury apartment and his campsite there has a 'space age' barbecue which rises hydraulically with an elaborate 'command system'. His toilet in the same campsite has a bank of electronic controls, and in a previously acquired private jet – a 707 in the early 1980s – he had his followers installed a gold toilet.

Behind the Scenes

Prem Rawat lives a life that is at complete variance to the renunciate style that he once recommended for his followers. It is tempting to compare the way that Prem Rawat conducts his life with that of a wealthy and reclusive celebrity; however, Rawat's own self-image suggests something closer to a 'Captain of Industry' – someone for whom the rewards of decision-making brings an entitlement to Rolls-Royces, an executive jet, an ocean going 'mega yacht', a personal chef, a branded watch collection and a mansion on every continent.

Prior to the inception of the Internet, most criticism made of Prem Rawat had come from the mainstream media and centered on Rawat's lifestyle. This criticism began in the early 1970s, when the press drew attention to Prem Rawat's liking for Baskin Robbins ice cream, cowboy boots and luxury cars.

The first 'inside' reports on Prem Rawat's lifestyle came in the year 1979. Bob Mishler, who had been fired as the President of the US Divine Light Mission Incorporated in January 1977 claimed in a radio interview that Prem Rawat had put his (Rawat's) own financial well-being ahead of his mission. His mental and physical health were intimately tied to his materialism and over-eating and the strain of acting out his role even hospitalised him with an ulcer when he was fifteen years old.

And for a few months, we tried to change things, and what it really came down to was that Maharaj Ji was not willing to take the financial risk involved. I had set up a programme to use the tax-free income that he was getting in gifts from the premies to create a programme of investments for him, so that ultimately he could live off his invested capital and no need to have the premies keep making incredible contributions to him – not need to have Divine Light Mission give so much of its money to him to maintain his lifestyle. . . . The programme never really got off the ground, because he was too worried about it. It meant that he would have to really compromise his lifestyle.

'By the time I left', Mishler said, 'he must have had at least three Mercedes, a couple of Rolls-Royces, and least three or four other luxurious automobiles in the 30 or 40,000 dollar range . . . Materialism is like a disease with him'.

Mike Finch writes of Rawat's first years in England: *I drove him to Harrod's often, which was his favourite destination, and several times we were there all day. He had a fascination for the watches department* (Without the Guru). Jos Lammers writes of Rawat's tours of Europe in the mid 1970s:

'He didn't have contact with the premies that welcomed him to their country, but if he went to see the city, which he liked to do, they had to come along. To pay. The watches in Switzerland, I still remember well. One shop after another. Together with the national general secretary I followed the small group that hung around Maharaj ji like a cloud on his tour of the shiny showcases. We didn't see much of him at all. We heard his voice though when he asked a shop assistant to get a watch from behind the bullet-proof glass. When he liked what he saw, Bob Mishler signaled in our direction. Pay. While we were still finishing up doing that, the cloud had already drifted into the next jewelry shop'. – (p. 69 Abandoned Roads)

Mishler also claimed Rawat had a serious drinking problem, an accusation corroborated by many others:

'Rawat drank heavily, to the point that he was stewed every evening. There was more than one occasion where we had to carry him to bed after he had passed out'.

By 1976, Rawat (then still known as Guru Maharaj Ji) had degenerated physically to the point that he was having these fainting spells, and we had had it diagnosed and found out that there was no physical cause for it, it was psychosomatic. It was just obvious that he was living with too much stress. He hated to hear about the premies. I felt that this burden of playing God for people was killing him, as well as being injurious to the premies, and we had agreed essentially to change things.

Mishler's claims had little effect on premies at the time, as few read the newspapers or listened to the radio programmes on which they were aired. Other close followers have confirmed Rawat's greed.

Prior to Mishler's departure from DLM, Canadian Michael Dettmers was appointed his deputy, Dettmer's was summarily sacked by Rawat as Mishler's deputy (despite Rawat having no legal power over DLM employment issues) but immediately given the position of Rawat's personal manager, a post he held until 1987. Dettmer's position as Rawat's 'right hand' brought with it the effective position of Divine Light Mission 'International President', a role previously accorded to Bob Mishler on the basis of his holding the joint positions of US DLM President and Prem Rawat's personal assistant. As the various National Divine Light Missions were separately constituted under differing legal regimes, no legally constituted positions of 'International President' in fact ever existed. Once Mishler had left, the role of President of the US DLM was downgraded, none of the subsequent incumbents ever having organisational primacy over Michael Dettmers.

Mishler died in a helicopter accident in 1979. But in 2002, Dettmers (by then no longer working for Rawat) went public with his recollections of their time together. He supported Mishler's view that Rawat was 'an alcoholic'. *When he gets drunk,* he stated, *he becomes very negative. He becomes abusive in the sense that he verbally trashes certain people.* Rawat, Dettmers added, had also been in the habit of smoking pot *four or five nights a week.* Dettmers arranged with premie women to provide Rawat with sexual favours. The women, he said, were invariably promptly dropped, which resulted in 'upset and confusion'.

According to Dettmers and other close aides from this period such as Michael Donner, North American DLM National Co-ordinator, Prem Rawat's lifestyle was shielded from premies by a system known as X-Rating. 'X-Rated' premies were those 'cleared' to become privy to Rawat's drinking, drug-taking, cigarette-smoking and sexual liaisons. But they were to keep their knowledge of these activities from Rawat's other devotees (most of whom were on low incomes or living monastic lifestyles – and frequently both).

'After a while', Dettmers said, *I concluded that there was a strong correlation between his failing mission and the fact that he was slightly inebriated, if not out-and-out drunk, five out of seven days of every week for years on end.* After twelve years as his right hand man, Dettmers left Rawat's service in 1987.

Although premies are not generally appraised of the extent of his assets, Rawat has never tried to hide that he lives very well. Most of Rawat's remaining followers believe he more than deserves his lifestyle, indeed some even express gratitude for the opportunity to give him money and gifts, believing the 'Knowledge' he has given them is priceless – something he has told them again and again.

The level of care afforded Prem Rawat by his personal staff, who must always strive to be impeccable, is exceptional and those working in the Rawat residences endeavour to move any object that Rawat might touch as close as possible to where he might be passing, to reduce his levels of exertion. According to a 2002 newspaper article, a team of women regarded as especially trustworthy 'shower and meditate' before scrubbing clean every inch of the backstage area used by Prem Rawat at the Ivory's Rock Conference Centre in Australia when he is in residence there.

The meat for Rawat's Amaroo barbecues comes from a calf chosen by premies as 'the one with the nicest nature' of the herd and is massaged before being slaughtered, to ensure maximum tenderness. The wood for the barbecue is stacked, with excruciating neatness, over several hours – including a heart-shaped hollow in the middle of the pile.

Sources of Criticism

Prem Rawat has been able to ride out media criticism of his lifestyle because the vast majority of his followers have simply not acknowledged it. Over time however a canon of more serious allegations has served to raise doubts, not only about Prem Rawat personally but also about the veracity of his teaching and the validity of the organisations that support him. The most consistent and seemingly unshakeable allegation is that Prem Rawat is a charismatic leader of a harmful cult.

Criticism of Prem Rawat has come from four broad sources:

- Family members of his devotees, who believe their loved ones have been exploited and 'brainwashed'.
- Media. Originally media criticism centered around Rawat's luxurious lifestyle and the attempted murder of an activist by a senior devotee in 1974. Since 2001, the media critique of Prem Rawat has become more comprehensive.
- Cult experts and psychologists, who claim Prem Rawat heads a personality cult.
- Former followers.

The first criticisms of Prem Rawat surfaced almost as soon as he had arrived in the West. Newspapers published stories sceptical of his claims to godhood, pointing to his ostentatious lifestyle and rapid accumulation of assets.

The Millennium '73 event, and its ensuing debts, created media interest which even reached to national magazines such as *Newsweek*. Following the Millennium fiasco, a mahatma named Fakiranand assisted by an American premie, carried out a near fatal attack on one of Rawat's media critics, a journalist named Pat Halley. ('Mahatmas' were Rawat's senior disciples and were regarded as holy men.) The attack created ugly headlines, as did a mass murder by a premie in Tallahassee, Florida, the following year. Michael Donner was a senior officer of the U.S. Divine Light Mission at the time of the Fakiranand attack. In

2002, he revealed that Prem Rawat, while ostensibly co-operating with the authorities over the Halley attack, had in fact ordered that Fakiranand should leave the United States, before any charges could be brought.

During 1976, Bob Mishler, a founding member of the US Divine Light Mission, and at the time President of the U.S. organisation, attempted to persuade Prem Rawat to devote less energy to accumulating assets and to scale down the personal 'idol worship' (as he described it) that Rawat was insisting upon. Rawat refused, and in January 1977, Mishler (who had often lived under the same roof as Rawat up to that point) was fired and parted company with Rawat and his organisations.

In 1979, Mishler spoke to the media after the Jonestown massacre when newspapers were interested in stories about cults. He claimed that Rawat had undergone a 'tremendous psychological deterioration' since 1971. Whilst the 'Perfect Master' had, he claimed, insisted on a renunciate lifestyle for many of his devotees, he had hidden his own growing opulence, drinking alcohol, anxiety and louche lifestyle. Mishler also drew attention to Rawat's bullying of his family and devotees and made public mention of his drinking:

He himself had tremendous problems of anxiety which he combated with alcohol . . . Unlike what he advocates, he is not capable of dealing with it by means of meditation. He ends up drinking excessively in order to cope with the stress. It was very sad to see him drinking himself into a stupor day after day.

By early afternoon, on a typical day, he was already drinking. And he drank heavily, not just beer or wine – he drank cognac, and he drank it to the point that he was stewed every evening. There was more than one occasion where we had to pick him up and carry him to bed after he had passed out . . . He used to have fainting spells sometimes, because his blood pressure would be so high – and he would just black out. Things like this to me were indicative of some deeper problems'.

Mishler was also concerned about the plight of the ashram premies, who were living on the edge of destitution – really out of the result of policies that he [Prem Rawat] dictated. Ashram premies were becoming socially and culturally inept, and the victims of economic exploitation, just because of his gluttonous appetite.

Many people – not everyone, but many people – were becoming less capable as individuals rather than becoming more capable, as we had purported that they would be as a result of realising this Knowledge. There were people who were being essentially psychologically and economically exploited. And I would bring these things to his attention, and he wouldn't want to deal with it. He would put it off for weeks, months – sometimes just not deal with it at all – and he would go and get drunk instead, almost on a daily basis.

Mishler also revealed that Divine Light Mission's religious status (it had been classed as a religion by the U.S. Internal Revenue Service) was used as a cover to garner personal funds and assets for Rawat. These were the charges made by Michael Garson that the DLM had attacked only a few years before:

> He has all these material belongings . . . He would find ways to charge off things that we'd bought – for him – to various Divine Light Mission departments so that they could be hidden within our financial status.

> Consumerism is like a disease with him. He no sooner has the object of his desire, whether it's a new Maserati or Rolls Royce or whatever – Aston Martin – he's thinking about the next thing: it's got to be a helicopter, it's got to be a Grumman Gulfstream 2, it's got to be this or that.

Mishler also disclosed that Rawat was sometimes abusive to those around him, including his wife:

> 'He would just verbally assault her for, like, an hour – and she would be reduced to tears. And it would be terrible, because she really wasn't guilty – of anything. But he would play upon that . . . that kind of propensity she had to be vulnerable at that level'.

The Mishler claims created a brief flurry of media interest. But Mishler died in a helicopter accident shortly afterwards, and public interest in Prem Rawat died with him. Though there was occasional criticism over the next two decades by the media, church groups and cult observing psychologists,

Rawat managed to avoid prolonged scrutiny by keeping a low (indeed virtually non-existent) public profile for twenty years.

Then Came the Internet.

Ex-premie.org was born in 1996, and for the first time, ex-premies were able to rebuild old connections and share their experiences. Information flooded in, beginning with the Mishler media interviews, which an ex-premie patiently transcribed from old audio tapes.

Considerable interest was created in 2001, when Michael Dettmers – Bob Mishler's successor as Prem Rawat's chief assistant – answered questions on an Internet Forum – both confirming and expanding on everything Mishler had claimed. Dettmers added that the 'Perfect Master' had instructed him to procure premie women to provide him with sexual favours. Rawat had quickly abandoned the women, he said, causing 'upset and confusion'.

Dettmers also described the process of X-Rating: where 'inner circle' premies were introduced to Rawat's lifestyle excesses but sworn to keep the information from the mass of premies. He also provided a description of how Rawat, whilst driving had caused the death of a cyclist in Delhi in the mid-1980s, and the subsequent arrangement that an Indian premie – a senior mahatma's house boy – took the blame.

In 2001, Prem Rawat's claim to a spiritual 'lineage' came under scrutiny and its authenticity was brought into doubt. Professor Ron Geaves, a long time devotee of Prem Rawat's confirmed Hans Rawat was part of the Advait Mat lineage from which the Rawat father and sons have sourced elements of their respective claims to spiritual authority in the Sant Mat traditions.

The issue raised on the ex-premie web site which caused Prem Rawat the most difficulty was the emotive subject of child sexual abuse. Mahatma Jagdeo, who had been one of Prem Rawat's closest advisers in the 1970s and 1980s, was claimed to have raped male and female children of premies. Some of the victims spoke out via the ex-premie web forums in 2000 and 2001.

Many of those still following Prem Rawat became deeply disillusioned when it emerged, that despite attempts by victims and their parents to alert Rawat to Jagdeo's paedophilia, Jagdeo had been left in a position of trust. Although Rawat's closest advisors and senior organisational officials were informed of Jagdeo's attacks over many years, Prem Rawat denied all knowledge of the issue prior to it being made public on the Internet. Jagdeo has never been brought to any trial and is apparently living freely in India.

Compounding this difficult phase, Prem Rawat's supporters put up web sites defaming Rawat's critics, characterising them variously as kidnappers, drug dealers and being mentally unstable, the latter being an attack returned to on various Elan Vital web sites in 2004.

In 2001, several Australian followers left Rawat, partly as a result of the 'trainings' that he had overseen at Amaroo and other places. It was reported that the trainings had been emotionally violent and manipulative, and that Rawat had 'descended into violent rages on small provocation'. One of the participants later wrote of his experience:

'I finally grasped that Maharaji thrives on the mixed message: independence/devotion, honesty/secrecy, trust yourself/trust the master. One half of the mixed message empowers and expands, the other half intimidates and reduces; one half provokes love, the other half fears; one half liberates, the other half enslaves. The mixed message thus strategically confuses'.

Critics of Rawat also complain, of his 'exclusive' meditation techniques, that they are available from hundreds of other teachers, and are from books. The unduly harsh treatment meted out to ashram residents when the ashrams were closed in 1982 and 1983 also comes in for criticism, chiefly from those who endured it.

Prem Rawat's personal philosophy has come in for as many attacks as his actions – most notably his belittling of human relationships and his claim to be the only source of real and true love in the world. Many ex-followers believe this undermining of 'normal' relationships has been either a deliberate or perhaps unconscious ploy to bolster his apparent 'personality cult', it certainly adds credence to the views about Rawat's own dysfunctionality. Key to the development of what serves as the Rawat 'cult of personality' are the claims to divinity, which Rawat expressly made in the early part of his career. These claims no longer form part of Rawat's public presentation and the blame for the 'misapprehensions' about Prem Rawat's 'godhood' is placed upon Rawat's first followers, but Prem Rawat has never addressed the issue directly and regularly states that he is in fact a unique person who can empower others in a way only possible if he is divine. He continually gives mixed messages.

The institutional burning of Divine Light Mission's magazines and promotional materials at the end in the early 1980s suggests to some sceptics that the organisation is prone to 'rewriting' its past, and to secrecy. The impression of secrecy was strengthened when darshan (foot-kissing) lines were revived in the late 1990s, but with Rawat instructing that the news be kept from outsiders and media. Elan Vital meetings, workshops and written materials now emphasise the ethic of 'confidentiality', and for the most part, information is now only shared among premies on a 'need to know' basis.

Many ex-premies see the sex and money scandals associated with Prem Rawat as only symptomatic of a larger problem – that of the emotional manipulation of vulnerable people. Most cult observing psychologists class Elan Vital as an 'exploitative cult', alongside Scientology and ISKCON (the Hare Krishna movement).

In one of his 1979 interviews, Bob Mishler said he believed Prem Rawat employed systematic 'thought reform'. He added:

'I don't even think that he is sincerely wrong. I think that he is deliberately deceiving people'.

Prem Rawat's Claim to Spiritual Ascendency.

Although Prem Rawat and his supporting organisations now deny the religious content of Rawat's earlier teaching, there has been no attempt by Rawat to renounce the process of religious ascendancy that saw him titled 'Guru Maharaj Ji'. Indeed without his inheritance of his religious ascendancy, it seems certain that Prem Rawat would have had no ability to create the basis of his success as the teenage 'Perfect Master' of Divine Light Mission and without that devoted following, it is certain that Prem Rawat would have had no success as a secular 'inspirational speaker' of 'Elan Vital' nor as the internationally respected Master of Peace or 'Words of Peace Global' he is trying to become.

The Teacher

Since the age of eight, Prem Rawat has claimed that he can show every human being the peace that *you are looking for, within yourself,* this peace being accessed via initiation into the practice of 'Knowledge'. In the early years of his 'mission', Prem Rawat employed the system of initiation developed by his father, in which the ritualistic transmission of meditation techniques was carried out by intermediaries who were initially supposed to be advanced 'great souls' called mahatmas, and later referred to as 'initiators', and were chosen from Rawat's most dedicated Western devotees and were believed to have some spiritual cachet and finally called 'instructors' and were no longer expected to have extra spiritual attainments.

Currently, Prem Rawat maintains an exclusive right to show the techniques of meditation and even forbids his followers from talking in any depth about 'Knowledge'. To learn about the meditation, interested people are instructed to watch videos of Prem Rawat speaking. The system is one in which there is a single teacher, Prem Rawat, and all others are students, to whom Prem Rawat ministers in didactic fashion.

The Perfect Master: An Ideology

By what authority does Prem Rawat claim qualification as a 'teacher', why is he the sole source of 'learning' and what special understanding did he possess at age eight that entitled him to embark upon the role of 'Guru'?

When Prem Rawat was eight years old, his father, self-proclaimed 'Perfect Master' Hans Ram Singh Rawat, known as Shri Hans Ji Maharaj, died. Despite general expectations that the eldest Rawat son, Bal Bhagwan Ji, would become the new master and despite much debate within the Rawat family and the senior followers of Shri Hans, the mantle of 'Perfect Master' or 'Satguru' was passed by some process of agreement to the youngest son, Prem Pal Singh Rawat then known as *Balyogeshwar* (born king of the yogis) or *Sant Ji* in the family circle.

Throughout the 1970s and early 1980s followers of the then Guru Maharaj Ji, were taught that there is always a Perfect Master walking the Earth. This perfect master is supposed to possess some special powers and is even considered to be God in human form. The reason for the perfect master's presence on earth is to reveal the sacred 'Knowledge' to human kind and thus offer salvation from a presupposed human condition of *suffering*, a condition often believed to exist by the young. Furthermore, all the past perfect masters are alive now and all their powers are united in the one person and power, Prem Rawat and a new world is coming:

'Jesus is living now, Ram is living now, Krishna is living now, Buddha is living now, but they all have been united. All their powers have been united into one very, very, very, very powerful power. And when this power spreads its hand, you know, something is going to happen. All the things that are going on wrong in this world are going to be abolished'. – The Sayings of Guru Maharaj Ji

Prem Rawat as Guru Maharaj Ji was claimed to be the perfect master of the time. Prem Rawat explicitly taught in his perfect master ideology that such great religious leaders and icons as Jesus Christ, Krishna and Buddha were also perfect masters and each in their own time revealed the same 'Knowledge' as that taught by Prem Rawat. From this point of view, the Perfect Master and his 'Knowledge' are considered in themselves not to be a religion but rather the source of and inspiration for all true religion.

Amongst the followers of Prem Rawat, the ideology was further developed to incorporate a critique of established religions which were judged as mere 'beliefs', lacking the one true motivating spiritual 'experience':

- that it is possible to 'know God' rather than just believe in God
- that belief is inferior to experience
- that religion is merely concerned with belief

These propositions provide the rationale behind Prem Rawat's much repeated claim that he teaches an experience and not a set of beliefs or a religion.

Once these filters of ideology and proposition are made explicit, it becomes easier to understand how Prem Rawat holds such complete control over all aspects of his teachings, the meditation and the organisations that support him.

Although Prem Rawat has publicly distanced himself from the perfect master ideology, understanding that ideology and the contexts in which it was previously presented is essential to answering the questions about Prem Rawat's qualification as a 'teacher', why is he the sole source of 'learning' and what special understanding he possessed on his assumption of the mantle of Satguru?

The perfect master ideology is by no means exclusively a Prem Rawat conception, it is common to many Indian belief systems and to New Age style beliefs in the West and was given some intellectual credibility by Aldous Huxley in his book *The Perennial Philosophy*. It is essentially a syncretic, and by allusion at least, mystical concept. The powers of the perfect master are rarely specified and although the 'living master' may be ascribed many fantastical qualities the process of transmission of his 'teaching' always remains vague. In this respect, Prem Rawat's story is typical of other perfect master ideologies.

To understand how the perfect master ideology provided Prem Rawat with his initial qualification as a teacher and how it continues to provide him with the authority to lead his followers it is useful to begin by asking, 'What exactly happened to Rawat at age eight when his father died? For instance, did some magical or divine power enter his body?' A belief that this was literally true was widely held by both Indian and Western followers in the 1970s, and Prem Rawat did nothing to dispel this belief. In fact, he told and retold a well-rehearsed story detailing the process and providing unusual and supernatural details including receiving instructions from the resurrected body of his father. A further compounding of the view of Prem Rawat's specialness is that the 'Knowledge' was considered to be intrinsically bound with Prem Rawat's person. He insisted upon this throughout his career.

This is the Knowledge that Jesus Christ gave, that Guru Nanak gave, that Krishna gave, that Ram gave, that Mohammed gave. And I am giving it. Supreme Knowledge. It is sacred. Top sacred! And it dwells within all of us. All human beings. And we are unable to know it without the help of the true master. – Prem Rawat, 11 August 1971

Because without Guru Maharaj Ji's Grace, you cannot understand Knowledge. – Prem Rawat, 7 January 1978 'you can experience the joy that is inside of you. And that transformation is not possible without Knowledge, and Knowledge is not possible without the Master'. – Prem Rawat, Long Beach, 5 December 1997

Whatever actually happened to Prem Rawat following his father's death, from the perspective of his followers and especially in relation to the authority that Prem Rawat holds over them, it is enough to note that many believed, and indeed many still believe, that Prem Rawat was divinely incarnated, manifested, and he is the embodiment of the formless Creator in a human form.

Krishna and Hinduism: An Abiding Reference

With the inception in 2002 of The Prem Rawat Foundation web site as the primary presentation of Prem Rawat's public image, the grounds seem to have been set for a total break with past imagery and Prem Rawat's transformation from Guru to 'inspirational speaker' made complete. However, Prem Rawat the 'inspirational teacher' continues to make reference in his speeches to supposed past perfect masters, the Hindu demigod Krishna and the Sant Mat Master Kabir.

The story of Krishna appears in an ancient scripture called the Bhagavad Gita, which is held by many to be the most sacred of Hindu religious writings. Within this scripture, Krishna reveals himself as the almighty creator of the universe, thus Krishna is characterised as an Avatar, a representation of God in human form. In the light of Prem Rawat's contention that he is not concerned with religion, the choice of Krishna and Hindu scripture as points of reference seems somewhat surprising, particularly given that the story of Krishna reintroduces the perfect master ideology. Even more contentious is the fact that in his earlier explicitly religious phase as Guru Maharaj Ji, Prem Rawat frequently dressed in a stylised Krishna costume while celebrating Hindu festivals with his followers.

Prem Rawat's consistent return to Hindu imagery begs a number of questions: Is Prem Rawat suggesting that Krishna really existed? Is he, as he sometime seems to be, comparing himself with Krishna? Is this a surreptitious attempt to introduce a religious theme where to be explicit has been deemed not 'business savvy'? It is difficult not to conclude that Prem Rawat is making an unequivocal link between himself as a revealer of 'Knowledge' and Krishna who reveals himself to be 'God'. Prem Rawat's desire to make this link should not be a surprise, it was explicit in the earlier and more successful days of his 'mission' and to reassert his 'lineage' would certainly serve to maintain his position as absolute and unquestioned spiritual leader of his remaining followers and the effective head of the organisations that support him.

A Tradition Is Passed On

Prem Rawat is a child of post-Imperial rule India, he was born in 1957, just ten years after independence from Britain. His schooling was in the English style and while his father pursued the very Indian career of 'religious teacher', the aspirations of the Rawat family seem to have been strongly informed by middle class Anglo/Indian attitudes. Prem was not only his father's favourite son, he was also a favourite of his father's followers and crucially of certain senior mahatmas. The conferring of his father's 'guru' mantle onto the eight-year-old Prem in 1966 was as much a political decision within the Divine Light Mission as it was a religious consequence.

Prem Rawat's work and mission were inherited in 1966 from his father, Shri Hans Ji Maharaj.

Hans Rawat began his career as a guru in the 1920s, in what is now Pakistan and began preaching in Delhi in 1930. Hans Rawat rejected India's caste system, and India's Brahmins (the priestly caste) tended to ignore him, as did Western-educated Indians. Hans Rawat placed great emphasis on the experience of the 'Knowledge' meditation techniques and little on rituals or learning. His devotees were chiefly from the urban middle classes.

Like his son after him, Hans Rawat laid down the three daily aspects of a devotee's life: satsang (sessions where premies gathered to talk of their experiences of 'Knowledge' and their devotion to their master), service (selfless voluntary work for the master), and meditation (upon the four techniques of 'Knowledge'). A fourth aspect – darshan, or seeing the master – was an occasional 'extra' and highly prized.

Hans Rawat established his promotional organisation, Divine Light Mission, in India in 1960. After a career lasting more than three decades, Hans Ji died in 1966.

According to former US Divine Light Mission President, Bob Mishler, Hans Rawat's widow had wanted her eldest son (now known as Satpal Maharaj) to inherit her husband's mantle. However, Mishler says, a group of mahatmas (senior devotees) loyal to Prem, her youngest son, crowned and enthroned him in the midst of discussions – thus pre-empting any decision by the family.

Prem Rawat claims to have been nominated by his father as his successor, by means of a letter written shortly before Hans Rawat's death, although this document has never been produced.

Claims that Hans Rawat bequeathed six million devotees to Prem have never been verified and in any event, the Indian adherents of both Hans and Prem Rawat should not be seen as an homogenous group, nor even as followers of a single teaching. Hans Rawat may have been the favourite guru of many Indian citizens but other traditions and practices, both local and regional in character, are likely to have informed their spiritual and philosophical outlook. In contrast, the Western Mission of Prem Rawat was defined by its character of exclusive attachment to its master.

Prem Rawat inherited the role of 'Perfect Master' at the age of eight. It was very much a part-time role for five years or so, whilst he pursued his schooling, at the Catholic St Joseph's Academy in Dehra Dun, now the capital of Uttarakhand state.

By 1969, several Westerners had visited Prem Rawat at Prem Nagar Ashram in Haridwar and had been taught the 'Knowledge' meditation techniques. In October of that year, a senior disciple, Mahatma Gurucharnanand, was sent to London to proselytise amongst the Indian expatriate community.

In 1970, Rawat, at the age of thirteen, held a massive public event he called the 'Peace Bomb' at India Gate, Delhi. A million people attended. This programme marked the peak of his popularity.

The Young Guru Maharaj Ji goes West

In 1971, some six months before his fourteenth birthday, Prem Rawat (Guru Maharaj Ji) travelled to England in the company of Mahatma Gurucharanand, ostensibly to follow up on Gurucharanand's earlier evangelism amongst Hindus in London. Supported by a few 'hippie' followers, Rawat gained some exposure within disaffected youth. Buoyed by this success Rawat applied for and was granted a visa to visit the United States after much waiting round in the US Consulate by Rawat, Bihari Singh and Mike Finch, who handled the bureaucratic badgering. Within months, further young refugees from the dying hippie movement had been recruited and a Divine Light Mission organisation able to widely promote Rawat was in existence. What followed was three years of considerable expansion of the promotion of Prem Rawat and his Western Divine Light Mission.

Prem Rawat (then known as Guru Maharaj Ji) first visited the West, to the surprise of a tiny band of Western followers, during his school holidays in June 1971. After a month in London, he went to the US west coast.

At the end of 1971, an organisation called Divine Light Mission Incorporated was registered in the United States as a non-profit Church, with Guru Maharaj Ji listed as its chief minister. A separate Divine Light Mission was created as a charity in the United Kingdom in 1972 and subsequently other Divine Light missions were created in Australia, South Africa and Canada, as well as in several European and South American countries. Rawat's senior Indian disciples – saffron-robed 'mahatmas' – were sent to support the fledgling organisations and a system of ashrams (houses where Rawat's devotees followed a monastic rule) was instigated.

At age fourteen, against his mother's wishes, Guru Maharaj Ji left school and in 1972, once again travelled westward where he attracted an increasing number of followers. At a single event in Montrose Colorado, 2,000 people were initiated into the 'Knowledge', according to Divine Light Mission statements at that time. The exact number of new followers during this period is unknown, although by 1975 the US DLM was claiming over 50,000 initiates.

His mother, Mata Ji, as she was known, and her three older sons known as the Holy Family duly followed Prem Rawat to the West. Within the evolving quasi hippified Hindu belief system of the Western Divine Light Mission Prem Rawat's brothers were considered incarnations of the three aspects of the supreme Hindu deity, while Prem embodied the whole though this was hardly a system developed with Jesuit rigour.

Amongst some premies, the eldest brother, Bal Bhagwan Ji (now known as Satpal Maharaj) was supposedly Vishnu, the 'operator' of the Universe. He was also claimed to be Jesus Christ. The second brother, Raja Ji, was supposedly Brahma, the 'creator' – as well as being the 'king of the world'. And the third, Bhole Ji, was meant to be Shiva, the 'destroyer'.

Guru Maharaj Ji himself was considered to be the Satguru or Perfect Master of the time. According to the Divine Light Mission belief system, there is always a perfect master who comes to Earth to reveal the 'Knowledge of all knowledges'. Jesus, Buddha, Krishna, and Rama were all claimed to be have been perfect masters, as was Prem Rawat's father, Hans Rawat and his guru, Swarupanand as well.

By the end of 1972, there were 45 Divine Light Mission centres across the United States catering to a claimed 15,000 members. The national headquarters was in Denver, Colorado. Growth was very fast. Early the following year, one author noted:

> The way Maharaj Ji's converts kept multiplying was almost unbelievable. By spring of 1973, there were 480 Divine Light Centres around the world and in every continent. The US membership had now grown to 35,000. By the end of the year, US membership had increased to 50,000. Similar patterns were observed around the West. – Those

Curious New Cults in the 1980s by William J. Petersen, pp. 149–150.

In 1974, Guru Maharaj Ji, then aged sixteen, was living in a luxury property, at Malibu Beach, California, and in May 1974, he married twenty-five-year-old Marolyn Johnson, an American airline stewardess and a premie after conducting an affair known only to his inner circle. His new secret lifestyle included meat-eating and drunkenness. The marriage was very much against the wishes of Prem Rawat's mother and eldest brother, and his new lifestyle was unacceptable to his family and Indian DLM administrators and mahatmas who believed he had been corrupted by his inner circle of Western devotees. Professor Tandon and Mata Ji even tried 'to rescue and free him' with the help of the Malibu police on the night of 23 November 1974. Donner, Dettmers and Mishler were at the centre of deceiving the premies about Rawat's lifestyle while his mother and his deceased father's senior devotees were telling the truth as the trio acknowledged years later. The dispute culminated in Mata Ji and two of Rawat's brothers and the Indian DLM administrators and mahatmas disinheriting him and deposing him as Satguru. In India, Mata Ji crowned Bal Bhagwan Ji (Satpal Maharaj) as the new 'Guru Maharaj Ji' leaving him the option of repenting and returning to the family but not as Satguru.

Virtually, all of the Indian premies went with Mata Ji and Bal Bhagwan Ji (who, after a protracted court case, won control of the name and property of Divine Light Mission in India). Outside of India, the split had little effect: premies wrote it off as a Prem Rawat lila – literally 'game of God', something which was beyond their mortal understanding.

Rawat renamed his wife Durga Ji, after an Indian goddess, and premies were told to call her 'Mom' and embarrassingly, many did. Over the next few years, four children were born to Prem and Marolyn Rawat – two boys and two girls.

From the early to mid-1970s period, Rawat had a high public profile. There was some praise – he received the keys to several U.S. cities though this is a meaningless honour and one such ceremony caused a lot of damaging media when an anarchist threw a shaving cream pie in Rawat's face and some high-status premies then tried to beat him to death with a hammer. Rawat was invited to speak to an extreme right wing lobby group at a bi-centenary dinner – hardly a high point on his resumé. The overwhelming numbers of media stories were highly critical. There were mostly sceptical articles in the press (especially the alternative press), and some well-publicised cases where premies were kidnappedy and 'deprogrammed' by distraught parents.

A sizeable minority of premies throughout North and South America, Europe, Africa and Australia moved into ashrams (group homes where a monastic rule was followed) and forswore drugs, alcohol, sex, 'idle talk or gossip', relationships and money. These rules were not always obeyed to the letter. Although many former residents today believe the ashrams deprived them of a normal youth, some others acknowledge that they did at least remove them from the era's drug culture though leaving the drug culture was a normal progression in non-DLM young people of the times. In fact, according to Rawat himself, the rules were hardly ever observed:

> Because I know, quite well that ashram rules, ashram guidelines, are really not being followed – that is an understatement. People are doing whatever they want to, you know. They go out; people go out, maybe get drunk. That is the time they should be sitting down and doing meditation. They come home to the ashram, they're zonked, and then they get up in the morning and say, 'Guru Maharaj Ji, I'm confused' – The Frankfurt Conference November 1976.

In this period of furious activity for Prem Rawat's devotees, numerous sub-organisations came and went:

> The World Peace Corps (WPC), begun in the West in 1972 and run by Rawat's brother Raja Ji, built stages for Rawat's programmes, painted newly rented ashrams and formed security teams for Rawat's protection. In London, the WPC bugged what it considered rival power bases within the Divine Light Mission and even undertook marching drills, taking on a decidedly paramilitary character. The WPC eventually drifted out of existence, although its culture of self-importance and propensity for intimidation was transmitted to the personal security team that became attached to Prem Rawat.

In 1973, Rawat announced the creation of Divine United Organization. This was supposedly a worldwide philanthropy project that would feed the world. Rawat's DUO Proclamation was as grandiose, as his acompanying speech was confused and incoherent.

Whereas, Knowledge of the aim of human life is being revealed to all people of the world by the living perfect master and spiritual head of Divine Light Mission, Paramhans Satgurudev Shri Sant Ji Maharaji, thus eliminating the cause of ignorance and misery. Therefore, the people who have experienced the Knowledge of Shri Santji Maharaj, with full awareness of the difficulties of living without knowing the aim of human life, are compelled to reach out to the rest of the struggling humanity to spread the solution to strife and suffering by a commitment to work in all fields of endeavour for the elevation of humanity, manifesting an exemplary alternative to be known as the Divine United Organization or DUO.

Numerous small companies did adopt the DUO name although few had any legal relationship to each other. Most existed only on paper or ceased to trade within a few years. DUO was the name of Prem Rawat's Delhi base, which he managed to retain control of in the feud with his brother Sat Pal. The Indian DUO has recently (2005) been renamed Raj Vidya Kender.

The World Welfare Association was supposedly founded to bring practical, charitable relief to the underprivileged – though it, too, quickly overreached itself and folded.

These various projects were funded by tithing through the 'Active Membership Programme' (AMP), through the collected wages of the ashram premies and through various business ventures such as 'Divine Sales', which sold second-hand goods collected door-to-door. Special cash collections raised hundreds of thousands of dollars for gifts to Rawat, such as a new Aston Martin car in 1976, and later the first of his many jets. 'Darshan lines' – a ritual where premies queued to kiss Rawat's feet and deposit a gift of cash or goods – also raised large sums.

Following the legal changes which saw Prem Rawat gain control of substantial personal wealth, in 1977 he embarked on a reassertion of his role as Guru, restating the importance of devotion to the 'Master' in the Hindu Bhakti tradition. As part of this restatement of devotion, the ashram system was reinvigorated after a period of decline; the restrictive life in an ashram was codified in the 'Ashram Manual' which required that members must 'observe a vow of poverty . . . personally possessing nothing'. All of Rawat's followers, even those with family commitments, were subject to stronger encouragement to enter the ashram system.

In 1979, the acquisition and customisation of a Boeing 707 for Prem Rawat's exclusive use became a dominant drive within the then Divine Light Mission. A 1961 vintage aircraft was acquired for US$ 1 million from an American Football Team. A business operation called the DECA Project based in Florida was set up with ashram residents drafted into all aspects of work on the plane itself as well as project management, most significantly – fund raising.

Like other expansive projects undertaken by Rawat's followers, DECA had no beneficial impact on the Rawat movement or its participants; however, DECA did provide a model for income generation, which was free of the costs and other considerations of the ashram system. Although dependant on the ashrams for its existence, DECA, or at least the funding expertise that it generated, can be seen as the development which allowed Rawat to dissolve the ashram system in 1982 and 1983 and to still maintain an income flow to his organisations.

Within the DECA facility, a range of activities took place that were focused on Prem Guru Maharaj Ji's interests – servicing of his Rolls Royces was undertaken there. The financial structure seems to have lacked commonly expected controls, and there have been accusations of inadequate and illegal work practices. Work on the Boeing 707 was completed in 1980 but the plane was only briefly used by Guru Maharaj Ji before being sold to Maharishi Mahesh Yogi, who had it flown to Malaysia where it rapidly fell into disuse because its emissions exceeded legal limits.

The DECA business sought development as a corporate jet customisation operation but proved unviable and was soon sold, being renamed Aircraft Modular Products (AMP). Some of Prem Rawat's followers gained employment with AMP but the company had no other links with Rawat or his organisations. AMP prospered and was sold for over US$ 100 million in 1998 by its then owner Roger Koch who had begun work as an unpaid premie volunteer in DECA in 1978. Roger made a US$ 5.5 million donation to Rawat in 2008 (though he was never informed how it was spent) and this gave him Major Donor status and the chance to get to know the Rawats better. In 2011, he apostatised and wrote a highly entertaining story of his journey.

It is unclear what happened to the receipts from the sale of the Boeing 707 and the DECA business. There appears to have been a chronic incapacity within Divine Light Mission to protect either its interests as a charity or the interests of those who voluntarily assisted it. Numerous business operations started by Prem Rawat's followers seem to have become absorbed into a quasi-corporate structure ostensibly to the benefit of Divine Light Mission, only to be 'demerged' to the sole benefit of subsequent owners.

Those individuals who achieved ownership of businesses started under the aegis of Divine Light Mission frequently retained close personal contact with Prem Rawat, and Rawat appears to have benefited financially from those contacts.

Maharaji and Elan Vital, the 1980s Image Makeover

The many contradictions of the Western Divine Light Mission inevitably led to conflict not only for the organisation but also for its adolescent 'leader'. As Prem Rawat grew to adulthood, he looked to fashion an image for himself and the mission that was more to his liking. The religious aspects of the early days became an encumbrance for Rawat and he sought the creation of an organisation that could deliver him as the 'branded' product. Spiritual teacher Guru Maharaj Ji became Maharaji 'humanitarian giver of a practical way to peace', this image served Rawat from the late 1970s through to the early 1990s when the 'inspirational speaker' label was subtly introduced.

Although it exists to this day in India as part of the Raj Vidya Kender organisation, at Maharaji's (Prem Rawat's) instruction the Divine Light Mission ashram structure in Western countries was dissolved during 1982 and 1983. According to former DLM administrators, Maharaji was becoming concerned about the financial liabilities that loomed as ashram residents aged, became unemployed and required increasing medical and dental care.

The closures caused considerable dislocation to many ashram premies, who had abandoned university, employment training and families to serve Prem Rawat. In one address, Maharaji complained angrily of learning that a U.S. ashram had handed each of its former residents US$ 100, with which to start new lives. A few ashram residents got subsistence wage jobs as Rawat's personal servants – valets, cleaners, gardeners and the like. A few others were kept on as administrators or as instructors (formerly 'initiators' formerly 'mahatmas'). But most began new lives in 'the world' – something which few were psychologically or practically prepared.

During the 1980s, Maharaji effected other transitions. The term mahatma had already been largely replaced with the term 'initiator' – referring to the task of 'initiating' new followers into the meditational practice that Maharaji calls 'Knowledge' in a ritualised Knowledge Session. All the 'mahatmas' had been Indian nationals except one British national, Mahatma Param Saphlanand but except for a handful these left Rawat and returned to the more familiar environment of the Indian ashrams, now controlled by the replacement Perfect Master, Satpal Maharaj. Rawat appointed increasing numbers of Americans and Europeans as initiators. The title 'initiator' was then dropped in favour of 'instructor'.

The closing of the ashrams and the other changes Rawat had made had halved the number of Westerners involved in Rawat's knowledge. Without enough funds to maintain full-time initiators and with no ashrams to use as their bases, Rawat decided he must heve been completely mistaken when he proclaimed that to be an initiator was a full-time job and it could not be done by part-timers. In 1986, he began a series of part-time instructors training conference in San Antonio, Texas, in 1986. These conferences, like all of Rawat's meetings, were mainly Rawat talking and everyone listening. Hundreds of instructors were soon appointed and were on hand for the Rejoice events that began in 1987 and continued up to 1993 in which Rawat taught an altered form of meditation techniques and tried to restart his following. While these were relatively successful, he has never been able to restore his pre-1983 number of followers.

In late 1980s and early 1990s, Maharaji to and froed with part-time and full-time initiators and no initiators, hiring and firing initiators at will. He had taken over the teaching of the meditation techniques exclusively. In 2000, he introduced his computer-based presentation of the techniques of Knowledge. It soon began to be used to teach the Knowledge techniques to new students. Rawat has always appeared to believe that only he has the charisma and skills and power to spread the Knowledge, he or a machine. Sometimes he tells his followers they are unnecessary and even a problem, other times he says the opposite. But in the end, he has an insatiable need for money so the fund-raising always has to continue.

Now there can be a happy culmination of both by merely having an instructor's phone number on a card that you can give to an interested person.

So then came a time when I said 'Please you know do me a favour don't say anything just pass on a video or something'.

'When it is my ball, why do I need you?' But I'm saying I need that support and I need that help'.

'I'll tell you this story that happened with Shri Maharaj Ji'. There were a few premies, and they said, 'Maharaj Ji, you cannot function without us', you know, 'we helped you a lot'. And he said, 'Oh yeah? That's what you think? I'll tell you', he says, 'all of you stay here, and let me go out'. – And It Is Divine, Volume 2, Issue 5

'From the time of Shri Maharaji whether he was sitting by his instructors, whether he's giving an event, it always took a team, it took a team effort to do it so let's not con ourselves into thinking it doesn't take a team'.

Although the name continued to be attached to a United Kingdom-based charity until 1995, from the early 1980s onwards, the various nationally based Divine Light Missions were progressively renamed as Elan Vital. Prem Rawat said the name Elan Vital had been given to him by his father, in a dream. In addition to changing the name of the organisation, Prem Rawat ceased to use the name 'Guru Maharaj Ji' and instead had himself styled 'Maharaji'. Westerners hearing this term for the first time would quickly relate it to 'Maharaja' but would not realise that Maharaji himself translates it as the Ultimate Ruler, which certainly shows what he thinks of himself or what he aspires to.

Maharaji also instigated changes both to the presentation of his message and to his relationship to his followers. Whilst teaching that devotion was the path to a joyful, fulfilled life, he now publicly denied that he personally was divine, blaming the mahatmas for introducing this 'misunderstanding' in the 1970s. Around the world, the nightly gatherings, called satsang, at which premies described their experiences and sang devotional songs were abolished. Thereafter, premies only gathered at events attended by Rawat or to watch videos of Prem Rawat speaking. Premies were instructed to hand in their 'devotional' magazines, books and tapes, which were then destroyed.

Maharaji's views about premies' lifestyles remained unchanged despite the abolition of the ashrams. In an interview, Rawat's personal assistant, Michael Dettmers, said:

> Dettmers: *Even as late as '85 he was still very strict about being vegetarian and abstaining from sex. He was very strict about that and absolutely believed in it.*

Interviewer: *But didn't follow any of that himself?*

Dettmers: *Oh no, of course not.*

Michael Dettmers replaced the departing Bob Mishler in 1976 and had become Maharaji's personal assistant and Rawat's voice to the wider Divine Light Mission/Elan Vital. Dettmers managed Rawat's assets, personal affairs and 'presentation to the world' from 1975 till 1987. More than anyone else, Dettmers has provided detailed testimony of what Prem Rawat is really like.

Although unknown to all but a select few 'inner circle X-rated' followers, Prem Rawat was drinking and smoking cigarettes and marihuana regularly in private and by 1985 with an 'open marriage'. On an Internet forum on 17 December 2000, Dettmers wrote:

> He told me that there was a particular premie woman he had in mind, and he asked me to arrange that they meet, which I did. Soon, thereafter, he asked me to arrange a meeting with another woman. In the meantime, the first person was left high and dry wondering what was going on. He cut off communication with her, and her only recourse was to contact me . . .

After three such incidents, I told him that his reckless behaviour was backfiring, and that I did not have the time to take care of the negative consequences it produced. He responded by agreeing that I had more important things to handle for him than procuring women, and that he would now take care of that task himself – meaning that he simply delegated the task to someone who was more amenable to it. He continued to have numerous 'affairs' of which I am aware'.

Roger Koch reported that his final disillusionment came closer when he heard about the sexual conquest of an old acquaintance by Mr Rawat. The idea that Rawat could seduce anyone who wasn't a devoted premie is so ludicrous as to not require any thought.

Gail Benton, an instructor, had witnessed Maharaji's drinking, smoking and the fact that he had a mistress and never disclosed any of it to anyone. She drew the line over his drug taking and getting his aides to procure premie women for sex. She thought that *the Lord Incarnate who is giving the Knowledge of all knowledges to transcend worldly attachment* shouldn't be doing such things. Most people would have thought the drinking, smoking and mistress were enough.

Until their closure, the Divine Light Mission ashrams had served as local centres for promoting Prem Rawat. There appears to have been no planned replacement for this promotion function and on an ad hoc basis, promotion devolved to small national offices of Elan Vital. Until Prem Rawat claimed the role exclusively for himself or at least a video of himself, instructors (most of whom were only part-time) revealed the four meditation techniques (the 'Knowledge') to small numbers of 'aspirants'.

Instructors were also now the only people authorised to speak publicly about Maharaji and his teachings. This ruling was soon applied even to private conversations: Rawat instructed that premies should not tell new people about him or the 'Knowledge' – but instead 'take them to a video event'. These 'video events', held in small local halls with no or minimal 'low key' advertising – which began in the mid-1980s – were still the staple for 'coming together' and 'propagation' for twenty years but have been progressively superseded by the Internet.

One of Maharaji's senior instructors in this period was Jagdeo, one of the original mahatmas from India, who conducted special 'children's satsangs' throughout the West. Several premie children of this era (now grown) attest that Jagdeo raped or otherwise sexually abused them. Their parents have stated that they sent word to Rawat of the abuse and were ignored. Jagdeo's misdeeds against children were fairly well-known within senior Elan Vital circles at the time. Prem Rawat's critics believe it is difficult to credit his claim that he knew nothing of them. It is important to emphasise that there is no evidence of widespread systemic child abuse in Prem Rawat's supporting organisations. Indeed, Jagdeo is the only 'senior' offender who has come to light. But because the paedophilia reports were apparently ignored by Rawat or at least those who advised Rawat, when the reports did surface in 2000, they caused enormous damage to Prem Rawat's standing among the small number of premies who heard about it.

While the abuse of children appears thankfully to have been rare within the Rawat organisations, there have been many reports of abusive behaviours by Mahraji himself, mahatmas, initiators and administrators against adult devotees. In the 1970s and 1980s, there was clearly inadequate protection of vulnerable people within Divine Light Mission/Elan Vital and associated organisations.

One of Prem Rawat's most remarkable claims was that you could meditate on this word twenty-four hours a day, sleeping, driving, walking and presumably doing anything as everyone had been in the womb before birth. Two days before he was acclaimed as the new Satguru, the young Rawat denounced Pandits as hypocrites, because they could not chant mantras while asleep as he claimed you could meditate on the Holy Name he revealed. He did teach that though Knowledge was free, there was one group of people who couldn't meditate constantly but needed to be alone in a quiet place: mothers with young children. Maharaji loves cars so it is perfect for him that this meditation can be done driving as he explained in Denmark, 'Because you can be eating, you can be driving, you can be sleeping – I mean, that sounds a little peculiar but you can be sleeping – and still meditate on this Name. It's so fantastic. I mean, people talk about concentration. And for reasons such as driving race cars their concentration should be completely straight. (I'll tell you one thing. There is one car that has been given to me by a premie in Boston. It's a real fast car. And it really needs good concentration.) But when you start meditating on this Knowledge, you could be going a hundred miles an hour in rush hour without hitting a car. It's so good. It's so beautiful. But then there's the crazy mind'. It seems that only the crazy mind is preventing people driving 100 mph in rush hour traffic, such a shame the problems the mind causes. It's a scary thought. That fat little toad who had the muscles of a blancmange sitting on a cushion behind the wheel of a very fast car and finally feeling the power flowing through him as he presses his flabby foot on the accelerator pedal.

In her Ph.D. thesis, Lucy Dupertuis recorded that many 1970s premies worked in mundane repetitive jobs so that they could keep concentrating on their breath as much as possible. Belief in the possibility that this would have dramatic effects in expanding consciousness waned after some years and in the 1980s, Rejoice meetings an older Rawat told his followers to stop trying to constantly meditate and to cut back their formal meditation to one hour a day from the two they were supposed to do but which they aspired to but which many never attained. The effect of this decade attempting to obey Rawat's instructions to constantly meditate and working in menial jobs could have terrible effects on their life-long prosperity. Rawat has never given the slightest appearance of knowing anything about meditation.

There are no published studies of Prem Rawat's followers as practitioners of meditation; however, investigations of comparable practices have relevance and certainly raise concerns. There have been a number of studies of the practitioners of Transcendental Meditation as taught by the Mahareshi Mahesh Yogi. TM is comparable to Prem

Rawat's prescribed techniques, both have a transcendental objective, both are described in mystical terms separated from religious context and both involve techniques of inward concentration. In the case of TM, this involves concentration on a mantra while in the Prem Rawat process, concentration is upon a set of physiological processes.

Although TM, along with other meditational practices are ascribed numerous beneficial outcomes there is now a substantial body of evidence for negative outcomes, chief amongst these are psychological changes typified by depersonalisation and dissociation. The characteristics of these psychological states are familiar to many who formerly followed Prem Rawat and are particularly and unhappily familiar to family and friends of those who continue to pursue the Prem Rawat techniques.

Of studies carried out on meditators, primarily TM practitioners, symptoms of depersonalisation, derealisation and dissociation have been widely reported. In a 1990 study, Richard J. Costello records *Individuals who practice the type of meditation designed to alter their consciousness may suffer depersonalization (loss of one's own reality or a loss of his own identity in relation to others around him) and derealization (change in one's perception of his environment) during meditation. Deikman (1963, 1966a) and Kennedy (1976) reported cases in which depersonalization and derealization occurred in individuals practising meditative techniques designed to alter consciousness* (Costello R. J. Psychiatry, Vol. 53, May 1990, pp. 158–167 Depersonalization

and Meditation.) Article available online at minet.org/
Documents/research.1990.castillo

Asharam Babu

Asaram (born 17 April 1941), also known as Asaram Bapu
('Father') by his followers, is a Hindu religious leader from
India. In early 1970s, Asaram built his first ashram on 4 ha
(10 acres) of land in Gujarat. By 2013, he had 400 major
and minor ashrams in India and abroad, with numerous
followers. In 2000s, several cases of land encroachment were
lodged against his ashrams in multiple states. In 2008, the
death of two boys at his Motera ashram led to public protests,
amid allegations that black magic was being practised at the
ashram. In 2013, Asaram was arrested when a sixteen-year-
old girl accused him of sexually assaulting her in Jodhpur.
He is currently in jail.

Early life

Asaram was born on 17 April 1941, in the Berani village
of the Nawabshah District in British India (present-day
Pakistan), to Menhgiba and Thaumal Sirumalani. His
birthname was Asumal Thaumal Harpalani or Asumal
Sirumalani.

After his father's death, Asaram dropped out of Jai Hind
High School, where he had studied till class III. According
to *Sant Asaramji ki Jeevan Jhanki*, a biography published
by his ashram, he ran away to an ashram in Bharuch at

the age of fifteen, eight days before his scheduled wedding. His family persuaded him to return, and he married Laxmi Devi. At the age of twenty-three, he again left home and wandered in pilgrimage places in Uttarakhand and Uttar Pradesh. He met the spiritual guru Lilashah in Nainital, wanting to be his disciple, but the guru sent him back home. Thirteen days later after the return, he left home for another Ashram but was sent back again. He then visited Lilashah once again, who accepted him as a disciple in Vrindavan. Lilashah named him Asaram on 7 October 1964.

Asaram and Laxmi Devi have two children: Narayan Sai and Bharti Devi.

Ashrams

According to *Sant Asaramji ki Jeevan Jhanki*, Asaram returned to Ahmedabad on 8 July 1971. On 29 January 1972, he built a hut at Motera, then a village on the banks of the Sabarmati. Although his official biography doesn't mention it, Asaram also lived in Motera's Sadashiv Ashram for two years, before setting up his own hut adjacent to it. He converted his hutment into an ashram in 1973, starting with five to ten followers. In 1981 and 1992, the Indian National Congress-led state government allotted the ashram 14,515 m^2 land. In 1997 and 1999, the Bharatiya Janata Party-led government allotted it 25,000 m^2 for expansion. Asaram had few followers in the beginning, but the numbers increased as local politicians became his devotees.

By 2013, Asaram had 400 major and minor ashrams in India and abroad, with numerous followers.

In 2000, Asaram's ashram was allocated about 10 acres (4 ha) of land in Bhairavi village of Navsari district by the Gujarat government. The ashram encroached on an additional 6 acres (6 ha), leading to protests in the local villages. On a complaint filed by locals, and after repeated notices were ignored, the district authorities with police assistance bulldozed the encroachments and took possession of the land.

On 8 January 2010, the Gujarat government took over 67,059 m^2 of land from Asaram's Ahmedabad ashram, stating that the ashram had encroached on it. The government also took over 70 acres of agricultural land bought by Asaram's family in Sabarkantha, arguing that the family had forged papers to show themselves as farmers.

Spiritual Teaching

Asaram has organised spiritual discourses all over India, including cities like Ahmedabad and Patna. His devotees are shown taking *diksha* (initiation by a guru) from him in these *satsang* programmes. Around 20,000 students visited his *satsang* in Ahmedabad in December 2001. He preaches the existence of *One Supreme Conscious* and citing Bhakti yoga, Gnana yoga and Karma yoga as influences. In August 2012, when he was reportedly to deliver a lecture in a local college, his helicopter crashed while landing at Godhra. Asaram, the pilot, and the other passengers survived.

In January 2013, while addressing a gathering of his followers, Asaram reportedly said that the victim of the 2012 Delhi gang rape was as guilty as her rapists. He is reported to have said: 'The victim is as guilty as her rapists . . . She should have called the culprits brothers and begged before them to stop . . . This could have saved her dignity and life. Can one hand clap? I don't think so. He is also reported to have said that he was against harsher punishments for the accused in the Delhi rape victim case, as the law could be misused. To support his point, he is said to have stated that, 'Dowry law in India is the biggest example of law is being misused'. This alleged blamed was widely criticised, including by politicians belonging to the two major political parties – Bharatiya Janata Party and Indian National Congress. Asaram later denied giving any statement blaming the victim and stated that his statement had been distorted and misrepresented. He announced a reward of Rs. 50,000 for anyone who could prove that he blamed the victim.

Gurukul deaths case

By 2008, forty of Asaram's ashrams had gurukuls (residential schools). The deaths of four boys at two of these Ashrams in 2008 led to allegations of black magic being practised there.

On 3 July 2008, two boys went missing from Asaram's residential school (gurukul) in Motera. On 5 July 2013, the boys' mutilated bodies were found on the banks of the Sabarmati river near the Ashram. The parents alleged that the police harassed them and refused to register a complaint against Asaram or the ashram administration. The incident led to public agitations, with allegations that the boys had been sacrificed by Asaram and his followers for black magic.

Two dead bodies were also found in Asaram's Chhindwara ashram, leading to protests by the local residents. On 29 July 2008, a nursery student was found dead in the ashram's toilet. The police initially suspected that he had slipped on the floor and died from injuries. On 31 July, another five-year old student was found dead in the toilet. A forensic examination revealed that the bite mark matched the teeth of a senior student. On 4 August, the senior student was arrested for the murders. According to the police, he lured the victims to the toilet with the chocolates and killed them. The parents of the boys' gave clean chit to Asaram.

The Narendra Modi-led Gujarat state government set up the Justice D. K. Trivedi Commission to probe the deaths in the Motera ashram. In 2009, Asaram's followers organised a rally, protesting against their alleged harassment by the Gujarat police. The protest turned violent, and over 200 supporters of Asaram were arrested after they attacked and injured twenty policemen. In 2012, when Asaram was summoned by the Trivedi Commission, he issued a threat to the Narendra Modi government, saying that any further 'suppression' of him and his followers would result in Modi being 'thrown out'.

Raju Chandak, a former aide of Asaram, told the DK Trivedi Commission that black magic and suspicious financial dools took place at the ashram. Mahender Chawla, secretary of Narayan Sai during 2001–2005, told the commmission that he had seen Sai performed black magic in presence of dead bodies. As an example, he stated that Sai had recited mantras over the body of child covered with black cloth at Kalyan Ashram in Jhabua district. Shekhar Kashmirilal Giridhar.

Arrest

In August 2013, a sixteen-year-old girl accused Asaram of sexually assaulting her at his ashram in Jodhpur on the pretext of exorcising her from evil spirits. The girl's parents filed a complaint with the police in Delhi, and a medical examination confirmed that she had been assaulted.

When Asaram did not appear for interrogation by 31 August, Delhi police booked him under sections 342 (wrongful confinement), 376 (rape), 506 (criminal intimidation) of the Indian Penal Code, sections of the Juvenile Justice Act, and the Protection of Children from Sexual Offences Act. Asaram remained inside his other ashram in Indore and avoided arrest while his devotees clashed with journalists and policemen outside. Eventually, the Jodhpur police arrested him on 1 September 2013 from his ashram.

Asaram dismissed the girl's allegations and claimed that the accusations were a conspiracy orchestrated by Sonia Gandhi and her son Rahul Gandhi of the then-ruling Congress Party. He had also claimed that he was impotent and not capable of sexual assault; however, this was proven to be a lie as tests showed him to be capable of the act. He has since been in jail and denied bail multiple times.

In December 2013, Asaram's son Narayan Sai was also arrested on charges of rape, after two sisters from Surat alleged that he and his father had raped them in Asaram's ashram during the mid-2000s. The elder sister accused Asaram of repeated sexual assaults during 1997–2006 at the Motera ashram. The younger sister accused Narayan Sai of sexually assaulting her during 2002–2005 at the Surat ashram. One of the sisters also alleged that Asaram's wife and daughter helped the two men exploit the girls.

Threats and Attacks

Asaram's followers have been accused of threatening and attacking those involved in the probe against him. In September 2013, the father of the sixteen-year-old girl who accused Asaram of sexually assaulting her alleged that he had received death threats from Asaram's followers. He submitted audio clippings of these threats to the court. In October 2013, Surat Deputy Commissioner of Police (DCP) Shobha Bhutada also alleged that Asaram's supporters had threatened her, and asked her to stop the probe against Asaram. On 14 September 2014, Rambabu Kori, a follower of Asaram made an anonymous call to ATC Udaipur, and threatened to disrupt flight operations if Asaram was not released within two weeks. He was arrested from Uttar Pradesh.

On 6 December 2009, a former aide of Asaram who alleged that black magic was performed at Asaram's ashram and suspicious financial deals also happened there was attacked. From 2014–15, there have been numerous attacks against various witnesses in the Asaram case. Amrut Prajapati, a personal aide of Asaram, who claimed to have been attacked multiple times before, was attacked and killed on 23 May 2014. Another associate Akhil Gupta was shot and killed on 11 January 2015.

Catholic Sex Abuse

The **Catholic sex abuse cases** are a series of allegations, investigations, trials and convictions of child sexual abuse crimes committed by Catholic priests, nuns and members of Roman Catholic orders against boys and girls, some as young as three years old, with the majority between the ages of eleven and fourteen. The accusations began to receive wide publicity in the late 1980s – many span several decades and were brought forward years after the abuse occurred. Cases have also been brought against members of the Catholic hierarchy who did not report sex abuse allegations to the legal authorities, moving sexually abusive priests to other parishes where abuse sometimes continued.

The cases received significant media and public attention throughout the world, especially in Canada, Ireland and the United States. Members of the Church's hierarchy have argued that media coverage was excessive and disproportionate. A critical investigation by *The Boston Globe* in 2002 led to widespread media coverage in the United States. By 2010, much of the reporting focused on abuse in Europe. From 2001 to 2010, the Holy See, the central governing body of the Catholic Church, considered sex abuse allegations concerning about 3,000 priests dating back up to fifty years. Cases worldwide reflect patterns of long-term abuse and the covering up of reports. Diocesan officials and academics knowledgeable about the Roman Catholic Church say that sexual abuse by clergy is generally not discussed, and thus is difficult to measure. In the Philippines, where, as of 2002, at least 85 per cent of the population is Catholic, revelations of child sexual abuse by priests followed the United States' reporting in 2002.

Studies have found that priests in the Catholic Church may not be any more likely than other men to commit abuse, and that the prevalence of abuse by priests had fallen sharply in the last twenty to thirty years. After the implementation of self-imposed transparency in abuse matters by Pope Benedict XVI, accusations of a sexual nature against Roman Catholic priests in the United States numbered eight in 2010.

International extent of issue.

The sexual abuse of children under the age of consent by priests has received significant media and public attention in Canada, Ireland, the United States, the United Kingdom, Mexico, Belgium, France, Germany and Australia, while cases have been reported throughout the world. Many of the cases span several decades and are brought forward years after the abuse occurred.

Although nationwide inquiries have only been conducted in the United States and Ireland, cases of clerical sexual abuse of minors have been reported and prosecuted in Australia, New Zealand, Canada and other countries. In 1994, allegations of sexual abuse on forty-seven young seminarians surfaced in Argentina. In 1995, Cardinal Hans Hermann Groër resigned from his post as Archbishop of Vienna, Austria, over allegations of sexual abuse, although he remained a Cardinal. Since 1995, over one hundred priests from various parts of Australia were convicted of sexual abuse.

In Ireland, the Commission to Inquire into Child Abuse issued a report which covered six decades (from the 1950s) and noted 'endemic' sexual abuse in Catholic boys' institutions, with church leaders aware of what was going on and government inspectors failing to 'stop beatings, rapes and humiliation'. The commission's report on church abuse ran to five volumes.

In Australia, according to Broken Rites, a support and advocacy group for church-related sex abuse victims, as of 2011, there have been over one hundred cases where Catholic priests have been charged for child sex offences. A 2012 police report detailed forty suicide deaths directly related to abuse by Catholic clergy in the state of Victoria. In January 2013, the terms of reference were announced for an Australian Royal Commission into institutional responses to child sexual abuse which would investigate institutional sexual abuse of minors related, but not exclusive, to matters concerning clergy of the Catholic Church.

Of the Catholic sexual abuse cases in Latin America, the most famous is arguably of the sexual scandal of Father Marcial Maciel, the leader of the Legion of Christ, a Roman Catholic congregation of pontifical right made up of priests and seminarians studying for the priesthood. This occurred after the Legion spent more than a decade denying allegations and criticising the victims who claimed abuse.

In Tanzania, Father Kit Cunningham and three other priests were exposed as paedophiles after Cunningham's death. The abuse took place in the 1960s but was only publicly revealed in 2011, largely through a BBC documentary.

Church officials and academics knowledgeable about the Third World Roman Catholic Church say that sexual abuse by clergy is generally not discussed, and thus is difficult to measure. This may be due in part to the more hierarchical structure of the Church in Third World countries, the 'psychological health' of clergy in those regions and because third word media, legal systems and public culture are not as apt to thoroughly discuss sexual abuse.

Academic Mathew N. Schmalz notes India as an example: 'you would have gossip and rumors, but it never reaches the level of formal charges or controversies'. Traditionally, the Roman Catholic Church has held tight control over many aspects of church life around the globe, including 'the words used in prayer', but left sex abuse cases to be handled locally. In 2001, sex abuse cases were first required to be reported to Rome. In July 2010, the Vatican doubled the length of time after the eighteenth birthday of the victim that clergymen can be tried in a church court and streamlined the processes for removing 'pedophile priests'.

In *A Perspective on Clergy Sexual Abuse* by Thomas Plante, the Augustin Cardinal Bea, S. J. University Professor of Psychology on the faculty of the Jesuit Santa Clara University, who specialises in abuse counselling and considered an expert on clerical abuse, he states 'approximately 4 per cent of priests during the past half century (and mostly in the 1960s and 1970s) have had a sexual experience with a minor'. According to *Newsweek* magazine, the figure is similar to that in the rest of the adult population.

Allegations of and convictions for sexual abuse by clergy have occurred in many countries. Although there are no figures available on the number of sexual abuse cases in different regions, in 2002, *The Boston Globe* reported 'clearly the issue has been most prominent in the United States'. The United States is the country with the highest number of Catholic Sex Abuse cases, leading Plante to surmise that the 'crisis in the United States reached epidemic proportions within the Church, the likes of which haven't been witnessed before'.

After the United States, the country with the next highest number of reported cases is Ireland. A significant number of cases have also been reported in Australia, New Zealand, Canada and countries in Europe, Latin America, Africa and Asia. In 2004, the John Jay report tabulated a total of 4,392 priests and deacons in the United States against whom allegations of sexual abuse had been made.

In response to the attention, members of the church hierarchy have argued that media coverage has been unfair, excessive and disproportionate. According to a Pew Research Center study, in 2002 the media coverage was focused on the United States, where a *Boston Globe* series initiated widespread coverage in the region. However, by 2010 the focus had shifted to Europe.

In September 2011, a submission was lodged with the International Criminal Court alleging that the Pope, Cardinal Angelo Sodano (Dean of the College of Cardinals), Cardinal Tarcisio Bertone (Cardinal Secretary of State), and Cardinal William Levada (then-current Prefect of the Congregation for the Doctrine of the Faith) had committed a crime against humanity by failing to prevent or punish perpetrators of rape and sexual violence in a 'systematic and widespread' concealment which included failure to co-operate with relevant law enforcement agencies. In a statement to the Associated Press, the Vatican described this as a 'ludicrous publicity stunt and a misuse of international judicial processes'. Lawyers and law professors emphasised that the case is likely to fall outside the court's jurisdiction.

Contemporary history of child sex abuse

Child sexual abuse is an umbrella term describing offenses in which an adult engages in sexual activity with a minor or exploits a minor for the purpose of sexual gratification. The American Psychiatric Association states that 'children cannot consent to sexual activity with adults', and condemns any such action by an adult as 'a criminal and immoral act which never can be considered normal or socially acceptable behavior'. Only at the beginning of the 1900s did Western society begin to regard children as fledgling citizens whose 'creative and intellectual potential require fostering' rather than 'cheap labor'. According to *The Atlantic*, 'the idea of the "modern child" was shaped by the same forces that shaped the rest of society: industrialization, urbanization, and consumerism'.

Child sex abuse has gained public attention in the past few decades and has become one of the most high-profile crimes. Since the 1970s, child molestation and the sexual abuse of children have increasingly been recognised as deeply damaging to children and thus unacceptable for society as a whole. While sexual use of children by adults has been present throughout history, it has only become the object of significant public attention in recent times. The first published work dedicated specifically to child sexual abuse appeared in France in 1857: *Medical-Legal Studies of Sexual Assault (Etude Médico-Légale sur les Attentats aux Mœurs)*, by Auguste Ambroise Tardieu, a noted French pathologist and pioneer of forensic medicine.

Roman Catholic cases

In the late 1940s, American Fr. Gerald Fitzgerald founded the Congregation of the Servants of the Paraclete, a religious order that treats Roman Catholic priests who struggle with personal difficulties such as substance abuse and sexual misconduct. In a series of letters and reports to high-ranking Catholic leaders starting in the 1950s, Fitzgerald warned of substantial problems with pedophile priests. He wrote, for example, '[sexual abuse] offenders were unlikely to change and should not be returned to ministry', and this was discussed with Pope Paul VI (1897–1978) and 'in correspondence with several bishops'.

In 2001, sex abuse cases were first required to be reported to Rome. After the 2002 revelation that cases of abuse were widespread in the Church, *The Dallas Morning News* did a year-long investigation. The results made public in 2004 showed that even after the public outcry, priests were moved out of the countries where they had been accused and were still in 'settings that bring them into contact with children, despite church claims to the contrary'. Among the investigation's findings is that nearly half of 200 cases 'involved clergy who tried to elude law enforcement'. In July 2010, the Vatican doubled the length of time after the eighteenth birthday of the victim that clergymen can be tried in a church court and streamlined the processes for removing 'pedophile priests'.

Public and political issues

The earliest medical studies of child sex abuse were published in France by Auguste Ambroise Tardieu (1818–1879), though his work was often received negatively or ignored by peers. Richard von Krafft-Ebing's *Psychopathia Sexualis*, first published in 1886 and subsequently revised and expanded several times, also discusses children as victims of sex crimes and uses the term 'paedophilia erotica' to describe a sexual preoccupation with children.

Some sources report that studies on child molestation were non-existent until the 1920s and that the first national estimate of the number of child sexual abuse cases was published in 1948. By 1968, 44 out of 50 U.S. states had enacted mandatory laws that required physicians to report cases of suspicious child abuse. Second-wave feminism (early 1960s to late 1990s) brought greater awareness of child sexual abuse and violence against women and made them public, political issues.

Legal action began to become more prevalent in the 1970s with the enactment of the Child Abuse Prevention and Treatment Act in 1974 in conjunction with the creation of the National Center on Child Abuse and Neglect. Since the creation of the Child Abuse Prevention and Treatment Act, reported child abuse cases have increased dramatically. The National Abuse Coalition was created in 1979 to create pressure in congress to create more sexual abuse laws. In 1986, Congress passed the Child Abuse Victims' Rights Act, giving children a civil claim in sexual abuse cases. The number of laws created in the 1980s and 1990s began to create greater prosecution and detection of child sexual abusers. Megan's Law, enacted in 2004, gives the public access to knowledge of sex offenders nationwide. Anne Hastings described these changes in attitudes towards child sexual abuse as 'the beginning of one of history's largest social revolutions'.

According to John Jay College of Criminal Justice professor B J Cling,

By the early twenty-first century, the issue of child sexual abuse has become a legitimate focus of professional attention, while increasingly separated from second-wave feminism . . . As child sexual abuse becomes absorbed into the larger field of interpersonal trauma studies, child sexual abuse studies and intervention strategies have become degendered and largely unaware of their political origins in modern feminism and other vibrant political movements of the 1970s. One may hope that unlike in the past, this rediscovery of child sexual abuse that began in the 1970s will not again be followed by collective amnesia. The institutionalisation of child maltreatment interventions in federally funded centres, national and international societies, and a host of research studies (in which the United States continues to lead the world) offer grounds for cautious optimism. Nevertheless, as Judith Herman argues cogently, 'The systematic study of psychological trauma . . . depends on the support of a political movement'.

United States

In the United States, which has been the lead focus of much of the scandals and subsequent reforms, BishopAccountability. org, an 'online archive established by lay Catholics', reports that over 3,000 civil lawsuits have been filed against the church, some of these cases have resulted in multi-million dollar settlements with many claimants. In 1998, the Roman Catholic Diocese of Dallas paid US$ 30.9 million to twelve victims of one priest (US$ 44.9 million in present-day terms). From 2003 to 2009, nine other major settlements involving over 375 cases with 1551 claimants/ victims resulted in payments of over US$ 1.1 billion. The Associated Press estimated the settlements of sex abuse cases from 1950 to 2007 totaled more than US$ 2 billion. Bishop Accountability puts the figure at more than US$ 3 billion in 2012. Addressing 'a flood of abuse claims' five dioceses (Tucson, Arizona; Spokane, Washington; Portland, Oregon; Davenport, Iowa, and San Diego) got bankruptcy protection. Eight Catholic dioceses have declared bankruptcy due to sex abuse cases from 2004 to 2011.

Although bishops had been sending sexually abusive priests to facilities such as those operated by the Servants of the Paraclete since the 1950s, there was scant public discussion of the problem until the mid-1960s. Even then, most of the discussion was held amongst the Catholic hierarchy with little or no coverage in the media. A public discussion of sexual abuse of minors by priests took place at a meeting sponsored by the National Association for Pastoral Renewal held on the campus of the University of Notre Dame in 1967, to which all U.S. Catholic bishops were invited.

Various local and regional discussions of the problem were held by Catholic bishops in later years. However, it was not until the 1980s that discussion of sexual abuse by Roman Catholic clerics began to be covered as a phenomenon in the news media of the United States. According to the Catholic News Service, public awareness of the sexual abuse of children in the United States and Canada emerged in the late 1970s and the 1980s as an outgrowth of the growing awareness of physical abuse of children.

In 1981, Father Donald Roemer of the Archdiocese of Los Angeles pleaded guilty to felonious sexual abuse of a minor. The case received widespread media coverage. In September 1983, the *National Catholic Reporter* published an article on the topic. The subject gained wider national notoriety in October 1985 when Louisiana priest Gilbert Gauthe pleaded guilty to eleven counts of molestation of boys. After the coverage of Gauthe's crimes subsided, the issue faded to the fringes of public attention until the mid-1990s, when the issue was again brought to national attention after number of books on the topic were published.

In early 2002, the *Boston Globe*'s Pulitzer Prize winning coverage of sexual abuse cases involving Catholic priests drew the attention, first of the United States and ultimately the world, to the problem. Other victims began to come forward with their own allegations of abuse, resulting in more lawsuits and criminal cases. Since then, the problem of clerical abuse of minors has received significantly more attention from the Church hierarchy, law enforcement agencies, government and the news media.

In 2003, Archbishop Timothy M. Dolan of the Roman Catholic Archdiocese of Milwaukee authorised payments of as much as US$ 20,000 to sexually abusive priests to convince them to leave the priesthood.

Second Warning is an Internal Revolution

World Bank and IMF are Construction of America and European Mind and they solve the problems of their own region rather than of developing nations, some of European countries have more debt more than their GDP. Policies of all the international organisations have been dictated by American and European alliance, and developing countries have no role to play; Even UN organisations are no exception.

The Fortune 500 companies earned a combined US$ 820 billion in profits in 2012, which represents a decline of just US$ 4 billion, or 0.5 per cent, from the all-time record, set in 2011. The world's 500 largest companies generated US$ 31.2 trillion in revenues and US$ 1.7 trillion in profits in 2014. Together, this year's Fortune Global 500 employ 65 million people worldwide and are represented by thirty-six countries.

Economic inequality. Some studies have emphasised inequality as a growing social problem. Too much inequality can be destructive, because income inequality and wealth concentration can hinder long-term growth. Early statistical studies comparing inequality to economic growth had been inconclusive, however in 2011, International Monetary Fund economists showed that greater income equality – less inequality – increased the duration of countries' economic growth spells more than free trade, low government corruption, foreign investment or low foreign debt. Economic inequality varies between societies, historical periods, economic structures and systems. The term can refer to cross-sectional distribution of income or wealth at any particular period or to the lifetime income and wealth over longer periods of time. There are various numerical indices for measuring economic inequality.

Measurement concepts

Economists generally think of three metrics of economic disparity: wealth, income and consumption. A skilled professional may have low wealth and low income as student, low wealth and high earnings in the beginning of the career, and high wealth and low earnings after the career. People's preferences determine whether they consume earnings immediately or defer consumption to the future. The distinction is also important at the level of economy:

There are economies with high-income inequality and relatively low-wealth inequality (such as Japan and Italy).

There are economies with relatively low-income inequality and high-wealth inequality (such as Switzerland and Denmark).

A study by the World Institute for Development Economics Research at United Nations University reports that the richest 1 per cent of adults alone owned 40 per cent of global assets in the year 2000. The *three* richest people in the world possess more financial assets than the lowest 48 nations combined. The combined wealth of the '10 million dollar millionaires' grew to nearly US$ 41 trillion in 2008. A January 2014 report by Oxfam claims that the 85 wealthiest individuals in the world have a combined wealth equal to that of the bottom 50 per cent of the world's population, or about 3.5 billion people. According to a *Los Angeles Times* analysis of the report, the wealthiest 1 per cent owns 46 per cent of the world's wealth; the 85 richest people, a small part of the wealthiest 1 per cent, own about 0.7 per cent of the human population's wealth, which is the same as the bottom half of the population. More recently, in January 2015, Oxfam reported that the wealthiest 1 per cent will own more than half of the global wealth by 2016. An October 2014 study by Credit Suisse also claims that the top 1 per cent now owns nearly half of the world's wealth and that the accelerating disparity could trigger a recession.

According to PolitiFact, the top 400 richest Americans have more wealth than half of all Americans combined. According to the *New York Times* on 22 July 2014, the 'richest 1 per cent in the United States now own more wealth than the bottom 90 per cent'. Inherited wealth may help explain why many Americans who have become rich may have had a 'substantial head start'. In September 2012, according to the Institute for Policy Studies, 'over 60 per cent' of the Forbes richest 400 Americans 'grew up in substantial privilege'.

The existing data and estimates suggest a large increase in international (and more generally inter-macroregional) component between 1820 and 1960. It might have slightly decreased since that time at the expense of increasing inequality within countries.

The United Nations Development Programme in 2014 asserted that greater investments in social security, jobs and laws that protect vulnerable populations are necessary to prevent widening income inequality . . .

There is a significant difference in the measured wealth distribution and the public's understanding of wealth distribution. Michael Norton of the Harvard Business School and Dan Ariely of the Department of Psychology at Duke University found this to be true in their research, done in 2011. The actual wealth going to the top quintile in 2011 was around 84 per cent, whereas the average amount of wealth that the general public estimated to go to the top quintile was around 58 per cent.

Global income inequality is decreasing, due to strong economic growth in developing countries. Income inequality is higher than it has ever been within OECD member nations and is at increased levels in many emerging economies. According to a June 2015 report by the International Monetary Fund:

> Widening income inequality is the defining challenge of our time. In advanced economies, the gap between the rich and poor is at its highest level in decades. Inequality trends have been more mixed in emerging markets and developing countries (EMDCs), with some countries experiencing declining inequality, but pervasive inequities in access to education, healthcare, and finance remain.

In October 2015, Credit Suisse published a study which shows global inequality continues to increase, and that half of the world's wealth is now in the hands of those in the top percentile, whose assets each exceed US$ 759,900.

Causes

- labour market outcomes
- globalisation
- suppressing wages in low-skill jobs due to a surplus of low-skill labour in developing countries

- increasing the market size and the rewards for people and firms succeeding in a particular niche
- providing more investment opportunities for already-wealthy people
- increasing international influence
- decreasing domestic influence
- policy reforms
- more regressive taxation
- plutocracy
- computerisation, automation and increased technology, which means more skills are required to obtain a moderate or high wage
- ethnic discrimination
- gender discrimination
- nepotism
- variation in natural ability
- neoliberalism
- Growing acceptance of very high CEO salaries, e.g., in the United States since the 1960s
- Land speculation: Followers of Henry George believe that landlords and land speculators derive excess wealth and income from the tendency of land to increase exponentially with development and at a much higher rate than population growth. Their solution is to tax land value, though not necessarily structures or other improvements. This concept is known as Georgism.

Labour market

A major cause of economic inequality within modern market economies is the determination of wages by the market. Some small part of economic inequality is caused by the differences in the supply and demand for different types of work. However, where competition is imperfect, information unevenly distributed, opportunities to acquire education and skills unequal, and since many such imperfect conditions exist in virtually every market, there is in fact little presumption that markets are in general efficient. This means that there is an enormous potential role for government to correct these market failures.

In a purely capitalist mode of production (i.e. where professional and labour organisations cannot limit the number of workers) the workers' wages will not be controlled by these organisations, or by the employer, but rather by the market. Wages work in the same way as prices for any other good. Thus, wages can be considered as a function of market price of skill. And therefore, inequality is driven by this price. Under the law of supply and demand, the price of skill is determined by a race between the demand for the skilled worker and the supply of the skilled worker. 'On the other hand, markets can also concentrate wealth, pass environmental costs on to society, and abuse workers and consumers'. 'Markets, by themselves, even when they are stable, often lead to high levels of inequality, outcomes that are widely viewed as unfair'. Employers who offer a below market wage will find that their business is chronically understaffed. Their competitors will take advantage of the situation by offering a higher wage to snatch up the best of their labour. For a businessman who has the profit motive as the prime interest, it is a losing proposition to offer below or above market wages to workers.

A job where there are many workers willing to work a large amount of time (high supply) competing for a job that few require (low demand) will result in a low wage for that job. This is because competition between workers drives down the wage. An example of this would be jobs such as dishwashing or customer service. Competition amongst workers tends to drive down wages due to the expendable nature of the worker in relation to his or her particular job. A job where there are few able or willing workers (low supply), but a large need for the positions (high demand), will result in high wages for that job. This is because competition between employers *for employees* will drive up the wage. Examples of this would include jobs that require highly developed skills, rare abilities or a high level of risk. Competition amongst employers tends to drive up wages due to the nature of the job, since there is a relative shortage of workers for the particular position. Professional and labour organisations may limit the supply of workers which results in higher demand and greater incomes for members. Members may also receive higher wages through collective bargaining, political influence or corruption.

These supply and demand interactions result in a gradation of wage levels within a society that significantly influence economic inequality. Polarisation of wages does not explain the accumulation of wealth and very high incomes among the 1 per cent. Joseph Stiglitz believes that 'It is plain that markets must be tamed and tempered to make sure they work to the benefit of most citizens'.

On the other hand, higher economic inequality tends to increase entrepreneurship rates at the individual level (self-employment). However, most of it is often based on necessity rather than opportunity. Necessity-based entrepreneurship is motivated by survival needs such as income for food and shelter ('push' motivations), whereas opportunity-based entrepreneurship is driven by achievement-oriented motivations ('pull') such as vocation and more likely to involve the pursue of new products, services or underserved market needs. The economic impact of the former type of entrepreneurialism tends to be redistributive, while the latter is expected to foster technological progress and thus have a more positive impact on economic growth.

Taxes

Another cause is the rate at which income is taxed coupled with the progressivity of the tax system. A progressive tax is a tax by which the tax rate increases as the taxable base amount increases. In a progressive tax system, the level of the top tax rate will often have a direct impact on the level of inequality within a society, either increasing it or decreasing it, provided that income does not change as a result of the change in tax regime. Additionally, steeper tax progressivity applied to social spending can result in a more equal distribution of income across the board. The difference between the Gini index for an income distribution before taxation and the Gini index after taxation is an indicator for the effects of such taxation.

There is debate between politicians and economists over the role of tax policy in mitigating or exacerbating wealth inequality. Economists such as Paul Krugman, Peter Orszag and Emmanuel Saez have argued that tax policy in the post–World War II era has indeed increased income inequality by enabling the wealthiest Americans far greater access to capital than lower income ones.

Education

Illustration from a 1916 advertisement for a vocational school in the back of a U.S. magazine. Education has been seen as a key to higher income, and this advertisement appealed to Americans' belief in the possibility of self-betterment, as well as threatening the consequences of downward mobility in the great income inequality existing during the Industrial Revolution.

An important factor in the creation of inequality is variation in individuals' access to education. Education, especially in an area where there is a high demand for workers, creates high wages for those with this education; however, increases in education first increase and then decrease growth as well as income inequality. As a result, those who are unable to afford an education, or choose not to pursue optional education, generally receive much lower wages. The justification for this is that a lack of education leads directly to lower incomes and thus lower aggregate savings and investment. Conversely, education raises incomes and promotes growth because it helps to unleash the productive potential of the poor.

In 2014, economists with the Standard & Poor's rating agency concluded that the widening disparity between the U.S.'s wealthiest citizens and the rest of the nation had slowed its recovery from the 2008–2009 recession and made it more prone to boom-and-bust cycles. To partially remedy the wealth gap and the resulting slow growth, S&P recommended increasing access to education. It estimated that if the average U. S. worker had completed just one more year of school, it would add an additional US$ 105 billion in growth to the country's economy over five years.

More of Barro studies also find that female secondary education is positively associated with growth. His findings show that countries with low female education; increasing it has little effect on economic growth; however in countries with high female education, increasing it significantly boosts economic growth. More and better education is a prerequisite for rapid economic development around the world. Education stimulates economic growth and improves people's lives through many channels.

By increasing the efficiency of the labour force, better conditions are created for good governance, improving health and enhancing equality. Labour market success is linked to schooling achievement, the consequences of widening disparities in schooling is likely to further increases in earnings inequality.

The United States funds education through property taxes, which can lead to large discrepancies in the amount of funding a public school may receive. Often, but not always, this results in more funding for schools attended by children from wealthier parents. As of 2015, the United States, Israel and Turkey are the only three OECD countries where the government spends more on schools in rich neighbourhoods than in poor neighbourhoods.

Economic liberalism, deregulation and decline of unions

John Schmitt and Ben Zipperer (2006) of the CEPR point to economic liberalism and the reduction of business regulation along with the decline of union membership as one of the causes of economic inequality. In an analysis of the effects of intensive Anglo-American liberal policies in comparison to continental European liberalism, where unions have remained strong, they concluded 'The U.S. economic and social model is associated with substantial levels of social exclusion, including high levels of income inequality, high relative and absolute poverty rates, poor and unequal educational outcomes, poor health outcomes, and high rates of crime and incarceration. At the same time, the available evidence provides little support for the view that U.S.-style labor-market flexibility dramatically improves labor-market outcomes. Despite popular prejudices to the contrary, the U.S. economy consistently affords a lower level of economic mobility than all the continental European countries, for which data is available'.

Sociologist Jake Rosenfield of the University of Washington asserts that the decline of organised labour in the United States has played a more significant role in expanding the income gap than technological changes and globalisation, which were also experienced by other industrialised nations that didn't experience steep surges in inequality. He points out that nations with high rates of unionisation, particularly in Scandinavia, have very low levels of inequality and concludes 'the historical pattern is clear; the cross-national pattern is clear: high inequality goes hand-in-hand with weak labor movements and vice-versa'.

A 2015 study by the International Monetary Fund found that the decline of unionisation in many advanced economies starting in the 1980s has fueled rising income inequality.

Globalisation

Trade liberalisation may shift economic inequality from a global to a domestic scale. When rich countries trade with poor countries, the low-skilled workers in the rich countries may see reduced wages as a result of the competition, while low-skilled workers in the poor countries may see increased wages. Trade economist Paul Krugman estimates that trade liberalisation has had a measurable effect on the rising inequality in the United States. He attributes this trend to increased trade with poor countries and the fragmentation of the means of production, resulting in low-skilled jobs becoming more tradeable. However, he concedes that the effect of trade on inequality in America is minor when compared to other causes, such as technological innovation, a view shared by other experts. Empirical economists Max Roser and Jesus Crespo Cuaresma find support in the data that international trade is increasing income inequality. They empirically confirm the predictions of the Stolper–Samuelson theorem regarding the effects of international trade on the distribution of incomes. Lawrence Katz estimates that trade has only accounted for 5 to 15 per cent of rising income inequality. Robert Lawrence argues that technological innovation and automation has meant that low-skilled jobs have been replaced by machine labour in wealthier nations, and that wealthier countries no longer have significant numbers of low-skilled manufacturing workers that could be affected by competition from poor countries.

Gender

The gender gap in median earnings of full-time employees according to the OECD 2008.

In many countries, there is a gender income gap in favour of males in the labour market. For example, the median full-time salary for U.S. women is 77 per cent of that of U.S. men. Several factors other than discrimination may contribute to this gap. On average, women are more likely than men to consider factors other than pay when looking for work and may be less willing to travel or relocate. Thomas Sowell, in his book *Knowledge and Decisions*, claims that this difference is due to women not taking jobs due to marriage or pregnancy, but income studies show that that does not explain the entire difference. A U.S. Census's report stated that in United States once other factors are accounted for, there is still a difference in earnings between women and men. The income gap in other countries ranges from 53 per cent in Botswana to – 40 per cent in Bahrain.

Gender inequality and discrimination is argued to cause and perpetuate poverty and vulnerability in society as a whole. Gender Equity Indices seek to provide the tools to demonstrate this feature of equity.

Nineteenth century socialists like Robert Owen, William Thompson, Anna Wheeler and August Bebel argued that the economic inequality between genders was the leading cause of economic inequality; however, Karl Marx and Fredrick Engels believed that the inequality between social classes was the larger cause of inequality.

Economic development

Kuznets curve

Economist Simon Kuznets argued that levels of economic inequality are in large part the result of stages of development. According to Kuznets, countries with low levels of development have relatively equal distributions of wealth. As a country develops, it acquires more capital, which leads to the owners of this capital having more wealth and income and introducing inequality. Eventually, through various possible redistribution mechanisms such as social welfare programmes, more developed countries move back to lower levels of inequality.

Plotting the relationship between level of income and inequality, Kuznets saw middle-income developing economies level of inequality bulging out to form what is now known as the Kuznets curve. Kuznets demonstrated this relationship using cross-sectional data. However, more recent testing of this theory with superior panel data has shown it to be very weak. Kuznets' curve predicts that income inequality will eventually decrease given time. As an example, income inequality did fall in the United States during its High School Movement from 1910 to 1940 and thereafter. However, recent data shows that the level of income inequality began to rise after the 1970s. This does not necessarily disprove Kuznets' theory. It may be possible that another Kuznets' cycle is occurring, specifically the move from the manufacturing sector to the service sector. This implies that it may be possible for multiple Kuznets' cycles to be in effect at any given time.

Individual preferences

Related to cultural issues, diversity of preferences within a society may contribute to economic inequality. When faced with the choice between working harder to earn more money or enjoying more leisure time, equally capable individuals with identical earning potential may choose different strategies. The trade-off between work and leisure is particularly important in the supply side of the labour market in labour economics.

Likewise, individuals in a society often have different levels of risk aversion. When equally able individuals undertake risky activities with the potential of large payoffs, such as starting new businesses, some ventures succeed and some fail. The presence of both successful and unsuccessful ventures in a society results in economic inequality even when all individuals are identical.

Wealth concentration

Wealth concentration is a theoretical process by which, under certain conditions, newly created wealth concentrates in the possession of already-wealthy individuals or entities. According to this theory, those who already hold wealth have the means to invest in new sources of creating wealth or to otherwise leverage the accumulation of wealth, thus are the beneficiaries of the new wealth. Over time, wealth condensation can significantly contribute to the persistence of inequality within society. Thomas Piketty in his book *Capital in the Twenty-First Century* argues that the fundamental force for divergence is the usually greater return of capital (r) than economic growth (g), and that larger fortunes generate higher returns.

Finance industry

Jamie Galbraith argues that countries with larger financial sectors have greater inequality, and the effects of inequality researchers have found include higher rates of health and social problems, and lower rates of social goods, a lower level of economic utility in society from resources devoted on high-end consumption, and even a lower level of economic growth when human capital is neglected for high-end consumption. For the top twenty-one industrialised countries, counting each person equally, life expectancy is lower in more unequal countries. A similar relationship exists among U.S. states.

2013 Economics Nobel prize winner Robert J. Shiller said that rising inequality in the United States and elsewhere is the most important problem. Increasing inequality harms economic growth. High and persistent unemployment, in which inequality increases, has a negative effect on subsequent long-run economic growth. Unemployment can harm growth not only because it is a waste of resources but also because it generates redistributive pressures and subsequent distortions, drives people to poverty, constrains liquidity limiting labour mobility, and erodes self-esteem promoting social dislocation, unrest and conflict. Policies aiming at controlling unemployment and in particular at reducing its inequality-associated effects support economic growth.

The economic stratification of society into 'elites' and 'masses' played a central role in the collapse of other advanced civilisations such as the Roman, Han and Gupta empires.

Third Warning is the Environmental Disturbances – the *Climate change* is a significant and lasting change in the statistical distribution of weather patterns over periods ranging from decades to millions of years. It may be a change in average weather conditions or in the distribution of weather around the average conditions (i.e. more or fewer extreme weather events). Climate change is caused by factors such as biotic processes, variations in solar radiation received by earth, plate tectonics and volcanic eruptions. Certain human activities have also been identified as significant causes of recent climate change, often referred to as 'global warming'.

Scientists actively work to understand past and future climate by using observations and theoretical models. A climate record – extending deep into the Earth's past – has been assembled, and continues to be built up, based on geological evidence from borehole temperature profiles, cores removed from deep accumulations of ice, floral and faunal records, glacial and periglacial processes, stable-isotope and other analyses of sediment layers, and records of past sea levels. More recent data are provided by the instrumental record. General circulation models, based on the physical sciences, are often used in theoretical approaches to match past climate data, make future projections, and link causes and effects in climate change.

Global Climate Changes

The most general definition of *climate change* is a change in the statistical properties of the climate system when considered over long periods of time, regardless of cause. Accordingly, fluctuations over periods shorter than a few decades, such as El Niño, do not represent climate change.

The term sometimes is used to refer specifically to climate change caused by human activity, as opposed to changes in climate that may have resulted as part of Earth's natural processes. In this sense, especially in the context of environmental policy, the term *climate change* has become synonymous with anthropogenic global warming. Within scientific journals, *global warming* refers to surface temperature increases while *climate change* includes global warming and everything else that increasing greenhouse gas levels will affect.

On the broadest scale, the rate at which energy is received from the sun and the rate at which it is lost to space determines the equilibrium temperature and climate of earth. This energy is distributed around the globe by winds, ocean currents and other mechanisms to affect the climates of different regions.

Factors that can shape climate are called climate forcings or 'forcing mechanisms'. These include processes such as variations in solar radiation, variations in the Earth's orbit, mountain-building and continental drift and changes in greenhouse gas concentrations. There are a variety of climate change feedbacks that can either amplify or diminish the initial forcing. Some parts of the climate system, such as the oceans and ice caps, respond slowly in reaction to climate forcings, while others respond more quickly.

Forcing mechanisms can be either 'internal' or 'external'. Internal forcing mechanisms are natural processes within the climate system itself (e.g. the thermohaline circulation). External forcing mechanisms can be either natural (e.g. changes in solar output) or anthropogenic (e.g. increased emissions of greenhouse gases).

Whether the initial forcing mechanism is internal or external, the response of the climate system might be fast (e.g. a sudden cooling due to airborne volcanic ash reflecting sunlight), slow (e.g. thermal expansion of warming ocean water), or a combination (e.g. sudden loss of albedo in the arctic ocean as sea ice melts, followed by more gradual thermal expansion of the water). Therefore, the climate system can respond abruptly, but the full response to forcing mechanisms might not be fully developed for centuries or even longer.

Internal forcing mechanisms

Scientists generally define the five components of earth's climate system to include atmosphere, hydrosphere, cryosphere, lithosphere (restricted to the surface soils, rocks and sediments) and biosphere. Natural changes in the climate system ('internal forcings') result in internal 'climate variability'. Examples include the type and distribution of species and changes in ocean currents.

Ocean variability

Pacific Decadal Oscillation 1925 to 2010

The ocean is a fundamental part of the climate system, some changes in it occurring at longer timescales than in the atmosphere, massing hundreds of times more and having very high thermal inertia (such as the ocean depths still lagging today in temperature adjustment from the Little Ice Age).

Short-term fluctuations (years to a few decades), such as the El Niño-Southern Oscillation, the Pacific decadal oscillation, the North Atlantic oscillation, and the Arctic oscillation, represent climate variability rather than climate change. On longer time scales, alterations to ocean processes such as thermohaline circulation play a key role in redistributing heat by carrying out a very slow and extremely deep movement of water and the long-term redistribution of heat in the world's oceans.

A schematic of modern thermohaline circulation. Tens of millions of years ago, continental plate movement formed a land-free gap around Antarctica, allowing formation of the ACC which keeps warm waters away from Antarctica.

Life

Life affects climate through its role in the carbon and water cycles and such mechanisms as albedo, evapotranspiration, cloud formation and weathering. Examples of how life may have affected past climate include glaciation 2.3 billion years ago triggered by the evolution of oxygenic photosynthesis, glaciation 300 million years ago ushered in by long-term burial of decomposition-resistant detritus of vascular land plants (forming coal), termination of the Paleocene-Eocene Thermal Maximum 55 million years ago by flourishing marine phytoplankton, reversal of global warming 49 million years ago by 800,000 years of arctic azolla blooms and global cooling over the past 40 million years driven by the expansion of grass-grazer ecosystems.

External forcing mechanisms

Increase in atmospheric CO_2

2 levels

Milankovitch cycles from 800,000 years ago in the past to 800,000 years in the future.

Variations in CO_2, temperature and dust from the Vostok ice core over the last 450,000 years

Orbital variations

Slight variations in earth's orbit lead to changes in the seasonal distribution of sunlight reaching the earth's surface and how it is distributed across the globe. There is very little change to the area-averaged annually averaged sunshine; but there can be strong changes in the geographical and seasonal distribution. The three types of orbital variations are variations in earth's eccentricity, changes in the tilt angle of earth's axis of rotation and precession of earth's axis. Combined together, these produce Milankovitch cycles, which have a large impact on climate and are notable for their correlation to glacial and interglacial periods, their correlation with the advance and retreat of the Sahara and for their appearance in the stratigraphic record.

The IPCC notes that Milankovitch cycles drove the ice age cycles, CO_2 followed temperature change 'with a lag of some hundreds of years', and that as a feedback amplified temperature change. The depths of the ocean have a lag time in changing temperature (thermal inertia on such scale). Upon seawater temperature change, the solubility of CO_2 in the oceans changed, as well as other factors impacting air–sea CO_2 exchange.

Solar output

Main article: Solar variation

Variations in solar activity during the last several centuries based on observations of sunspots and beryllium isotopes. The period of extraordinarily few sunspots in the late seventeenth century was the Maunder minimum.

The s is the predominant source of energy input to the earth. Both long- and short-term variations in solar intensity are known to affect global climate.

Three to four billion years ago, the sun emitted only 70 per cent as much power as it does today. If the atmospheric composition had been the same as today, liquid water should not have existed on Earth. However, there is evidence for the presence of water on the early earth, in the Hadean and Archean eons, leading to what is known as the faint young Sun Paradox. Hypothesised solutions to this paradox include a vastly different atmosphere, with much higher concentrations of greenhouse gases than currently exist.

Over the following approximately 4 billion years, the energy output of the sun increased and atmospheric composition changed. The Great Oxygenation Event – oxygenation of the atmosphere around 2.4 billion years ago – was the most notable alteration. Over the next five billion years, the sun's ultimate death as it becomes a red giant and then a white dwarf will have large effects on climate, with the red giant phase possibly ending any life on earth that survives until that time.

Solar output also varies on shorter time scales, including the 11-year solar cycle and longer-term modulations. Solar intensity variations are considered to have been influential in triggering the Little Ice Age, and some of the warming observed from 1900 to 1950. The cyclical nature of the sun's energy output is not yet fully understood; it differs from the very slow change that is happening within the sun as it ages and evolves. Research indicates that solar variability has had effects including the Maunder minimum from AD 1645 to 1715, part of the Little Ice Age from AD 1550 to 1850 that was marked by relative cooling and greater glacier extent than the centuries before and afterward. Some studies point towards solar radiation increases from cyclical sunspot activity affecting global warming, and climate may be influenced by the sum of all effects (solar variation, anthropogenic radiative forcings, etc.).

Interestingly, a 2010 study *suggests*, 'that the effects of solar variability on temperature throughout the atmosphere may be contrary to current expectations'.

In an August 2011 Press Release, CERN announced the publication in the *Nature* journal the initial results from its CLOUD experiment. The results indicate that ionisation from cosmic rays significantly enhances aerosol formation in the presence of sulphuric acid and water, but in the lower atmosphere where ammonia is also required, this is insufficient to account for aerosol formation and additional trace vapours must be involved. The next step is to find more about these trace vapours, including whether they are of natural or human origin.

Volcanism

In atmospheric temperature from 1979 to 2010, determined by MSU NASA satellites, effects appear from aerosols released by major volcanic eruptions (El Chichón and Pinatubo). El Niño is a separate event, from ocean variability.

Volcanic eruptions release gases and particulates into the atmosphere. Eruptions large enough to affect climate occur on average several times per century and cause cooling (by partially blocking the transmission of solar radiation to the Earth's surface) for a period of a few years. The eruption of Mount Pinatubo in 1991, the second largest terrestrial eruption of the twentieth century (after the 1912 eruption of Novarupta[j]) affected the climate substantially. Global temperatures decreased by about 0.5 °C (0.9 °F). The eruption of Mount Tambora in 1815 caused the Year Without a Summer. Much larger eruptions, known as large igneous provinces, occur only a few times every hundred million years, but may cause global warming and mass extinctions.

Volcanoes are also part of the extended carbon cycle. Over very long (geological) time periods, they release carbon dioxide from the earth's crust and mantle, counteracting the uptake by sedimentary rocks and other geological carbon dioxide sinks. The US Geological Survey estimates are that volcanic emissions are at a much lower level than the effects of current human activities, which generate 100–300 times the amount of carbon dioxide emitted by volcanoes. A review of published studies indicates that annual volcanic emissions of carbon dioxide, including amounts released from mid-ocean ridges, volcanic arcs and hot spot volcanoes are only the equivalent of three to five days of human caused output. The annual amount put out by human activities may be greater than the amount released by supererruptions, the most recent of which was the Toba eruption in Indonesia 74,000 years ago.

Although volcanoes are technically part of the lithosphere, which itself is part of the climate system, the IPCC explicitly defines volcanism as an external forcing agent.

Plate tectonics

Over the course of millions of years, the motion of tectonic plates reconfigures global land and ocean areas and generates topography. This can affect both global and local patterns of climate and atmosphere–ocean circulation.

The position of the continents determines the geometry of the oceans and therefore influences patterns of ocean circulation. The locations of the seas are important in controlling the transfer of heat and moisture across the globe and therefore, in determining global climate. A recent example of tectonic control on ocean circulation is the formation of the Isthmus of Panama about 5 million years ago, which shut off direct mixing between the Atlantic and Pacific Oceans. This strongly affected the ocean dynamics of what is now the Gulf Stream and may have led to Northern Hemisphere ice cover. During the Carboniferous period, about 300 to 360 million years ago, plate tectonics may have triggered large-scale storage of carbon and increased glaciation. Geologic evidence points to a 'megamonsoonal' circulation pattern during the time of the supercontinent Pangaea, and climate modelling suggests that the existence of the supercontinent was conducive to the establishment of monsoons.

The size of continents is also important. Because of the stabilising effect of the oceans on temperature, yearly temperature variations are generally lower in coastal areas than they are inland. A larger supercontinent will therefore have more area in which climate is strongly seasonal than will several smaller continents or islands.

Human influences

Global warming

In the context of climate variation, anthropogenic factors are human activities which affect the climate. The scientific consensus on climate change is 'that climate is changing and that these changes are in large part caused by human activities, and it "is largely irreversible".'

'Science has made enormous inroads in understanding climate change and its causes, and is beginning to help develop a strong understanding of current and potential impacts that will affect people today and in coming decades. This understanding is crucial because it allows decision makers to place climate change in the context of other large challenges facing the nation and the world. There are still some uncertainties, and there always will be in understanding a complex system like Earth's climate. Nevertheless, there is a strong, credible body of evidence, based on multiple lines of research, documenting that climate is changing and that these changes are in large part caused by human activities. While much remains to be learned, the core phenomenon, scientific questions, and hypotheses have been examined thoroughly and have stood firm in the face of serious scientific debate and careful evaluation of alternative explanations'.

United States National Research Council, *Advancing the Science of Climate Change*

Of most concern in these anthropogenic factors is the increase in CO_2 levels due to emissions from fossil fuel combustion, followed by aerosols (particulate matter in the atmosphere) and the CO_2 released by cement manufacture. Other factors, including land use, ozone depletion, animal agriculture[54] and deforestation, are also of concern in the roles they play – both separately and in conjunction with other factors – in affecting climate, microclimate and measures of climate variables.

Physical evidence

Comparisons between Asian Monsoons from AD 200 to 2000 (staying in the background on other plots), Northern Hemisphere temperature, Alpine glacier extent (vertically inverted as marked) and human history as noted by the U.S. NSF.

Arctic temperature anomalies over a 100-year period as estimated by NASA. Typical high monthly variance can be seen, while longer term averages highlight trends.

Evidence for climatic change is taken from a variety of sources that can be used to reconstruct past climates. Reasonably complete global records of surface temperature are available beginning from the mid-late nineteenth century. For earlier periods, most of the evidence is indirect – climatic changes are inferred from changes in proxies, indicators that reflect climate, such as vegetation, ice cores, dendrochronology, sea level change and glacial geology.

Temperature measurements and proxies

The instrumental temperature record from surface stations was supplemented by radios on de balloons, extensive atmospheric monitoring by the mid-twentieth century, and, from the 1970s on, with global satellite data as well. The $^{18}O/^{16}O$ ratio in calcite and ice core samples used to deduce ocean temperature in the distant past is an example of a temperature proxy method, as are other climate metrics noted in subsequent categories.

Historical and archaeological evidence

Climate change in the recent past may be detected by corresponding changes in settlement and agricultural patterns. Archaeological evidence, oral history and historical documents can offer insights into past changes in the climate. Climate change effects have been linked to the collapse of various civilisations.

Decline in thickness of glaciers worldwide over the past half century

Glaciers

Glaciers are considered among the most sensitive indicators of climate change. Their size is determined by a mass balance between snow input and melt output. As temperatures warm, glaciers retreat unless snow precipitation increases to make up for the additional melt; the converse is also true.

Glaciers grow and shrink due both to natural variability and external forcings. Variability in temperature, precipitation and englacial and subglacial hydrology can strongly determine the evolution of a glacier in a particular season. Therefore, one must average over a decadal or longer time-scale and/or over a many individual glaciers to smooth out the local short-term variability and obtain a glacier history that is related to climate.

A world glacier inventory has been compiled since the 1970s, initially based mainly on aerial photographs and maps but now relying more on satellites. This compilation tracks more than 100,000 glaciers covering a total area of approximately 240,000 km², and preliminary estimates indicate that the remaining ice cover is around 445,000 km². The World Glacier Monitoring Service collects data annually on glacier retreat and glacier mass balance. From this data, glaciers worldwide have been found to be shrinking significantly, with strong glacier retreats in the 1940s, stable or growing conditions during the 1920s and 1970s and again retreating from the mid-1980s to present.

The most significant climate processes since the middle to late Pliocene (approximately 3 million years ago) are the glacial and interglacial cycles. The present interglacial period (the Holocene) has lasted about 11,700 years. Shaped by orbital variations, responses such as the rise and fall of continental ice sheets and significant sea-level changes helped create the climate. Other changes, including Heinrich events, Dansgaard–Oeschger events and the Younger Dryas, however, illustrate how glacial variations may also influence climate without the orbital forcing.

Glaciers leave behind moraines that contain a wealth of material – including organic matter, quartz and potassium that may be dated – recording the periods in which a glacier advanced and retreated. Similarly, by tephrochronological techniques, the lack of glacier cover can be identified by the presence of soil or volcanic tephra horizons whose date of deposit may also be ascertained.

This time series, based on satellite data, shows the annual Arctic sea ice minimum since 1979. The September 2010 extent was the third lowest in the satellite record.

Arctic sea ice loss

The decline in Arctic sea ice, both in extent and thickness, over the last several decades is further evidence for rapid climate change. Sea ice is frozen seawater that floats on the ocean surface. It covers millions of square miles in the polar regions, varying with the seasons. In the Arctic, some sea ice remains year after year, whereas almost all Southern Ocean or Antarctic sea ice melts away and reforms annually. Satellite observations show that Arctic sea ice is now declining at a rate of 11.5 per cent per decade, relative to the 1979 to 2000 average.

Vegetation

A change in the type, distribution and coverage of vegetation may occur given a change in the climate. Some changes in climate may result in increased precipitation and warmth, resulting in improved plant growth and the subsequent sequestration of airborne CO_2. A gradual increase in warmth in a region will lead to earlier flowering and fruiting times, driving a change in the timing of life cycles of dependent organisms. Conversely, cold will cause plant bio-cycles to lag. Larger, faster or more radical changes, however, may result in vegetation stress, rapid plant loss and desertification in certain circumstances. An example of this occurred during the Carboniferous Rainforest Collapse (CRC), an extinction event 300 million years ago. At this time, vast rainforests covered the equatorial region of Europe and America. Climate change devastated these tropical rainforests, abruptly fragmenting the habitat into isolated 'islands' and causing the extinction of many plant and animal species.

Satellite data available in recent decades indicate that global terrestrial net primary production increased by 6 per cent from 1982 to 1999, with the largest portion of that increase in tropical ecosystems, then decreased by 1 per cent from 2000 to 2009.

Pollen analysis

Palynology is the study of contemporary and fossil palynomorphs, including pollen. Palynology is used to infer the geographical distribution of plant species, which vary under different climate conditions. Different groups of plants have pollen with distinctive shapes and surface textures, and since the outer surface of pollen is composed of a very resilient material, they resist decay. Changes in the type of pollen found in different layers of sediment in lakes, bogs or river deltas indicate changes in plant communities. These changes are often a sign of a changing climate. As an example, palynological studies have been used to track changing vegetation patterns throughout the Quaternary glaciations and especially since the last glacial maximum.

Top: Arid ice age climate
Middle: Atlantic Period, warm and wet
Bottom: Potential vegetation in climate now if not for human effects like agriculture.

Precipitation

Past precipitation can be estimated in the modern era with the global network of precipitation gauges. Surface coverage over oceans and remote areas is relatively sparse, but, reducing reliance on interpolation, satellite data has been available since the 1970s. Quantification of climatological variation of precipitation in prior centuries and epochs is less complete but approximated using proxies such as marine sediments, ice cores, cave stalagmites and tree rings.

Climatological temperatures substantially affect precipitation. For instance, during the Last Glacial Maximum of 18,000 years ago, thermal-driven evaporation from the oceans onto continental landmasses was low, causing large areas of extreme desert, including polar deserts (cold but with low rates of precipitation). In contrast, the world's climate was wetter than today near the start of the warm Atlantic Period of 8,000 years ago.

Estimated global land precipitation increased by approximately 2 per cent over the course of the twentieth century, though the calculated trend varies if different time endpoints are chosen, complicated by ENSO and other oscillations, including greater global land precipitation in the 1950s and 1970s than the later 1980s and 1990s despite the positive trend over the century overall. Similar slight overall increase in global river runoff and in average soil moisture has been perceived.

Ice cores

Analysis of ice in a core drilled from an ice sheet, such as the Antarctic ice sheet, can be used to show a link between temperature and global sea level variations. The air trapped in bubbles in the ice can also reveal the CO_2 variations of the atmosphere from the distant past, well before modern environmental influences. The study of these ice cores has been a significant indicator of the changes in CO_2 over many millennia and continues to provide valuable information about the differences between ancient and modern atmospheric conditions.

Animals

Remains of beetles are common in freshwater and land sediments. Different species of beetles tend to be found under different climatic conditions. Given the extensive lineage of beetles whose genetic makeup has not altered significantly over the millennia, knowledge of the present climatic range of the different species and the age of the sediments in which remains are found past climatic conditions may be inferred.

Similarly, the historical abundance of various http://en.wikipedia.org/wiki/Fish species has been found to have a substantial relationship with observed climatic conditions.

Changes in the primary productivity of autotrophs in the oceans can affect marine food webs.

Sea level change

Current sea level rise is about 3 mm/year worldwide. According to the US National Oceanic and Atmospheric Administration (NOAA), 'this is a significantly larger rate than the sea-level rise averaged over the last several thousand years', and the rate may be increasing. Sea level rises can considerably influence human populations in coastal and island regions and natural environments like marine ecosystems.

Between 1870 and 2004, global average sea levels rose to a total of 195 mm (7.7 in) and 1.46 mm (0.057 in) per year. From 1950 to 2009, measurements show an average annual rise in sea level of 1.7 ± 0.3 mm per year, with satellite data showing a rise of 3.3 ± 0.4 mm per year from 1993 to 2009. The reason for recent increase is unclear, perhaps owing to decadal variation. It is unclear whether the increased rate reflects an increase in the underlying long-term trend.

There are two main mechanisms that contribute to observed sea level rise: (1) thermal expansion: ocean water expands as it warms and (2) the melting of major stores of land ice like glaciers and ice sheets.

Sea level rise is one of several lines of evidence that support the view that the global climate has recently warmed. The global community of climate scientists confirms that it is very likely human-induced (anthropogenic) warming contributed to the sea level rise observed in the latter half of the twentieth century.

Sea level rise is expected to continue for centuries. In 2007, the Intergovernmental Panel on Climate Change (IPCC) projected that during the twenty-first century, sea level will rise another 18 to 59 cm (7.1 to 23.2 in), but these numbers do not include 'uncertainties in climate-carbon cycle feedbacks nor do they include the full effects of changes in ice sheet flow'. More recent projections assessed by the US National Research Council (2010) suggest possible sea level rise over the twenty-first century of between 56 and 200 cm (22 and 79 in). The Third National Climate Assessment (NCA), released on 6 May 2014, projects a sea level rise of 1 to 4 feet by 2100.

On the timescale of centuries to millennia, the melting of ice sheets could result in even higher sea level rise. Partial deglaciation of the Greenland ice sheet, and possibly the West Antarctic ice sheet, could contribute 4 to 6 m (13 to 20 ft) or more to sea level rise.

Work by a team led by Veerabhadran Ramanathan of the Scripps Institution of Oceanography suggests that a quick way to stave off impending sea level rise is to cut emissions of short-lived climate warmers such as methane and soot.

Fourth Danger is the war. The two important wars on Afghanistan and Iraq has cost America 6 Trillion dollars and still nothing has changed much in these countries for last ten years. A recent report suggests that taken together, the Iraq and Afghanistan conflicts will end up costing somewhere between US\$ 4 and US\$ 6 trillion. This includes long-term medical care and disability compensation for service members, veterans and families, military replenishment and social and economic costs. About 4,488 US soldiers were killed in Iraq war alone and among the 180,000 Iraqi deaths almost 80 per cent were civilians. The United States has done the same mistake long back with Vietnam War in which 58,000 American soldiers and millions of Vietnamese died.

Wars in Middle East, Israel, Palestine, Ukraine, Syria are killing more civilians than soldiers. There is always possibility that a full-fledged Third World War may erupt by 2019. Our chances of survival is weak, and we may become less human.

The United Nations defines 'major wars' as military conflicts inflicting 1,000 battlefield deaths per year. In 1965, there were ten major wars under way. The new millennium began with much of the world consumed in armed conflict or cultivating an uncertain peace. As of mid-2005, there were eight major wars under way (down from fifteen at the end of 2003), with as many as two dozen 'lesser' conflicts ongoing with varying degrees of intensity.

Most of these are civil or 'intrastate' wars, fueled as much by racial, ethnic or religious animosities as by ideological fervour. Most victims are civilians, a feature that distinguishes modern conflicts. During World War I, civilians made up fewer than 5 per cent of all casualties. Today, 75 per cent or more of those killed or wounded in wars are non-combatants.

Africa, to a greater extent than any other continent, is afflicted by war. Africa has been marred by more than twenty major civil wars since 1960. Rwanda, Somalia, Angola, Sudan, Liberia and Burundi are among those countries that have recently suffered serious armed conflicts.

War has caused untold economic and social damage to the countries of Africa. Food production is impossible in conflict areas, and famine often results. Widespread conflict has condemned many of Africa's children to lives of misery and, in certain cases, has threatened the existence of traditional African cultures.

Conflict prevention, mediation, humanitarian intervention and demobilisation are among the tools needed to underwrite the success of development assistance programmes. Nutrition and education programmes, for example, cannot succeed in a nation at war. Billions of dollars of development assistance have been virtually wasted in war-ravaged countries such as Liberia, Somalia and Sudan.

Fifth warning is the famine: World population has grown at alarming rate, the seventh billion has come in just twelve years. It is interesting to know that 15 per cent population of world (Europe and USA) control 45 per cent of World GDP, on other hand, Africa's 15 per cent of world population has to satisfy with 5 per cent of World GDP. Every year many African countries still had to go through hunger and death.

World Bank and IMF are constructions of America and European mind, and they solve the problems of their own region; some countries have more debt than GDP. Policies of all the international organisations are being dictated by American and European alliance, and developing countries have no role to play, Even UN organisations are no exception.

Sixth warning is earthquake: There has been increase in the earthquake eruptions, Nostradamus predicted many earthquakes near France and Italy. Tsunami was among the deadliest natural disasters in human history, with at least 290,000 people killed or missing in fourteen countries. The 2004 Indian Ocean earthquake was an undersea mega thrust earthquake that occurred at 00:58:53 UTC on Sunday, 26 December 2004, with an epicentre off the west coast of Sumatra, Indonesia.

Another 6.8-magnitude earthquake has hit Japan's northern coast near the nuclear power plant in the 2011 earthquake and tsunami.

The 2011 Japan disaster killed about 19,000 people. That disaster also triggered multiple meltdowns at the Fukushima plant. More than 100,000 people are still unable to go home due to fear of radiation contamination from the plant.

Last **and Seventh Biblical Warning is Plague:** Most of the infection diseases are under control at least in developed nations and developing economies. Many infectious disease like smallpox has been eradicated and polio is on the verge of eradication from the globe. But non-communicable silent diseases have overtaken the world for the last fifteen years at alarming rates, this includes cardiovascular problems, cancer, diabetes and obesity. Developing and emerging economies have been more affected by these conditions and 65 per cent cause of death. As per WHO, 85 per cent of all the non-communicable diseases are preventable can be prevented and delayed with good lifestyle and adopting good healthy diet including less carbohydrate and refined fats and more of fibre, mineral, vitamin rich vegetables and fruits.

On average, an American takes 265 litres of soft drinks every year.

The world has a burgeoning appetite for meat. Fifty years ago global consumption was 70 m tonnes. By 2007 – the latest year for which comparable data are available – it had risen to 268 m tonnes. In a similar vein, the amount of meat eaten by each person has leapt from around 22 kg in 1961 to 40 kg in 2007. Tastes have changed at the same time. Cow (beef and veal) was top of the menu in the early 1960s, accounting for 40 per cent of meat consumption, but by 2007 its share had fallen to 23 per cent. Pig is now the animal of choice, with around 99 m tonnes consumed. Meanwhile, advances in battery farming and health-related changes in Western diets have helped propel poultry from 12 per cent to 31 per cent of the global total. Although populous middle-income countries such as China are driving the worldwide demand for meat, it is mainly Western countries, who still eat most per person. Luxembourgers, who top this chart, are second only to Argentinians in beef consumption. Austrians are the keenest pig-eaters, wolfing down 66 kg every year – just more than Serbians, Spaniards and even neighbouring Germans. At the other end of the scale, cow-revering Indians eat only 3.2 kg of meat each, the least of the 177 countries assessed.

CHAPTER 3

ADVENT OF III ANTICHRIST: PROPHECY OF NOSTRADAMUS

1.1

Estant afsis de nuict fecret eftude Seul repose fur la felle d'aerain: Flame exigue fortant de folitude Fait pfperer qn'eft a croire vain.	At night, sitting secretly in study, he (GOD) rest on brass tripod. A flame comes out of nothingness, making successful which had been in hurry.

Divine Power takes control of his mind (For the Second Birth of Avatar) into trance and prepare his mind by divinisation for forecasting the world future events, he is sitting in night study, out of emptiness comes a voice making trance possible for third antichrist (Divine).

What is Second Birth of Spirit, First birth from the womb of mother in physical form, all of us come this way in physical life form. Even Jesus came this way. Second birth is the birth in spirit through divinisation, or popularly called DIKSHA or NAAM or Shabd or AUM or *Omen* or Kalma by a *guru* or saints in India or around the world.

Unless you are born of water and spirit, you cannot enter in the kingdom of God – Jesus Christ.

Verily Verily I say unto thee except a man be born again (Second birth), he cannot enter the kingdom of God.

Again in Bible same words are repeated that you will have to be born in spirit and water (Light which is seen by a devotee when he or she meditates between two eyes and at forehead, and hear sound and vibration, under the instruction of a holy *guru* or saint.

The said the Jesus unto them, when ye have lifted up the son of man then shall see know that I am He.

To those who are chosen one, *God* sends saints or Prophet to bring back lost sheeps to the kingdom of *God* and this is the reason he creates two type of *Godhood* entity one is *Guru* or Prophet who is the Mercifull and competent to take his disciple back to kingdom of *God* and other is avatar which is seen in Hindu traditions through ages. He is God personified and fully competent to take souls back to *God* but he is also commissioned for additional work of punishing the wicked and people going against the law of nature. Therefore, he rules the nation with his punishment policy and persecutes the Earthly king with his divine weapon which is given to him by Cosmic Government. He works through his one essential rule punishment of accumulated bad karma by nations, religions, society, sects, castes, group of people, organisation or individuals, leaders for their wrong policy, head of nations, political leaders and bureaucratical structures.

And the Word was made flesh and Dwelt among us.

This is cosmic Vibration Devotee hear this sound also see light at the forhead and between eyes when she or he is initiated by GURU(Holy Master) under his holy instructions.

This is type of divinization technique, divine power (GOD) uses for the astral birth of Antichrist (Avatar), Nostrademus uses the word third antichrist in the line of Nepolean and Hitler for start of Ist and IInd World War and IIIRD antichrist for the start of IIIrd World War, secondly I will make it clear that He will persecute the church as Church do not follow doctrine of rebirth and law of karma which is seen in Hinduisim, Budhuisim and various religion of East. Even our old and orthodox religious activity and various religious Groups are under persecution because of the bad karmic reaction. This is the form of GOD shown to Avatar, He wears long heavy Rob and He (GOD) sprinkles with water(Bose-Einstein condensates) his garment and foots, after he puts a wand in the tripod made by legs, a voice with fear going through whole body, a lightening of lifetron, astral body of antichrist(AVATAR) is thus born. This is how the Lifetronic body of Astral light body behave, past life births also comes to the memory of Avatar. I will emphasise it again and again GOD Discloses who will be the Avatar or IIIrd Antichrist to the heaven and Earth. He have been decided thousands years back who is the AVATAR and GOD shows him his various births through animal kingdom as different species and final birth as human being. He shows Evolutionary cycle of soul from lower species to human being. This is the warning to those saints and GURUs(Masters) who declares themselves as Avatar or IInd coming of Christ. Anybodies Who has gone under this divinization and GOD has come to him in this form is Avatar.

I. XXIX

Quand le poiffon tereftre & aquatique, For forte vague au grauier fera mis: Sa forme eftrange fuaue & horrifique, Par mer aux murs bien toft les ennemis.	A Fish which travels over land when cast upon the sea reach to seashore, its shape horrible & foreign. Enemies soon reach the walls.

A fish (GOD) by power of his subtle matter produce great waves on sea, like Tsunami a supernatural Power given to antichrist, he soon reaches the foreign country by invasion through sea route

This is the Great Power given to Avatar, He invades the Nation through sea route, will be a very powerful Avatar, he will be given 64 SuperNatural power by GOD. Some of the Power will be:

To Him that overcome will I Grant to sit with me on my throne, even as I also overcome, and sitting with my father on his throne.

1. The power of making ones body or anything else as small as possible.

2. The power making ones body or anything else as large as possible.
3. Power of becoming lord over everything.
4. Power of satisfying all the desire, kama by will.
5. Power of bringing anything under control.
6. Power of obtaining anything he or she likes.
7. Power of making one body as heavy as he likes.
8. Power of making ones body as light as possible.
9. Power of creating fire or lightening in sky.

Inspite of all the Power mentioned above he will be given A divine Sword which will emenates from his Two below and two above Incisor tooths (Subtle astral Body of AVATAR).

I. XXXIX

De nuict dan le lict le supresme estrangle
Pour trop auoir subiourné blond esleu
Par trois l'Empire subroge exancle,
A mort mettra carte, pacquet ne leu.

At night the final (claimant) one will be strangled in his bed because he became too involved with the blond heir elect. The Empire is enslaved and three men substituted. He is put to death with neither letter nor packet read.

Thia is the failed Qutrain, Claimant is the Disciple of Kirpal Singh Ji Maharaj who see and hear during his astral travel in meditation, he is too much involved with Sister of Avatar, Loi Ji Turk(she is Blond and American in this birth & Jerry astra Turk has adopted as her daughter) & supposed to be elected President of America, Avatar will strangle man in his bed at night, a failed future event.

Loi Ji Turk used to sent letters and Booklets to her Brother AVATAR in India, but she did not know that He has to Implement the law of Justice on earth and heaven, selected by Cosmic Government(Aliens). This is failed an she left for heaven.

I. XL. I

Siege en Cité & de nuict assaillie
Peu eschappez non loing de mer conflit,
Femme de ioye, retours fils defaillie,
Poison & lettte cachée dans le olic.

The city is besieged and assaulted by night;
few have escaped; a battle not far from the sea.
A woman faints with joy at the return of her son,
poison in the folds of the hidden letters.

This again failed Quatrain, The besieged city is florida where Jerry astra Turk and loi Ji Turk used to lived, now both are diseased. A Women, Jerry Astra Turk faints as she sees return of her son appointed AVATAR by cosmic Govt. As I have mentioned variously Jerry astra son Julius Caesar Scaliger is reborn as AVATAR in india, both Mother and son has met in astral world by Arrangement by the mercy of GOD. She used to sent him letters, poisoned means he will not be able to follow her mother as he has been taken by GOD for his own Purpose. He has been choosen as IIIrd Antichrist to start War on earth and ultimately bringing Peace on Earth. Cosmic Govt has arranged for war starting from 1992 but Cosmic Govt delayed the war by 22 years and I expect Preparation for war will start by 2014 and Ultimately AVATAR will make his Physical Appearance by 2019.

I. LXXXIIII

Lune obscurcie aux profondex tenebres,
Son frere passe de couleur ferrugine:
Le grand caché long temps soubs les tenebres,
Tiendra fer dans la playe sanguine.

The moon eclipsed in great gloom,
his brother becomes the colour of blood.
The great one hidden for a long time in the shadows,
will hold the blade in the bloody wound.

Brother(Appointed AVATAR) of Loi Ji turk will soon becomes the color of blood as he will start war and there will be many who try to kill him.

I. XCIIII

Au port Selin le tyran mis à mort,
La liberté non pourtant recouuree
Le nouueau Mars par vindicte & remort,
Dame par la foere de frayeur honoree.

The tyrant Selim will be put to death at the harbor
but Liberty will not be regained, however.
A new war arises from vengeance and remorse.
A lady is honored through force of terror.

Again the failed Quatrain, American top Leader will be put
to death by AVATAR and Loi Ji Turk American Sister of
AVATAR will be made President of USA by force of terror.
A future which never took place as Aliens had to change
their mind as per the World situation.

II. V

Qu'en dans poiffon, fer & letter enfermee, Hors fortira qui puis fera la guerre: Aura par mer fa claffe bien ramee, Apparoiffant pres de latine terre.	The weapon and secrete document are kept in fish, Out of which will come a man who will later on make war Fleet have taken him to appear near Italian shore.

The divine weapons & secrete document of war are kept in
fish(Soul), out of it will come a Avatar who will makes war
of Truth, at that time his Soul has appeared near Italian
shore(Because of his strong Karmic connection of his past
life with italy & france). Divine Power has called him for
the purpose and therefore has attached in his astral body
various type of Divine Weapon which he will uses to renew
the Earth.

IIIrd Antichrist was Born as Julius Caesar Scaliger in his
8 birth before Present birth in Italy on 1484, and lived in

france as Philospher and Physician, His astral body was taken to Italian shore because of his Memory of his birth attached to this region.

I. L

De l'aquatique triplicate naiftra, D'vn qui fera le ieudy pour fa fefte: Son bruit, loz, regne, fa puiffance Croiftra, Par terre & mer aux Oriens tempefte.	From three water signs will be born a man who will make Thursday his feast day, His renown, power, praise and rule will increase by land & Sea.

A country surrounded by Water on its three side, i.e INDIA, will be born a man who will makes thursday as its feast day, In India hindus makes Thursday, day of Vishnu workship, Muslim make Friday as their day of workship & Christian Sunday, this indicating clearly the birth of Vishnu Avatar, Avatar. Even the layman in india know the day of workship of Vishnu is thursday.

His power, praise and rule will increase by land and sea. This is very clear Qutrain for All of us on earth, how the GOD Predict through Nostrademus 500 before of Coming of his Representative in the form of Avatar, That GOD is Beyond Comprehension and All powerful, Even he takes Human Soul his Incarnates No power on earth comes in his way.

Kal Yuga of 4800 is ending and Satya Age is about to begin, is Awaiting for his Coming as king and Mighty Powerful

Being with Divine Weapons to Balance the Wheel of karma, Avatar Incarnates is not known to Western World, therefore this prophecy indicates clearly the advent of Last Avatar of Vishnu Kalki Avatar, who is suppose to come at the end of present kal yuga.

He will start his war from East.

In the 1992 he was informed and the number 7 given to him of about his final coming in 1999 by Helping king of Mangol to bring back to his seat.

GOD has changed his mind and finally 20 years delay was announced by Heaven as there was much complication in heaven created by Astral GODS. We are expecting his holy war starting in final war in 2019.

II. XIII

Le corps fans ame plus n'eftre en facrifice, lour De la mort mis en natiuite: l'esprit diuin fera l'ame felice, Voyant le verbe en fon eternite.

The body without soul cannot be of use in sacrificing, when the body dies it comes to rebirth at the same day. Divine spirit rejoice the incarnated soul seeing the miserable state of world.

A body without Soul is of no use, it cannot be used even for sacrifice, when the body dies it comes to rebirth, a concept found in eastern religion from ancient time, divine spirit rejoice the soul whom GOD has choosen to be coming Avatar, as its sees worldly leaders rule badly & in state of violence & atheism.

As per Hinduisim and various religion of Eastern World, rebirth has been advocated by all saints and holy scriptures, Through this quatrain cosmic Government see the state of Earthly kingdom so miserable, Social, economical, environmental and political imbalance is at its height, therefore GOD takes control of his choosen Avatar on earth and Broadcast to the world about his coming.

Doctrine of rebirth is being rediscovered by certain Western Gurus like DavidIcke, Rupert Sheldrake, Deepak Chopra, Amit Goswami and many more.

II. XLV

Trop le ciel pleure l'androgyn Pocree, Pres de ciel fang human refpandu, Par mort trop tard grand people recree. Tard & toft vient le fecours attendu.	The heaven cry too much at the birth of androgyny; Human blood spread upto heaven, Nations could not be Revived because of great death of People, though helps come late.

As heaven weeps so much when they saw the Birth of Androgyn(Qualities of both male & female, electric and magnetic Property in equal proportion), Word Androgyn her denote him to Quality wise both male and female character. As lower heaven is always busy in sexuality,

Money, Fame, anger, jealousy, they saw their downfall, even Devi and Devta are worst affected by Jealousy and thus blood was seen in heaven because of war started by Avatar. Earthly nations will see great war but help will come late. Human blood spread to the heaven denotes so many false saints earth is flooded with them. In India and also in west around 500 saints have claimed themselves to be Avatar in past 500 years, but no one can prove themselves to be Avatar, like Prem Rawat Ji Maharaj(Brother of Satpal Ji maharaj of India) also known as Maharaj Ji of india, In 80's he also claimed himself be Avatar, Saint Satya sai also once told that he is kalki, Kalki Bhagwan in Satya lok of south india at present also call himself to be Avatar and had larger followers, not only this there is cult of false GURU which has become very Popular not only in east but also in west now, Swami ram(Dehradun) sex cultism, miracle of various type has cheated there devotes and now his successors in his name are earning donations and continue with bad karma, Swami ram and other false saints and their dovotees are creating a negative Morphogenic field in astral world & they cannot save themselves from its effects through down causation of consciousness.

II. XXVII

Le diuin verbe fera du ciel frappe, Quine Pourra proceder plus auant: Du referent le fecret eftoupe, Qu'on marchera par deffus	Divine Voice will be struck from the heaven & will not be able to continue until the revelation, so people will & daunt. walk above their head.

Divine call will be struck from heaven but he(GOD) will not continue to enlighten him unless he(GOD) reveals his purpose & revelation to Incarnated one.

Divine Voice will Appoint Jerry Astra Turk (A devotee of Kirpal Singh Ji Maharaj) son of Past Birth as Avatar,(Julius Caesar Scaliger was the son of Jerry Astra Turk born in 1484 in Italy, In present birth in America Miss Jerry was the Devotee of Kirpal Singh(a True Saint), same Julius Caesar Scaliger is born as Avatar in present birth), Heaven was confused with the Appointed one, therefore heaven shows him Revelations related to IIIrd World War, War of Justice from heaven.

III. II

Le diuin verbe Donrra a la fubftance, Caprins ciel terre, or occult au laict myftique. Corps, ame, efprit ayant toute puiffance,	The divine words will be give to earth and heaven, Occult gold in mystic act, Body, mind & Soul all powerful, Tant foubz fes pied everything below his feet at the seat of heaven.

The Divine message will be given to heaven & earth, A supreme mystical act will be shown to Avatar in the form that everything on earth & heaven moves by the power of GOD & everything Is below his (GOD) feet. There are different type of divinization method GOD uses for Avatar, Showing him different layers of soul(Spirit), innermost layer is golden and GOD gives him freedom after removal of his layer.(He is declared as immortal without birth and death) Soul is covered by five Coverings:1. Annamayakosha, which is dependent on food we takes.2. Pranamayakosha, which is life forces helps in digestion, assimilation, Excretion and circulation.3. Manomayakosha, Sense vision, hearing, touch, taste, smell..4. Gyanamayakosha,(Third Eye or Divya Shakshu) see What is truth, Inteligence or Budhi and judge what is truth & false.5. Anandmayakosha, innermost covering which is bliss without thought. This is the last covering of Soul which is when removed Soul regain its status as pure soul or spirit and fully competent to Initiate devotee after truth, such soul is appointed by GOD as Satguru or Saints. Earth is full of false Gurus and light and sound they provide it to their devotes cannot take them to Paradise or Satloka, a True abode abode of Soul. Even this type of soul is not GOD or have GOD substance. Most of Learned Personality and saints equates soul merzes with the oversoul and become GOD is not True.

GOD is Separate from Soul and makes 6th substance even beyond Consciousness, This has been mentioned as Purusha, Atmavatattvam(Upanishada). GOD is a all Powerful and not present in the universe either in matter or living being. Its very sad that Saints in past and present equates soul with GOD which is not true. GOD is mllions time more Powerful than Soul. All the Yoga Practice and Meditation, Spirtuality is concern with SOUL or Spirit which under the instruction of GURU or saints leads to NIRVANA or MOKSHA not subject to birth and death cycle and such soul is now called Jivanmukta. Soul is the son of GOD and that why Jesus was called son of GOD. Jesus was also born in the womb by Fertilization process not Immaculate conception Bird of Paradise (Soul) is shielded by these 5 coverings.

GOD is even Beyond Soul and different entity, altogether is million type more powerful compare to soul. GOD is ParamTattwa and do not have any resemblance to the soul or Atma. GOD does not remain in the universe in any living being. Paramtattwa or paramatma or Puroshotma or atmattatwam is Supreme being cannot be compare with anything in the universe. He is even Beyond Consciousness. He is not even present in saints, they are purest form of Soul or spirit but not GOD itself. In Past GOD is only revealed in AVATAR, In satya age, its was only VISHNU Who was AVATAR of GOD, In treta Yuga and Dwapara Yuga RAMA and KRISHNA were only AVATAR and now at the end of Kalyuga, Kalki will be only AVATAR of GOD. They are also GOD Personified and Commissioned from GOD to work the WILL of GOD on Earth and heaven. They generally take charge of National & International Karma and Punish them very badly once they manifest(Publicly come in Picture). AVATAR look like human being but Charged with the Power of GOD to Settle the bad Pralabhda karma of earth. They are like Superman and leads the army of Aliens on Earth and astral World. They have divine weapon with them, which cannot been seen by earthly human being but they can sense its effects. At Present Nostrademus has clearly written the Prophecy related to Birth and work of Kalki avatar who is supposed to have taken divine Incarnation in 1969 and will manifest himself by 2019.

IV. XXIIII

Ouy foubs terr faincte dame voix fainte, Humaine flamme pour diuine voir luire. Fera des feuls de leure fang terre tainte. Et les faincts teples pour les impurs deftruire.

Faint voice of a woman is heard under holy Ground, A human flame lights up for divine voice, this will cause the earth to be Stained with the blood of celibate. and ruined the temples by the celibate.

A low pitch women voice(Avatar mother of past birth) is heard calling her son to be holy one, this human flame lights for divine voice, her son will cause earth to be stained with bloody war not seen before, this so called Celibate son of a holy women will destroy material temples of GOD on earth.

Jerry Astra Turk Past Mother of Avatar, called her son to become disciple of Saint Kirpal Singh Ji of India, Kirpal made various tour of America from 1955 onwards and initiated various disciple in Surat Shabd Yoga called Santmanth. Miss Jerry astra Turk of America was one of Disciple Initiated by him during his visit(Even Jerry Astra used to see his Master kirpal in her inner vision even before she met her GURU because Jerry was very important Personality and gave birth to Julius Caesar Scaliger in 1484 in Italy and this same Person is going to be born as AVATAR. In 1992 Jerry Distributed some Books and his teaching manual of his Guru to her son of Past life to be appointed as Avatar. GOD Chooses her son to be Avatar and He will stain the Earth with IIIrd World War and will Destroy the Physical Temples.

Celibacy is unknown in west, and this is the main reason of downfall of Western Occult & religion, Sex is taken as means to enjoyment and excitement, but if preserved it is source of kandalini Power when aroused under a competent Master can lead us to a pious life full of energy and lead us into the mystery of our past and Universe. Some of Saints like Swami Ram, Prem Rawat (Balyogi of india) has used this Kundalini energy in negative way, like Gratification of Senses & Money.

Let me make it clear, mere manifesting this divine light & Sound in oneself does not give foolproof of being a True Master, even some body who can shows us this light and sound Principle does not mean that they are Satguru or True Master. So called Guru like Satpal Ji maharaj, his bother Balyogi Prem Rawat can show us light but cannot take us beyond High heaven(Astral World).

Swami Ram was a Sex maniac & had physical relationship with his many Women Disciple, He used to show us various type of Miracles to attract Disciple & Money in west and india.

I do agree these Masters gives Peace and Fullfill desire of their devotes upto a limit but cannot takes us to GOD or kingdom of GOD, as neither they are near to GOD nor they are Appointed by GOD Power to Work as SatGuru or Master on Earth or heaven. As the GURU will be so will be disciple, there is no excuse in this arena.

Even Indian GODS and goddesses, Like Vaisno devi, Durga, kali, Bhairva, Akhori babas, Brahm kumaris are different cultism and not pure spiritual entity and cannot be above law of karma, they are also punished time to time for their activities which increase violence and giving knowledge beyond what they know.

Even Master cannot make his son or nephew Masters. GOD Power or Cosmic power Decides who will be Satguru or True Master on Earth and Astral World.

Here again one thing I would like to Mentioned who is Satguru or True Master.

Satguru is the Master who has completed his full development of SOUL and reached to kingdom of GOD which All the religion in present and past has longed for, But Even they are not GOD, GOD is million times more Powerful and Creative than Perfect Master, Therefore even Masters are under his control. GOD is different Substance altogether & cannot be thinked at all.

There is massive confusion about Sat Guru and fake gurus, who pose themselves as Satguru

VIII. XV.

Vers aquilon grands efforts par hommaffe, Prefque l'europe & l'vniuers vexer, Les deux eclypfes mettra en telle chaffe,	A great advancement of a Man-women to vex whole of Europe and all universe.

Again it is shown here a Women(who is in heaven) & man(Avatar on earth) attachement due to their many reincarnation as mother & son on earth, taking charge of whole Europe & almost all of Universe, GOD is creating a powerful force by making them mother & son in their past lifes then separating them and again reuniting of Mother and a son through nature law of holography & Conscious Counter Computation and thus controlling whole of the universe.

This Young man has been born to Women in East for many births and Women in West(Jerry Astra Turk has given birth to same man as Julius Caesar Scaliger in Italy on 1484 AD, and same Jerry Astra Turk was born in New York around 1910 and Become Disciple of Saint Kirpal Singh Ji Maharaj of India, I would like to say one important Issue here is that, Jerry's Guru Kirpal Singh used to come to in her Trance before she met with him, GOD was showing Clearly to humanity that he is using Kirpal singh as his medium and because of his son a very important future Avatar.

Please be informed that Women who bear Avatar in her womb is very Important Entity, because Avatar are most Dear to their Mother. if we takes away Avatar Mother from her physical frame, you Creates state of War in his mind, he becomes very irritable and ready to go for War on earth.

Therefore GODS Shows through this Quitrain, A women, Avatar Mother & Avatar Vexing Europe and Whole Universe.

IV. XXV

Corps fublimes fans fin a l'oeil vifibles. Obnubiler viendront par ces raifons, Corps, front comprins, fens chief & Inuifibles. Diminuant les facrees orafons.

The heavenly bodies comes to Mind endlessly for their own concern, The forehead, body, and Senses all hiding, as the sacred prayer return.

GOD takes his astral body which passes through heavenly bodies to Superstring universe,

He sings the sacred prayer during this journey.

His Astral body & Mind taken to 10th Door called Dasam Dwar or Boundary between Astral and Swarga 3rd and 4th Creation, So many heaven bodies in astral universe come in contact with Subtle body, divine light with Sound illuminate the subtle body, and finally his subtle body end up in Golden Egg(and this way divinization process of his(Avatar) body take place. GOD seems to show to mankind about his different Layer of creations and how the divinization is possible and how he can contact his touch with humanity at large.

He is feared looking at all the wonderful heavenly bodies and therefore he recite the holy prayer to GOD. GOD Takes full charge of his Astral body and start his process of Divinization & Welcome his entry in heaven.

These heavenly bodies are visible and made up of tiny strings in spiral form and gets uncoiled as it strike with heavenly matter. Strings are coiled up mostly at head and antistring is present at Muladhra(at the base of spine), therefore when Kundalini at the based are aroused, called antistring raises up and meets string at head, matter collides with antimatter and pure energy in the form of illumination is the result.

IV. XLIX

Nay fouz les vmbres & iournee nocturne Sera en regne & bonte fouueraine, Fera renaiftre fon fang de l'antique vrne, & Renouullant fiecle d'or pour l'aerain.

he is born in shadow on a dark day, he will be sovereign both in his rule goodness. He will cause ancient truth to renewing the century for brass.

As per his horoscope in his birth chart, he is born on dark day, not a auspicious day but he will be good in his rule & conduct. he will renew ancient truth & value system based on ethics & code of conduct. He will renew the Eastern System of Yoga & Meditation as mentioned by Ancients Philosophy & Religion. He will introduce Religion of one GOD.

IV. XXXI

La Lune au plain de nuict fur le haut mont, Le nouueau fophe d'vn feul cerueau l'a veu, Par fes difciples eftre immortal Femond, Yeux au midy, en feins Mains, corps au feu.

In middle of night, moon over the high mountain only the young wise man alone in his mind has seen it, invited by his disciple to become immortal, his eyes to the south, his hand over his chest & his body on fire.

This young wise man only has seen moon over high mountain, his eyes to south, his hand over His chest and his body feels lot of heat. As Moon is lead by its Angel Great changes on Earth and heaven is expected. The one who has seen this vision in his trance is the Avatar, this vision clearly appoint that person as Avatar & non other, if anybody who claims to be Avatar is false one, because more than thousands people who have claimed to be Messiah or Avatar or 2nd coming of Christ in last 500 yrs. To avoid any confusion this is prophecy for the choosen one. GOD has shown to heaven & Earth He has selected a young Man on Earth as Messiah who had been appointed as Avatar and latter this young man, who is physician by his profession will make his appearance & this is how people will recognize him. Below Quatrain will illuminate upon his Profession.

VI. XVIII.

Par les phifiques le grand roy delaiffe, Par fort non art de l'ebrieu eft en vie, Luy & fon genre au regne hault pouse, Grace donnee a gent qui chrift enuie.

Great king deserted from the lives of Physician, not the upbringing of jews. He & his people sitting in high posts But pardon given to race who deny Christ.

This Quatrain clearly tells about his career or Profession, He is physician by Profession(not belong to any main religion of world) & He is not Jew or belong to any Major Religion of Today, he is more interested in knowledge of other sciences,(this is his taste) not a Jew or Christian, he & his coutrymen citing high in Political Posts. He pardon those Who deny Jesus Christ. He will extend his religion to other part of world.

Christianity has lost it touch with humanity, it does not believe in rebirth, it does not practice Meditation as light & sound principle as taught by Jesus Christ, Unless you are born of Light you cannot see GOD, this light Jesus talked is about light at the forhead and mind of Man & Women.

These truth have been lost and Christanity has now become theoretical.

Law of karma & Rebirth are two important law of Religion as per the Eastern Philosphy & Science, which seems to be absent in Christianity. Christian believe Jesus Christ is the only son of GOD and conceived through Immaculate Conception which is against the law of Universe and not truth.

Therefore Appointed Avatar will change theses law and Substitute with his new law of Reincarnation, Law of forward motion of Matter Consciousness and Backward movement of Matter-Consciousness called Complementary Consciousness or reduction or manifestation of reality.

Consciousness is primal stuff which creates matter and energy and Universe is born with various strings with 10 Dimension of space and one dimension of time, time go in forward and backward direction, In forward direction time runs to future quantum states where entropy increases and in backward direction replay of past events take place and Previous quantum states are reduced into low entropy states and information which is created in forward direction are erased in backward reduction of Matter Consciousness in the presence of Observer i.e object and subject comes in marriage sort of union or monism and Reduction of Events take place, Consciousness is felt as global event involving several area of Brain in unison called Qualia. The philosopher called this hard problem.

I. LIII

Las qu'on verra grand people tourmente, El la loy faincte en totale ruine: Par autres loix toute la chreftiente, Quand d'or, dargent trouue nouuelle Mine.	Sadly, We shall see great nations troubled & holy law in utterly spoiled, Christianity taken by all other laws, when new source money and Gold discovered.

We will see great nations troubled and holy laws destroyed, the christianity taken by law of karma, cause and effect principle(Quantum mechanics & Consciousness) this is new source of money & Gold,

Gen theory of relativity (Albert Einstein) & quantum Mechanics are two important discovery which have changed thinking about the events & universe behaviour in very different & bizarre way.

20 century has given rise to Quantum theory which is one of the precise scienctific theory, even Einstein was surprised

with the result of Quantum Mechanic experiments, to this Einstein said GOD Does not Play dice.

General theory of Relativity is a classical theory but Quantum theory does not follow the rules of classical physics. Quantum theory has following Postulates.

1. Objects and Particles can exist in multiple locations at the same time.
2. Objects or Particles can be reduced or unified by single wave function if are disturbed or observed, though the distant object are connected to one other by a single entity and reduced when observer or microstructure of planck scale become sensitive to its own sensitivity(Pensrose-Hameroff Model of ORs Consciousness).
3. Particle Spatially separated are unified through non locality through Quantum Entanglement.

Quantum Mechanics and Consciousness:

a. Observer phenomena shows that observer consciousness collapse/reduce to definite state(Classical or Cognitive state) and location simultaneously.
b. Copenhagen interpretation also states that Consciousness of observer cause collapse/reduce the quantum superpositions.
c. David Bohm Propose that wave function does not collapse but Consciousness involve active information.

d. Everett avoids collapse/reduction by involving infinite minds of observer.

e. Stapp's(1993) identifyreduction/collapse but does not identify cause of this phenomena.

f. Roger Penrose Objective reduction Ors identify consciousness as the cause of collapse/reduction and also specify cause and limiting threshold which connects to fundamental space-time geometry, including non-computable platonic influences. This connects to us the philosophical occasion of consciousness movement with discrete quantum events. Observer role is limited in collapse/reduction of wavefunction in Penrose model and relies totally on the Quantum gravity effect.

II. XLVI.

Apres grat troche humain plus grad s'apprefte, Le grand moteur les fiecles renouuelle. Pluye, fang, laict, famine, fer & pefte. Au ciel veu feu, courant longue eftincelle.

The Great misery for the mankind, even Greater one approaches, when great Cycle of earth is on renewal. Over the sky will be seen fire dragging tail.

We expect a great misery for mankind as great Cycle of Earth (Present Kal yug) will be renewed

And changed to satya (Golden) age as per hinduisim 4 Cycle of 12000 years is completing and satya age(Golden Age)of 1000 years is waiting to begin.

I. XCI

Les dieux feront aux Humains apperence, Ce qu'ilz feront auteurs de grand conflict: Auant ciel veu ferein efpee & lance, Que vers main gauche fera plus grand afflict.

GOD will make to mankind that they are planner of this war. Suddenly in the sky will be seen fighter planes and weapons. Greatest demage will be done on the left side of globe.

GOD will Show clearly that they are the author of this III rd World war, great war of century, as suddenly you will see fighting fighter plane in sky, though their was no sign of war before. After this war greatest demage will take place on left side (America & Europe) of globe.

I. LII

Les deux malins de Scorpion conioint, Le grand Seigneur meurtry de dans *fa falle* Pefte à l'Eglife par le nouueau Roy ioint. L'Europe ba*ffe*, & Septentrionale.

Two evil influences in conjunction in scorpio. The Great lord is murdered in his room. A newly Appointed King Persequtes the Church in lower part of Europe and North.

The great lord here is POPE in Europe will be murdered before Newly appointed king, Avatar Will persecute the Church in throught Europe as church does not teach law of rebirth and law of karma, a doctrine known to East from time Immemorial. As Man of east appointed by

Cosmic Government will regulate Dharma, therefore he will Persecute wrong teaching of Christianity.

I. LVI

Vous verrez to*f*t & tard faire grand change, Horreurs extremes & vindications. is Que *f*i la Lune conduite par *f*on ange, Le ciel s'approche des inclinations.

Soon you will see changes made, the Dreadful horrors and vengeances, as moon lead my its Angel, the heaven draw nearer to balance.

Libra is the sign of Balance which will soon rule the heaven as moon is ruled by its Angels, Century is renewed and Imbalance of planets and Vernal Equinoxe will be restored by Libra.

The difference between the East and West as per Socio-economic status is huge, the balance will be restored by Libra through war. Horrors Deeds will be seen in land & water.

Earth Structure geographically and Nation wise will change a lot because of earthquakes and comet str iking on earth.

XLI.

Siege en Cité & de nuict assaillie Peu eschappez non loing de mer conflit, Femme de ioye, retours fils defaillie, Poison & lettte cachée dans le olic.

The Besieged city is assaulted by night, few escape, a battle not far from the ea. A women faints with joy at the return of her son, poison in the fold of the letter

The besieged city is Miami beach, florida near sea, is attacked in night by Avatar along with alien astral army(Failed Quatrain). Miss Jerry Astra turk faints with joy, as she saw return of his son, the present incarnated one was born as his son in 1484 in Italy with the name of Julius Caesar Scaliger, As her son was selected for Avatar in this birth. In 1992 both son and mother was brought in there astral body through quantum consciousness reduction of their morphogenic field created by them in Italy as son & mother in 14th century.

Jerry astra turk in 1992 invites his son of past birth to come to Miami beach, florida to take care of her Satsangh of her GURU Kirpal singh Ji maharaj of India, As jerry was disciple of kirpal singh ji maharaj and was initiated by him during his visit to America in 1955.

But the GOD has Different Plan for him, he need him to go for war as Avatar, therefore GOD is giving her poison so that she may not interfere in his working. Concept of Avatar and War is unknown to her, she only know yoga and way to reach GOD as per Instruction of her GURU kirpal singh

Ji maharaj. She used to send lot of letter and books of yoga to her son in india.

So therefore GOD gave very little time to Jerry & her son to meet only in astral Morphogenic field for some time.

Here I would like to mention that Avatar is the GOD Creation and therefore GOD shows to mankind his relation to his mother, who she is, when he took birth in her womb and where and when. GOD will make it seems to mankind that, Avatar is most sacred and powerful forces present in our universe and GOD can use him for his purpose.

I. XCII.

Souz Vn la Paix par tout fera clamee Mais non long temps pille & rebellion: Par refus ville, terre, & mer entamme, Mors & captifs le tiers d'vn million	Under one man will Peace will be Proclaimed Everywhere, before that will be looting and rebellion. Because of that town, land & water will Split, A third of million will be Captured and dead.

Soon you will see Everything will be controlled & peace will be achieved under one Man(Commissioned Avatar on earth) WILL. But before that there will be looting, rebellion and due to this land and water will be split, over more than million will captured or dead.

Commissioned from cosmic Government "he will bring peace to Earth", He will unite all the regions of earth under his WILL and put Unbeliever and will bring ksunamic like waves on the surface of Earth. He will put unbeliever in Jails.

The order of Vishnu's ten main avatars has significance in the sense that the avatars evolve from simplistic life forms to more complex life-forms in a definitive order. Therefore, it is speculated that the Dasavatara story is a symbolization of the modern theory of evolution (Darwin Theory).

- Matsya - fish, the first life in water.
- Kurma - amphibians, living in both water and land.
- Varaha - wild land animal.
- Narasimha - beings that are half-animal and half-human.
- Vamana - short, premature human beings.
- Parasurama - early humans living in forests and using weapons.
- Rama - humans living in community, beginning of civil society.
- Krishna - humans practicing animal husbandry, politically advanced societies.
- Bhuddha - humans finding enlightenment.
- Kalki - advanced humans with great powers of destruction.

I. XCVI.

Celuy qu'aura la charge de deftruire Temple fectes, changez par fantafie: Plus aux rochier qu'aux viuans viendra Nuire, par langue ornee d'oreilles reffafie.

A man will be charged with annhilation of temples & sects, He will changed by his visions. He will harm non living things rather than living; he will deliver such Loud speeches.

A man(Incarnated one) will be charged with destruction of temples & sectarianism,(All the religions will be unified & combined with science, he will be guided by his visions. He will make such louded speeches.

Temple of God is Body of man not the outside physical temple, churches, mosques, therefore may destroy physical structure and let the mankind remember that temple of GOD is body and Mind, highest structured and developed monument of evolution in nature.

II. IX

Neuf ans le regne le maigre en paix tiendra
Puis il cherra en soif si sanguinaire
Pour luy grand peuple sans foy & loy mourra,
Tué par vn beaucoup plus debonnaire.

For the nine years the reign of the slim thing will continue,,
Then it will fall into a very bloody thirst that
a great lawless nation will die because of it,

Killed by one far more good-natured man.

AIDS Disease will continue upto 9 years, then a lawless Nation(USA) will be greatly troubled by it, Better natured person is AVATAR here who will kill it.

As his coming is delayed this is again a failed Quatrain.

II. XXIX

L'oriental fortira de fon fiege, Paffer les monts apennins voir La gaule. Tranfpercera le ciel les eaux & neige, Et vn chafcun frappera de fa gaule.	Eastern man will come from his country and will cross the appenine to france, He Travel over land,, sea, snow and will strike people with his rod.

Eastern Man (Avatar) will come from his country and cross mountain to france, he will travel over land, sea, snow & will strike people with his rod (A divine weapon).

He(Avatar) was born as Julius Caesar Scaliger in Italy 500 yrs before and became famous as Physician and Phylospher in france. This is the same man reborn as Avatar, His karma of past life in france has taken his astral body to france (in trance).

He(Avatar) will be given various type of divine weapon and he will strike with his weapon to wicked rulers of all the Nations.

IV. XLVII

Le noir farouche quand aura effaye. Sa main fanguine par feu, fer arcs tendus. Treftout le peuple fera tant effraye, Voir les plus grans par col & pieds pendus.

when dark ferocious one will have exercised his hand through fire, sword, drawn bow all the nation so terrified to see the great Ones hanging by their neck & feets.

When Dark Ferocious (Avatar), he is not white skinned, but dark(Asian) will exercise his divine weapon i.e, Sword, Drawn bow and fire. All the nations will be so terrified when they will see earthly big politicians, Capitalist & rulers will be hanged by their neck & feets.

Last & tenth Incarnation of Vishnu, will Rule the nation with his rule of Punishment, He will Punish the wicked and reward the Righteous life on Earth.

V. LIII

La loy du sol, & venus contendens, Appropriant l'efprit de prophetie, Nel'vn ne l'autre ne feront entendus, Par sol tiendra la loy du grand meffie.

The law of Sun comprising with venus, forcasting the spirit of prophecy, neither the one nor the other will know, law of great Messiah retained through the Sun.

The Law of Sun (Dharma) i.e 21st Century with Libra(venus) balance, eternal cycle of justice reinforcing the spirit of prophecy, Law of Great Messiah will be retained through SUN.

Law of Sun is purity, truth, pure science of Quantum mechanics, Consciousness will be restored.

Quantum Mechanics and General theory of relativity is the major discovery of 20th Century, how they will be united into theory of one, and with Consciousness will open the door to GODHOOD.

Science will come to rescue religion and they will be united into unification which is unique to 21st Century(Century of SUN).

Book of Enoch, second coming of Jesus(Bible), Imam mehdi(Kuran), Maitreya Budha and Avatar as per puranas, has been Prophecied in holy books of all the major religion of today, that he will come to restore the balance of good over bad karma and will usher the kingdom of GOD on earth & heaven.

V. LX

Par tefte rafe viendra bien mal eflire, Plus que fa charge ne port paffera, Si grand fureur & raige fera dire, Qu'a feu & fang tout fexe trenchera.

Through the shaven heads he(Antichrist) will seems to be elected wrongly, he is so burdened with load he cannot lift and he will be in such great hurry & rage that entire Sexuality will be killed into pieces & on fire.

Through the Muslims, he will be seen to elected wrongly, he is overburdened with heavy load, He will be in such hurry to eliminate and put into pieces & fire, the bad aspect of venus i.e immensce sexuality, violence & lust prevalent in present society. He will Strike the Rampant Sexuality in Society very hard. He will pass so many laws related to Immorality in Society and that will be dealt with fine & Exile. You will see Great lady will fall from their immense name & Fame.

Those man who comes to protect them will not be spared.

This is about Rama AVATAR in Treta Yuga around 7200 Years before Rama Was born, He gone for war against Ravana, he was asked how he will defeat Ravana, to this Rama Told my two feets are Satya(Truth) and Ahinsa(Non violence) and Arrow I have is dipped in the Poison of lust not only one I can kill thousands of Ravana.

V. LXV

Subit venu l'effrayeur fera grande, Des principaux de l'affaire caches, El dame en braife plus ne fera en veue, Ce peu a peu feront les grans faches.

Suddenly appeared, A great terror, hidden (Antichrist), Women on charcoal(SEX) will no longer be seen more, thus earthly king (leaders) slowly will get angered.

Suddenly appeared he will be volatile, women on charcoal(sex) will not been seen more, and there after Earthly kings(leaders & Politicians) will get angered. There will be many debates in media and Society about sexual freedom and sexual crimes This century is going through its immence sexuality, showism & immorality which breeds violence, capitalism is gaining upper hand, gap between poor & rich is widening, earth is suffering from severe environmental disturbances, Cosmic Govt is inciting him(Avatar) to go for War, planets are changing their path, widening affects of earth and other planet will creates severe cold in winter & Severe rise of temperature in summer(NASA IS HIDING THIS INFORMATION).

SEX will be targeted by him, Women Nudity and Obscene Culture will be Punished greatly by him, therefore suddenly Great one (Politicians & Bureaucracy) will get angered, Mass Sexuality will be penalized by him(Avatar).

Modern Culture or Western Culture is bringing Negative occult Venus Character through Print media, Mass Media. This going to be Disasterous as this negative force were responsible for the extinction of many Civilization including Atlanteans in the west.

He will Bring Society to morality and Set of Code of conduct. Therefore Women on sex will be feared so much so that you will not see sex for sale. Even Great Man who come forward to protect so called liberty of sex, they will be exiled & put under execution.

Sex in Society is subject of debate in Different Culture & Religion. As per present Western Cultural Effect of SEXUAL Freedom on Eastern Culture & lifestyle is great. Many Western Countries have high divorce rate, Teenage

Pregnancy, Many sexual Partners, Homosexuality is on rise leading to unrest and breaking in Society.

V. LXX

Des regions fubiectes a la balance, Feront troubler les monts par grande Guerre, Captifz tout fexe deu & tout bifance, Qu'on criera a l'aube terre a terre.	The regions which will be balanced will trouble a mountain with war. The entire sex will be exiled with Byzantium, at morning they will call each other from land to land.

The region under balance will trouble a mountain with war, entire sex will be exiled with Byzantium. In morning they will find there near & dear from place to place.

Again Mass sexuality (Negative energy of Venus or out of phase viberation) will be harmed by him, Outward sexual energy is to be controlled so that we can see our own bad karmic reaction,

This is the only way that we can take correct Path (Path of meditation & self introspection).

Law of Consciousness-matter movement through its Complementary action, forward and backward Action will be advocated.

V. LXXIII

Perfecutee fera de dieu l'eglife, Et le fainctz temples feront expoliez, L'enfant la mere mettra nud en chemife, Seront arabes aux polons raliez.

The temple of God will be executed & churches will be destroyed, Mother will keep the child away, The arabs will joins with poles.

The temples of God will be destroyed, Mother & child will be separated due to war, The Arab nations will join with Russia & China.

Physical temple, churches and Holy places of worship will be destroyed as Body is the Temple of GOD, He will rule under this Doctrine.

V. LXXVIII

Les deux vnis ne tiendront longuement, Et dans treze ans au barbare satrappe, Aux deux coftez seront tel perdement, Qu'vn benyra le barque & fa cappe.

The two will not remain joined for long, in thirteen years they are taken by barbarian power, there will be such a loss on both Sides, that one will blame the other.

The two, USSR & USA will not be able remain allied for long, they will be ruled by barbarian (INDIA), there will be loss on both side West & East both side so that one will blame each other for the War. As this is divine war Planned in Heaven, Earthly power will blame each other, West will blame to the east and east to the West.

India was not the country which was their in Nostrademus mind at that time and this is the reason he has called Indian as barbarians.

V. LXXIX

La facree pompe viendra baiffer les aifles, Par la venue du grand legiflateur, Humble haulfera vexera les rebelles, Naiftra fur terre aucun aemulateur.	The sacred pomp will come to lower its wings, in time of great law giver, he will make humble and trouble the rebellious, His like will not occur on earth again.

The Holy Power, Christianity will lower its wings, at the time when Great one(Avatar) will gives its law, he will be humble & rebellious both while implementing his laws of spirtual evolution.

His like will be rarely seen on earth again.

He will give the world his law Rebirth (at the day of death body comes to rebirth again) of Eastern Yoga and Philosophy and unite Quantum Mechanics with sacred law of Universe. Body & Mind will be the True lab of Mankind and body will be workshipped rather than the physical so called religious places. Those who will not abide by his law will not be tolerated & persecuted.

XXIX.

La vefue saincte entendant les nouuelles,
De ses rameaux mis en perplex & trouble,
Qui sera duict appaiser les querelles,
Par son pourchas des razes fera comble.
The holy widow hearing the news
Of her offspring placed in perplexity and trouble:
He who will be instructed to appease the quarrels,
He will pile them up by his pursuit of the shaven heads.

Holy Widow here is the wife of Sant Darshan Singh Ji Maharaj son of Sant kirpal Singh Ji Maharaj of India sees the Downfall of his Succssesor Rajender Singh Ji Maharaj, she piles up Sikh Disciple Against Avatar, a failed Quatrin.

VI. LXX

Au chef du monde le grand chyren fera, Plus oultre après ayme, craint, redoubte, Son bruit & loz les cieux furpaffera, Et du feul titre victeur fort contente.

The great Chyren will be the supreme of the world, loving, feared and dreaded. His fame & renowen beyond the heaven & he will be greatly satisfied with the title of Victor.

The Chyren (Holding Golden chain in his hand), Nominated by Cosmic Govt (Aliens) will be the Supreme Power of the world. He is loving, polite at the same time will create fear & Dread on earth.

His fame will be seen in all heaven & earth, He will be solely satisfied with the title of Victor only.

There will not be many who will appreciate him, so he will be satisfied with the title of Victor. As he is divine AVATAR, his divinity will be reflected in his work & Rule, Nations will be forced to follow his laws, he will be supported by Divine Aliens army, those who will not follow him will be exiled and Persecuted in front of Great one.

VI. L. XXX

De fez le regne paruiendra a ceux d'europe, Feu leur cite & mer a grand d'afie terre & mer a grand troupe, Que bleux, pers, croix, a mort dechaffera.	From fez the kingdom will stretch out to Europe. The land blazes with sword. The great man of Asia with great Troops by land & sea and through Perse, blue, will drive out cross to Death.

From Asia & Middle east his kingdom will stretch to Europe. He will Execute with his divine blazing sword (Rider of white horse with the Sword as prophecied in bible). This great man of asia will drive out the Cross (Christian) nations to death through Persia(Middle east).

He will change Christian theory and Practice, he will bring the rule of Karma and Rebirth theory in mainstream science and unite Quantum theory with body & Mind. New theory of Consciousness will be implemented in Globe with Pure Spirtuality not spirtualism.

VI. XCVII

Cinq & quarante degrez ciel bruslera,
Feu approcher de la grand cité neuue,
Instant grand flamme esparse sautera,
Quand on voudra des Normans faire preuue,

At forty-five degrees the sky will burn,
Fire to approach the great new city:
In an instant a great scattered flame will leap up,
When one will want to demand proof of the Normans.

This is September 11 attacks (also referred to as September 11, September 11th, or 9/11) were a series of four coordinated terrorist attacks launched by the Islamic terrorist group al-Qaeda upon the United States in New York City and the Washington, D.C., metropolitan area on Tuesday, September 11, 2001. The attacks killed almost 3,000 people and caused at least $10 billion in property and infrastructure damage.[2]

Four passenger airliners were hijacked by 19 al-Qaeda terrorists so they could be flown into buildings in suicide attacks. Two of those planes, American Airlines Flight 11 and United Airlines Flight 175, were crashed into the North and South towers, respectively, of the World Trade Center complex in New York City. Within two hours, both towers collapsed with debris and the resulting fires causing partial or complete collapse of all other buildings in the WTC complex, as well as significant damage to ten other large surrounding structures. A third plane, American Airlines Flight 77, was crashed into the Pentagon (the headquarters of the United States Department of Defense), leading to a partial collapse in its western side. The fourth plane, United Airlines Flight 93, was targeted at Washington, D.C., but crashed into a field near Shanksville, Pennsylvania, after its passengers tried to overcome the hijackers. In total, almost 3,000 people died in the attacks, including the 227 civilians and 19 hijackers aboard the four planes. It also was the deadliest incident for firefighters and for law enforcement officers in the history of the United States, with 343 and 72 killed respectively.

Suspicion quickly fell on al-Qaeda. Although the group's leader, Osama bin Laden, initially denied any involvement, in 2004, he claimed responsibility for the attacks. Al-Qaeda and bin Laden cited U.S. support of Israel, the presence of U.S. troops in Saudi Arabia, and sanctions against Iraq as motives for the attacks. The United States responded to the attacks by launching the War on Terror and invading Afghanistan to depose the Taliban, which had harbored al-Qaeda. Many countries strengthened their anti-terrorism legislation and expanded law enforcement powers. Having evaded capture for years, bin Laden was located and killed by U.S. forces in May 2011.

The destruction of the Twin Towers and other properties caused serious damage to the economy of Lower Manhattan and had a significant effect on global markets, closing Wall Street until September 17 and the civilian airspace in the U.S. and Canada until September 13. Many closings, evacuations, and cancellations followed the attack, either out of fear of further attacks or respect for the tragedy. Cleanup of the World Trade Center site was completed in

May 2002, and the Pentagon was repaired within a year. Numerous memorials have been constructed, including the National September 11 Memorial & Museum in New York, the Pentagon Memorial, and the Flight 93 National Memorial in Pennsylvania.

On November 18, 2006, construction of One World Trade Center began at the World Trade Center site. As of September 2013, the new tower›s concrete construction was largely complete, and will officially open when the installation of podium glass and interior construction is completed, estimated 2014

VI. C

Qui legent hosce versus, maturé censunte:
Prophanum vulgus & inscium ne attrectato:
Omnesque Astrologi, Blenni, Barbari procul sunto,
Qui aliter faxit, is rité sacer esto.

May those who read this verse think upon it deeply, let the Profane and ignorant herd keep away, let all the astrologers, idiots and barbarians stay far off. He who does otherwise, let him be priest to rite.

Nostrademus Expain and warns those learned people who thinks and take astrology lightly and he warns the Priest also who thinks astrology as easy science and he again warns people his work should not be taken lightly.

VII. XII

Le grand puisnay fera fin de la guerre.
Aux dieux assemble les excusez:
Cahors, Moissac iront long de la serre,
Reffus Lestore, les Agenois rasez.

The great younger son will make an end of the war,
he assembles the pardoned before the gods;
Cahors and Moissac will go far from the prison,
a refusal at Lectoure, the people of Agen shaved.

VIII. XV.

Vers Aquilon grands efforts par hommasse
Presque l'Europe & l'vniuers vexer,
Les deux eclypses mettra en telle chasse,
Et aux Pannons vie & mort renforcer.

Great exertions towards the North by a man-woman
to vex Europe and almost all the Universe.
The two eclipses will be put into such a rout
that they will reinforce life or death for the Hungarians.

Here again its clear that A women and Man (Jerry Astra
Turk and AVATAR) both born as Mother and as Son(Julius
Caesar Scaliger born 1484 to Jerry Astra Turk in france), now
Jerry astra Turk born in New York in 1910 and AVATAR
born in India in 1969), theirfore GOD is trying to show
Mankind that he select AVATAR long before and give him
order to execute law of universe as the time approaches, law

of Justice and Mercy go side by side, this is the holy war which ultimately will bring peace to earth. GOD is using them for his use.

VIII. LXXVIII

Vn Bragamas auec la langue torte
Viendra des dieux le sanctuaire,
Aux heretiques il ouurira la porte
En suscitant l'eglise militaire.

A soldier of fortune with twisted tongue
will come to the sanctuary of the gods.
He will open the door to heretics
and raise up the Church militant.

His divine weapon sword is attached to his tongue, sanctuary of gods is the higher astral world where gods and goddesses resides, He AVATAR will opens his door to holy human beings and will be against churches.

VIII. XCVII

Aux fins du Var changer le Pompotans,
Prés du riuage les trois beaux enfans naistre,
Ruyne au peuple par aage competans
Regne au pays charger plus croistre.

At the end of the Var the great powers change;
near the bank three beautiful children are born.

Ruin to the people when they are of age;
in the country the kingdom is seen to grow and change more.

This Descibes the the fate of America in 21ˢᵗ Century, kingdom will change Greatly and will Ruin the Country where Kennedy three brothers are Born.

IX. LI

Contre les rouges sectes se banderont,
Feu, eau, fer, corde par paix se minera,
Au point mourir ceux qui machineront,
Fors vn que monde sur tout ruynera.

Against the red ones sects will conspire,
Fire, water, steel, rope through peace will weaken:
On the point of dying those who will plot,
Except one who above all the world will ruin.

Against Red ones Russia and china, European alliance will unite, those who plot will be troubled by AVATAR, those who will not listen to him, ultimately will destroyed by him.

IX. LV

L'horrible guerre qu'en Occident s'apprefte!
L'an enfuiuant viendra la peftilence
Si fort terrible, que ieune, vieil, ne befte.
Sang, feu, Mercu. Mars, Iupiter en France.

The horrible war which is being prepared in the West,
The following year will come the pestilence
So very horrible that young, old, nor beast,
Blood, fire Mercury, Mars, Jupiter in France.

This IIIrd World War is Prepared and planned in West with the help of Jerry Astra Turk, because his son(born in france as Julius Caesar Scaliger in 1484, is now born in india has been selected by Cosmic Govt as AVATAR who will make War and will end war and untimatley bring peace on earth.

IX. LXXXIII

Sol vingt de Taurus si fort terre trembler,
Le grand theatre remply ruinera,
L'air, ciel & terre obscurcir & troubler,
Lors l'infidele Dieu & saincts voguera.

Sun twentieth of Taurus the earth will tremble very mightily,
It will ruin the great theater filled:
To darken and trouble air, sky and land,
Then the infidel will call upon God and saints.

This is the theatre Jerry Astra turk uses to teach the teaching of his Guru Kirpal Singh Maharaj, will suffer a earthquake and thunder as to punish those disciple who do not follow holy teaching, reaction of his (Kirpal) disciple will be arrogant on saint as well as GOD. This is again failed Quatrain and GOD did not showed in action.

Law of Justice and law of Mercy, these are the two law which Governs the life in our universe, Saints are love personified and they come to earth to bring back the souls to kingdom of GOD those who have completed their cycle of numberless birth and karma bad and good.

Other power which comes from GOD is to implement the law of Justice so that GOOD human can be saved and wicked Human with bad karma can be punished, AVATAR is such Personality appointed by cosmic government to Execute Divine Weapons on earth and heaven. Justice fall in his domain and he is charged with power of Justice so that Earth and heaven can be saved and law of Universe can be implemented. He is supported by Aliens and Divine beings and ultimately bring peace to earth. Earthly powers ultimately surrenders to him.

X. XXX

Nepueu & sang du sainct nouueau venu,
Par le surnom soustient arcs & couuert
Seront chassez mis à mort chassez nu,
En rouge & noir conuertiront leur vert.

Nephew and blood of the new saint come,
Through the surname he will sustain arches and roof:
They will be driven out put to death chased nude,
Into red and black will they convert their green.

Saint Rajender Singh Ji Maharaj is Nephew of Saint Kirpal Singh Ji Maharaj of India, was not nominated by by Kirpal

Singh Ji but through his surname his son Darshan Singh Ji Maharaj become self claimed Guru, will be able to sustain their order but will be chased out through death or seat.

X. LXV.

O vafte Romme ta ruyne s'approache, Non de tes murs de ton fang & fuftance, L'asper par lettres fera fi horrible coche, Fer poinctu mis a tous iufques au manche.

O great Rome, your destruction comes soon, not of your walls but of your blood & substance, the harsh Statement in fold of letters, with a pointed Steel all in the sleeves.

The great Rome your destruction comes very soon not of your matter but of your barbaric laws (culture), pointing steel rod (divine weapon of Avatar) with letters of destruction.

Rome will suffer from severe Earth quake along with Italy & France. You will see Great Earth Quake in Italy and France and later on War. Pointed steel like weapon under his sleeves have been seen. Along with ulna bone part of his right arm is attached a divine weapon in his astral body which is used to hit wicked person or a part of land on Earth & heaven.

He is charged and commissioned with the power of Justice and Work with the "Principal of Rewarding Good Ones and Punishment for Unjustice on Earth". He is more mysterious and powerful than science fiction and any avatar in past on the Earth & heaven.

X. LXX

Lœil par obiect fera telle excroissance,
Tant & ardente que tombera la neige,
Champ arrousé viendra en decroissance,
Que le primat succombera à Rege.

Through an object the eye will swell very much,
Burning so much that the snow will fall:
The fields watered will come to shrink,
As the primate succumbs at Reggio.

A Comet will enters the earth and burn so much in the earth atmosphere that this will cause so much heat in the atmosphere that neaby water will shrink.

X. LXXI.

La terre & l'air gelleront fi grand eau, Lors qu'on viendra pour ieudi venerer, Ce qui fera iamais ne feut fi beau, Des quatre pars le viendront honnorer.

The earth & atmosphere will freez water when they comes to worship on Thursday, he who will come will not be as fair as few Partner will come to honor him.

The atmosphere will be so much clouded (Environmental changes will be severe) & you will see no sun, therefore air will freeze water, & this will happen when They(Avatar) & his follower come to workship on Thursday(day of Vishnu God workship in India).

Earth Motion around sun will be more Eliptical and this will cause more temperature in summer & Very cold during winters as Earth will be further away from sun compare to previous year. You will see very cold climate like -60(Degree Celcius) to -90 in Western(Left) side of Globe.

Earth Axis will be reversed by strike of Comet on Northern hemisphere, when this will occurs not certain but may be between 2020 to 2027 AD, By this way earth will come closer to sun and elipiticity of earth will be corrected, Magnetic field of earth will be reversed and this keep on going every 24,000 to 26,000 of when Zodiac Equinox complete cycle. After this event Earth will become smaller place to live and Population of Earth may go down to around 500 million.

The awaited one will not be simple as Few partners country will come to honour him & Support him. At the time of his appearance some of countries of East will come to make alliance with him.

X. LXXIII

Le temps prefent auecques le paffe, Sera iuge par grand louialifte, Le monde tard luy fera laffe, Et defloial par le clerge iuriste.

The present time and that of past will be judged by the great man of Jupiter. soon the world will be tired of him, Disloyal after oath taking clergy.

Present time & that of Past(bad karmic load) will be judged by great man of Jupiter(stands for Thursday as his day of rest,

As per Hindu Philosphy and Mythology records there are 10 Avatars,9th Avatar Budha and others have been Incarnated till now,10th Avatar of Vishnu called Kalki Avatar is Expected to come, this also show that Jupiter is Ascendant in his birth chart). Soon world will be tired of him. As Per International Karma is Concerned, accumulated Karma(Pralabda karma, stored karmic astrogenic field will be heavy for past 5000 years). Jupiter is for Cosmic cycle of Dharma which rotates by 4800-5000 years as kalyuga. Kalyuga is completing its Age and Golden Cycle called Satya Age will begin at the end of War which is expected to last one to two decades.

There are two Movement of Matter-consciousness, one is Gross physical movement in upward or forward way, where entropy of Matter-consciousness increases from past to future and we remember the events in past not in future, other movement of Matter-Consciousness is Backward, i.e Subtle matter –consciousness in astral World and in Astral subtle body(Subtle body is Overlap with Gross body and its matter is fine, tiny coiled strings. This backward movement or complementary movement of matter is with respect to forward movement of matter, this is also called manifestation or Matter Consciousness reduction backward in nature where entropy is reduced, i.e We remember from future to past, therefore we can remember future and this is called precognition or presentiments.

Backward Movement of Matter-Consciousness is very important as far as Karmic reaction is concerned where Future and past comes together on equal footing in the form of Complementarities where Past is erased and Preserved in more subtle form. Therefore information is not lost totally but information is reduced to low level and preserved in Subtle form in Casual world. Information is lossed in black whole and a part come out & preserved in other universe out of black hole. and Black whole as a whole will evaporated & ultimately universe will returned to low entropy as before and new cycle of universe will start again. Roger Penrose has explained his theory of cyclic universe where universe start with low entropy goes through high entropy by forming black hole and creating more information and ends again ends into low entropy through alking evaporation of black hole and loss of information. String Model has been able to explain loss of information more beautifully where half of information which goes into black hole is lossed and half information is preserved in other universe, there for universe has history and events history of world events are preserved in other astral universe through holography, quantum gravitational effect. Past is not lossed fully but a part of past is preserved in more subtle form in astral and casual world. String model explained this more aethetically and beautifully as we go from one string to other string as Ice is changed into water and water into water vapours but basic constituent of matter is H2O.

In the ends all the particle evaporates and become zero mass particle with no time to feel. As per Einstein theory in order to pass time particle should have mass.

No phenomena in the world leads to decrease in Entropy Except Quantum-Consciousness Reduction in the form of complementarily. This is called oneness of Consciousness

& Duality Disappear into Unity. Ancients Seers & Saints in all the religion have mentioned this state unification of Dual Matter state into single event called Manifestation and Principle of Oneness.

All the Veda, Vedanta, Upanishad have mentioned this state where opposite or Dualism merges into Unity of Consciousness.

Western Philosopher in present & past have try to separate matter and consciousness as independent entity and therefore they were unable to unite them into single entity. In Eastern Philosophy & Religion both are not independent but are doomed to be separated. We cannot separate Consciousness from matter but we can unify them in Complementarily as a whole undivided Truth.

Brain is a Quantum Computer, As a classical Computer its very Weak but As a Quantum Computer it has Parallel Processing in the Dendrites of Neurons where thousands of Neurons in the form of Qualia, along with their Dendrites Synchronously take part in Quantum activity and Consciousness take over & Reduces into classical state (Learned state). It reduced into one of the learned state as recognition which is different than cognition.

A new theory called Orchestrated Objective reduction(Orch OR), was introduced some 25 years back by Roger Penrose a famous British Mathematician & anesthesiologist stuart Hameroff, Center of Consciousness studies, university of Arizona, Tucson. They concluded that Quantum

Computations in microtubules play important role in generating Consciousness.

Information is created first by Brain in microtubules through Quantum Synchrony(Parallel Process of dendrites and then reduces into one of classical state learned by Brain through objective reduction, this creates dualism one in Quantum Mind of Individual and other in Astral Universe (Astrofield), these two fields again unite through backward movement of Consciousness and results into Synchrony, replay of past memory and ultimately reduction & Evaporation of most of memory, this final state is low in entropy and goes from high entropy to low entropy Field(Backward or Complementary). This state has been mentioned as the Monistic or Advaita Eastern Philosphy where dualism of objective and subjective merges into oneness and unity, therefore brain consciousness creates duality or multiplicity in the world through Hemroff-Penrose orchestrated objective reduction(ORs) and creates future quantum states where entropy in Mind(Astral Mind) decreases because of creating information but entropy as a whole in environment increases, inflated future is created, which in turns bring duality in objective world(Subtle World or Astral World) and subjective mind. Dualistic, subjective(astral mind) and Astral world are connected through non local interaction. Human brain and astral Mind are superimposed and communicate with each other through Orchestrated Objective reduction(ORs), classical information is created in objective brain and astral subjective mind.

Other process is where matter consciousness goes backward and object and subject is united through synchronicity of global quantum states in the presence of subjective consciousness and this sort of marriage bring oneness of stream of consciousness with the replay of past quantum states and evaporation of memory. This is the unique features of Consciousness where individual merges with the global consciousness and consciousness of nature or fine Prakriti (Vedanta). Here total entropy of system decreases not increases as in penrose reduction, matter is converted into energy. Veda describes such as macrocosm is in microcosm. We cannot separate consciousness from matter or energy, we feel consciousness when matter is fine, discrete and gives rise to synchrony or bose-Einstein statistics, Consciousness is primary and integral part of matter, when we break the matter into fine and finer particles and ultimately into strings consciousness supervene and matter consciousness soap governs the very febric of our cosmos, any theory of matter is unable to explain the universe because theory of Consciousness is essential in understanding how the universe and matter was created, mind creates the matter not vice versa.

We cannot have separate theory for matter and consciousness but we have theory which merges matter and consciousness, separate existence for Either of them is impossible and only there is refuge only in the union of both.

In the beginning was the word(Viberation), and world was with the GOD and word was GOD...Bible

When the world will end all the particles and matter will be converted into massless particle like photon, graviton with zero mass, this means they will not feel time as per the Albert Einstein General theory of relativity, Cyclic Conformal Model of universe by British Mathematician Roger Penrose have shown that this condition is akin to pre-big bang period, cyclic model is very successful in explaining why the universe will continue to expand and IInd law of thermodynamics gives arrow to time.

X. LXXIIII

Au reuolu du grand nombre feptiefme, Apparoiftra au temps leux d'hacatombe, Non efloigne du grand eage milliefme, Que les entres fortiront de leur tombe.	The year of seventh number finished, He will appear at the game of slaughter in the great millennium when dead Will come out of their graves.

The great number seven which is shown to him in 1992 (Avatar), which will be given final time for initiation of war in 1999, he will appear when earthly leaders will rule badly without any insight from the point of economic & social justice. This is Failed Quatrain as per timing His war is delayed by Cosmic Government by 20 Years. This will happen when dead will come out of their graves(this is prophecy of holy kuran which says Allahtalla(GOD) will come to earth to do justice and all the dead people will come out of their graves: means that body dies but not the soul but karma done by bodied in each birth will be accumulated & will be judged by him.

Early Muslims & Sufi Saints know about the rebirth phenomena, not only this Christian mystics before Jesus

Christ knows of rebirth. Christ lived long before Jesus. Jesus
came to india in kashmir and lived there for many years.

X. LXXII

L'an mil neuf cens nonante neuf sept mois
Du ciel viendra vn grand Roy d'effrayeur
Resusciter le grand Roy d'Angolmois,
Auant apres Mars regner par bon heur.

The year 1999, seventh month,
From the sky will come a great King of Terror:
To bring back to life the great King of the Mongols,
Before and after war reigns happily.

In this quatrain as 7 number was shown to him in 1992, i.e
In 1999 and seventh month from sky will come a Divine
AVATAR, he will bring back king of Mongol back to his
seat and after war reign happily. This is failed Quatrain as
Cosmic Govt decided to postpone war untill 2019.

X. LXXV.

Tant attendu ne reuiendra iamais, Dedans l'europe, en afie apparoiftra, Vn de la ligue yffu du grand hermes, Et fur tous roys des orientz croiftra.

Awaited for longtime, he will not appear in Europe but will appear in asia & he will grow above all other power in east, as revelation issued from heaven.

Appointed Avatar will grow above all other power in East, a Vision appeared in heaven.

His War will Start in Asia and will be Governing Power in nearby Countries.

He will start his war from East and will be involved in Middle East and will attack Europe with Middle East nations & Asia.

Heaven is waiting for Avatar's arrival, Long awaited he will not return in Europe (his soul taken to Europe because of his strong past birth karma in france & Italy, where he was born in 1484 as Julius Caesar Scaliger to a American Women known as Miss Jerry astra Turk(Present Birth new york city, around 1910), but will grow above all other Power in East, a vision appeared in heaven.

He will make Powerful Alliance with Asia and will attack through sea Route.

X. XCVI

Religion du nom des mers vaincra, Contre la fecte fils adaluncatif, Secte obftinee deploree craindra, Des deux bleffez par aleph & Aleph

A religion called by the name of sea will overcome, against the seat of the son Adaluncatif. A stubborn lamentable sect, two men harmed by alpha & alpha.

A religion called by name of Sea i.e Hindustan (Indian Ocean), will defeat Pakistan, a Stubborn sect, i.e Islam, harmed by Alpha & alpha(Antichrist or Coming Avatar).

Son Adaluncatif here refer to Pakistan as it was separated from India during Independence, but this has not resulted into Well being of Pakistan even after 65 years of Independence, There had been two to three war Between India & Pakistan and nothing was gained after the war, Pakistan had been Problem son of India and has contributed to the World Network of Terrorist Activities, It has Continued its Terror activities with various Jihadis Groups in India & other Countries.

India is a Secular state & never invaded any country in her past history.

Coming Avatar will unite Pakistan into India. Creating the Pakistan as separate Country has not given anything to world except violence and weak economy in the Region.

India is a Secular state & never invaded any country in her past history. Truth & Non violence are the two great pillar where its strength lies. Indian civilization is the most Ancient Civilization on earth which have survived against all the odds, This Region has given birth to Sages & Seers, Indian civilization is also known for its rich Heritage & Culture, Ancients Text of Veda & Upanishads were written in this land. This Country is also known for lineage of Avatars in different Yugas.

Secular & Democratic Process of its Constitution gives place to all the religions of world.

Asia need to be united in future and will creates a very Powerful alliance of Russia, china, india including other countries of South asia, southeast asia and central Asia.

He (Avatar) will creates Powerful influence in the middle east and alliance with the OPEC Nations.

X. LXXXIX

De brique en marbre serôt les murs reduicts,
Sept & cinquante années pacifique,
Ioye aux humains, renoüé l'aqueduict,
Santé, grands fruits, joye & temps melifique.

The walls will be converted from brick to marble,
Seven and fifty pacific years:
Joy to mortals, the aqueduct renewed,
Health, abundance of fruits, joy and mellifluous times.

This is the Peaceful world Nostrademus envisages after the war of 27 years on earth for 75 years. Earth will have good health to its people, Environment will become abundantly greenish and people will enjoy healthy times, world will becme a Global Village.

LXIX.

Le fait luysant de neuf vieux esleué,
Seront si grands par midy Aquilon,
De sa seur propre grandes alles leué:
Fuyant murdry au buisson d'ambellon.

The shining deed of the new old one exalted will be great in the south and north, raised by his own sister, Great crowds arise. when fleeing, is murdered in the bushes at Ambellon.

This is description about AVATAR his work will be Great in Norther Nation and South national under his control, raised by her sister(Loi Ji Turk), loi Ji who is Born in this life time in US and Adopted Daughter of Jerry Astra Turk is also Disciple of Saint Kirpal Singh Ji Maharaj, this is failed quatrain because loi J Turk and Jerry astra turk left this earth, but this quatrain clearly shows Lo Ji Turk is a sister of AVATAR and connected on astral world to her brother.

VIII. LXXXVII

L'antechrist trois bien tost annichilez,
Vingt & sept ans sang durera sa guerre,
Les heretiques morts, captifs exilez,
Son corps humain eau rougie gresler terre.

The antichrist very soon annihilates everything
twenty-seven years his war will last.
The unbelievers are dead, captive, exiled;
with blood, human bodies, water and red hail covering the
earth.

The Power of AVATAR is immense, his war will last after 27
years, Its seems he finally destroy everthing with his divine
weapons and what we see is human dead bodies and red hell
covering the entire earth.

What Kind of Alien Craft Did Neil Armstrong See on the Moon`

when Neil Armstrong was on the moon he reported seeing
something Spectacular, Was told to go back. We know
whats there, who was he talking to in Houston? Maybe
someone should find out and talk to him, as he obviously
knows something. A story that has been circulating for
decades and the confirmation of this can be traced back
to two ex-NASA employees in particular—Otto Binder and
Maurice Chatelain.

According to Binder, unnamed radio hams with their own
VHF receiving facilities that bypassed NASA's broadcasting

outlets picked up the following exchange: NASA: What's there? Mission Control calling Apollo 11… Apollo: These "Babies" are huge, Sir! Enormous! OH MY GOD! You wouldn't believe it! I'm telling you there are other spacecraft out there, lined up on the far side of the crater edge! They're on the Moon watching us.

Maurice Chatelain In 1979, Maurice Chatelain, former chief of NASA Communications Systems confirmed that Armstrong had indeed reported seeing two UFOs on the rim of a crater. "The encounter was common knowledge in NASA, but nobody has talked about it until now." Soviet scientists were allegedly the first to confirm the incident. "According to our information, the encounter was reported immediately after the landing of the module," said Dr. Vladimir Azhazha, a physicist and Professor of Mathematics at Moscow University.

"Neil Armstrong relayed the message to Mission Control that two large, mysterious objects were watching them after having landed near the moon module. But his message was never heard by the public-because NASA censored it." According to another Soviet scientist, Dr. Aleksandr Kazantsev, Buzz Aldrin took color movie film of the UFOs from inside the module, and continued filming them after he and Armstrong went outside. Dr. Azhazha claims that the UFOs departed minutes after the astronauts came out on to the lunar surface.

Maurice Chatelain also confirmed that Apollo 11's radio transmissions were interrupted on several occasions in order to hide the news from the public (this can actually be confirmed because recordings exist in the public domain of these radio 'blackouts'). He went on to claim that "all Apollo and Gemini flights were followed, both at a distance and sometimes also quite closely, by space vehicles of extraterrestrial origin-flying saucers, or UFOs, if you want to call them by that name. Every time it occurred, the astronauts informed Mission Control, who then ordered absolute silence." So….was it confirmed? Yes, if you believe Binder, Chatelain, Azhazha and Kazantsev.

But is there any PROOF in the form of recordings? Sadly, no. NASA even managed to lose most of the Apollo 11 mission tapes never to be recovered. I do find it very interesting that Armstrong initially refused to participate in any of NASA's 40th celebration ceremonies. He's certainly a man of integrity, and perhaps that's why he refused to be put into situations where he might be forced to lie about UFO's and a possible alien presence on moon? At a conference presented to new NASA apprentices which was aired on CSPAN, Armstrong first compared himself and the other astronauts to a parrot before claiming that parrots don't fly too well (but they do repeat what they are told). Armstrong then went on to state that 'there are great freedoms available to those who could strip away one of truth's protective layers.' Was this a reference to the disinformation surrounding the UFO topic? Either way, it's a fascinating story that–if true– will probably never be disclosed to the public.

Thanks to http://uk-ufo-aliens.blogspot.com

WWW.WORLDUFOPHOTOS.ORG

CHAPTER 4

CHAOS IN THE WORLD AND TECHNOLOGICAL DECEPTION BY ELITE NATION

Economy of Drug, Addiction, Entertainment & Prostitution

Elliott R Morris, Phd of www.morssglobalfianance.com has done Excellent Research on the Economy of Entertainment Industry and its long term Implications.

The Totals

The total sales by category are presented in the following table. Details on how these numbers were developed are presented in the remainder of the article

Entertainment Category	(in bil. US$)
Alcohol	1,163
Beer	614
Spirits	299

Wine	250
Entertainment Drugs	546
Cannabis	410
Cocaine	122
Ecstasy	14
Prostitution	400
Restaurants	183
Movies	180
Gambling	110
Pornography	97
Sports	63
Computer Games	54
Live performances	35
Tourism	25
Music	7
Total	2,862

For purposes of this study, both cigarettes and heroin are considered primarily as addictive drugs and not entertainment items. Cigarette sales are estimated at $336 billion annually, and global heroin sales are approximately $126 billion annually.

Alcohol

The Beverage Industry estimates global distilled spirits sales at $299 billion in 2008. Data from the Beverage Information Group and the Brewers Association of Japan indicates global beer consumption to be $614 billion. According to The

International Organization of Vine and Wine and IWSR, global wine consumption was $250 in 2008.

Drugs – Cannabis, Cocaine, and Ecstasy

According to the UNODC 2008 Annual Report, 3.9% of the world's population between 15-64, or 166 million people use cannabis. Worldwide, there are 41,000 metric tons of cannabis produced annually. At $10/gram, that generates $410 billion annually. Most of the high grade cannabis produced in the United States is grown in hidden fields or indoors. The number one producer is California with an annual revenue of nearly $14 billion.

According to the same report, 16 million people or 0.4% of the global population between 15-64 use cocaine. 994 metric tons of cocaine were produced in three Latin American countries (Bolivia, Colombia, and Peru). Most of this was probably sold in the US market. US retail prices fluctuate, but a recent estimate for a "pure" grain of cocaine in New York City was $123. That means the retail value of 994 metric tons is $122 billion.

Only 0.21% of the global population, or 8.4 million people aged 15-64 use Ecstacy. The UN report estimates global Ecstacy consumption to be 131 metric tons. At a recently estimated $25 per tablet price, this works out to approximately $13.8 billion in sales (8.4 million).

Prostitution

Prostitution is one of the largest entertainment industries in the world. In 1994, the industry generated revenues of more than $30 billion in only 4 Southeast Asian countries (Indonesia, Malaysia, Philippines, and Thailand) (ILO study). In Thailand alone, the study estimated it generated incomes of $22-24 billion.

These four countries constitute only 6.1% of the global population. If prostitution were practiced at the same rate per capita in the rest of the world, revenues from it 1994 would be over $360 billion. And they most certainly have grown since 1994. I have found no complete global survey, but particular country evidence suggests that prostitution revenues are large:

- Japan, earnings from prostitution in 1998 were estimated at $3.1 billion.
- German prostitution revenues have been estimated at $8.4 billion EURs;
- Zurich and Amsterdam have 11 prostitutes per 1,000 population;
- Spain has 500,000 prostitutes earning $54 billion annually;
- In Hungary, prostitution revenues exceed $1 billion;
- Iran is estimated to have 300,000 prostitutes.

My guess is that there is more prostitution per capita in the 4 countries reference above than worldwide. That suggests perhaps $300 billion worldwide in 1994. But prostitution revenues have definitely increased since 1994. I believe a conservative estimate of prostitution revenues in 2009 is $400 billion.

Prostitution is probably like alcohol and drugs in that it will continue, legal or not. In fact, evidence suggests that legalizing and regulating prostitution can help in reducing HIV/AIDS infections.

Restaurants

People enjoy eating out. A recent estimate of global restaurant revenues was $550 billion. Not all of this can be attributed to entertainment. First, people need to eat to live. Let us assume that the entertainment component of eating out is 50% of restaurant revenues: that is, for entertainment reasons, people are willing to pay twice as much for food as they would have to pay if they ate at home. That gives us $275 billion. Of that amount, another third should be deducted for the eating out that was done for convenience/necessity reasons, *e.g.,* lunch at work. That leaves $183 billion that is probably a pretty good estimate of the entertainment value of restaurants.

Movies

According to Screen Digest, 3,000 films are produced annually. Box office ticket revenues were $26.8 billion in 2008, with overall revenues amounting to $180 billion. Strategy Analytics has just published a report saying that for the first time, digital revenues from media and entertainment exceeded revenues from movie theaters and home video.

Gambling

According to a Pricewaterhouse Coopers report released in June 2007, worldwide gambling revenue is expected to climb from $101.6 billion in 2006 to $144 billion by 2011 as the large Macau casino investments come into play. US gambling revenues are projected to increase 6.7% per year, from $57.5 billion to $79.6 billion. The Asian Pacific region, fast becoming the world's second biggest casino market, can expect 15.7% growth in the 2006 to 2011 period from $14.6 billion to $30.3 billion.

Internet gambling revenue for offshore companies was estimated to be $5.9 billion in 2008 from players in the United States and $21.0 billion from players worldwide, according to H2 Gambling Capital. Internet gambling is anticipated to grow rapidly over the coming years.

Overall, I estimate gambling revenues at $110 billion in 2009.

Pornography

Global pornographic revenues are approaching $100 billion (Top Ten Reviews). The sale and rental of videos is still the top revenue generator, but it will shortly be eclipsed by online sales and pay-per-view. Already, 12% of all web sites (4.2 million) are porn. Pay-per-view makes the major hotel chains some of the largest distributors of pornography. Pornographic production is a large business: in 2005, the US producers released 13,500 new films.

Sports

Major sports include World Football (soccer), US Football, Baseball, Basketball, and Hockey. Revenues on these sports are provided in a series done by Forbes magazine and are presented below.

In US Football, *Forbes* covers only the National Football League. College games and a professional league in Canada with slightly different rules also generate considerable revenue. I estimate that taken together, US football generates US$ 10 billion.

Forbes only covers the top 25 professional teams in World Football. When receipts from World Football played in the rest of the world are added in, revenues are probably US$ 20 billion.

Major professional baseball leagues operate in the United States and Japan. Forbes only covers US major league baseball. Baseball is played throughout Latin America as well. Globally, I estimate baseball revenues at US$ 7 billion.

Basketball is gaining popularity throughout the world. In addition to the NBA in the United States, professional leagues exist in Europe and Asia. *Forbes'* data only covers the NBA. I estimate global revenues at US$ 5 billion.

Hockey is played in the United States, Canada, Europe and Asia. *Forbes* covers only the NHL. I estimate global hockey revenues at US$ 4 billion.

There are various auto racing venues like Formula One, NASCAR. Formula One racing is probably the largest in terms of revenue generated and viewers. For major events, it has 55 million viewers that make it second only to the Olympics in terms of viewers – see http://en. wikipedia. org/wiki/Formula_One. Reuters estimates Formula One revenues at US$ 2.2 billion annually. Building on this, I estimate global auto racing revenues at US$ 7 billion.

There are many other sporting events that people pay to see – horse racing, cricket, rugby, polo. I estimate the revenues from these events at US$ 10 billion.

Overall, I estimate sports revenues at US$ 63 billion. These data are summarised in the table below.

Sport	Forbes Revenues	Est. Global Revenues
	(in US$ billions)	
World Football (soccer)	6.9	20
US Football (NFL)	7.1	10
Baseball	5.8	7
Auto racing		7
Basketball	3.8	5
Hockey (NHL)	2.7	4
The rest		10
Total	**23.6**	**63**

Computer Games

Computer games, a form of interactive entertainment, are growing rapidly. Revenues from software sales are estimated at US$ 34.6 billion in 2009, with hardware sales generating another US$ 18.9 billion.

Live Performances

Here, I include music, theatre, opera, dance and celebrity performances. Totals here are difficult to find. A recent study found that:

The Boston Symphony Orchestra is the world's largest orchestral operation. Attendance at all BSO and BSO-produced concerts is estimated at nearly 1.5 million, with an annual budget now exceeding US$ 80 million. BSO.org, considered the most *successful orchestral web site in the country, launched in 1996 and currently receives approximately 7.6 million visits a year. Since the time of its launch, the site has generated US$ 40 million, with US$ 37 million generated over the last seven years. In 2007, bso.org brought in a record US$ 5.8 million in revenue, a figure that is expected to be surpassed in 2008. Web sales make up about 30 per cent of the organisation's overall ticket revenue, with online sales for Tanglewood reaching 40 to 45 per cent.*

Let us assume there are another 200 entities globally, with each generating $80 million in receipts. That would total $16 billion. How about the celebrity performers? The record for a concert series was US$ 558 million by the Rolling Stones' 'Bigger Bang' tour over the 2005–2007 period. Madonna has the record for a single performer with her 'Sticky' concert series in 2008. I estimate overall celebrity performer revenues at $10 billion. Overall, I estimate live performer revenues at US$ 35 billion.

Tourism

According to the World Travel and Tourism Council's (WTTC) Tourism Satellite Account (TSA), world travel and tourism is expected to generate in excess of US$ 7 trillion in 2007, rising to over US$ 13 trillion in 2017. However, most of this involves flying to and from the tourist site and accommodations at the site. I do not consider flying somewhere and staying in a hotel as entertainment. And most of the entertainment activities at the site, such as eating in restaurants and gambling, have been estimated separately.

The only item not included elsewhere is 'scenic and sightseeing transportation services'. This item constituted less than 1 per cent of the WTTC's $7 trillion, or $25 billion.

Music

According to the Recording Industry Association of America, sales of music totalled US$ 7.1 billion in 2008. That included physical sales of US$ 5.5 billion and digital sales of US$ 1.6 billion. Physical sales continue to decline from their high of US$ 14.6 billion in 1999.

Cigarette

According to the Tobacco Atlas, 5.6 trillion cig, 1.3 billion people or about 17 per cent of the world's population smoke cigarettes. Smoking is extremely addictive. 5.4 million people died from smoking in 2005. Information on cigarettes sold and revenues of the four leading cigarette companies globally, China National Tobacco Company, Phillip Morris British American Tobacco, and Japan Tobacco International, are provided by this source. From this information, it is reasonable to assume the average global sale price for a cigarette is US$ 0.06. This would mean annual cigarette sales of US$ 336 billion.

Conclusions

On one hand, the findings tell a pretty sorry tale about the human race: the leading entertainment items we purchase are alcohol, drugs and prostitution. They are all escapes from everyone's daily reality. But I want to emphasise that the above are the *purchased* entertainment items. Much of what entertains and gives us joy costs very little: taking a walk, socialising with friends, etc.

In doing work on this project, I was continually reminded of the move from physical to digital information transfer: consider what I reported on movies, music and the growing importance of video games.

Healthcare:

Few complaints about the U.S. healthcare system are as common as the claim that we spend too much on healthcare and get too little for all that spending in return – especially compared to other industrialised nations.

A new Commonwealth Fund report is the latest to indict U.S. healthcare. It pegs the American system dead last in a survey of eleven developed countries.

But like virtually every other study that trashes the U.S. healthcare system, Commonwealth's rankings rely on questionable assumptions, like giving weight to those systems that treat people equally rather than well. At the same time, Commonwealth ignores the problems that countries with socialised healthcare systems have actually treating people once they're sick.

And on that metric – that is, actually delivering care to those who need it – the United States is without peer.

The Commonwealth Fund report begins by asserting that the U.S. healthcare system 'is the most expensive in the world'.

It's true that the United States spends a larger share of its Gross Domestic Product – 17.9 per cent, or almost \$3 trillion – on healthcare than other countries. But by itself, that statistic means nothing.

The United States also happens to be one of the richest countries in the world. Once basic needs are taken care of, an increasing share of each extra dollar will go to what were once considered luxuries. You can only spend so much on food, after all.

That's borne out by national spending data. Between 1990 and 2012, for example, spending on healthcare climbed 290 per cent, significantly faster than overall GDP growth of 171 per cent.

But household spending on pets climbed 353 per cent over those same years; on live entertainment, it went up more than 500 per cent. Americans spend 639 per cent more on telephones and 900 per cent more on computers.

By the Commonwealth Fund's logic, America also faces a petcare spending crisis.

In contrast, spending on staples like food, clothing, housing and furnishings all climbed more slowly than overall GDP.

The Commonwealth Fund concludes that the United States 'underperforms relative to most other countries on most other dimensions of performance' despite having the most expensive healthcare system in the world.

But a closer look at those 'dimensions' calls that claim into question.

Take infant mortality rates, where the United States typically places far down the list behind France, Greece, Italy, Hungary, even Cuba.

This comparison is notoriously unreliable, because countries either use different definitions of a live birth – or fudge their numbers.

The United States, for example, counts every live birth in its infant mortality statistics. But France only includes babies born after twenty-two weeks of gestation. In Poland, a baby has to weigh more than one pound, two ounces to count as a live birth.

The World Health Organization notes that it is common practice in several countries, including Belgium, France and Spain, 'to register as live births only those infants who survived for a specified period beyond birth'.

What's more, the United States has significantly more preterm births than other countries. That fact alone accounts for 'much of the high infant mortality rate in the U.S.', according to a report from the Centers for Disease Control and Prevention (CDC).

The CDC found that if the United States had the same preterm birth rate as Sweden, our infant mortality rate would be cut nearly in half.

What about life expectancy, where the United States ranks below its peers as well?

International measures of longevity typically fail to account for differences in obesity, accidental deaths, car accidents, murders and the like, all of which shorten lives no matter how good a nation's healthcare system is.

The U.S. murder rate, for example, is more than four times the United Kingdom's – and far higher than all the other countries in the Commonwealth Fund study. The United States has a worse highway death rate than all but one of them. And U.S. obesity rates are more than double Canada's and more than four times Switzerland's.

A far more meaningful comparison of international health systems would take stock of how people afflicted with diseases such as cancer fare in different countries. And on this measure, there's no question the United States stands above the rest.

Five-year survival rates for breast cancer are higher in the United States than England, Denmark, Germany and Spain, according to the American Cancer Society.

In the United States, the survival rate for prostate cancer is 99.1 per cent. In Denmark, it is 47.7 per cent.

For kidney cancer patients, the survival rate here is 68.4 per cent. It is just 45.6 per cent in England, which the Commonwealth Fund ranked as the number one healthcare system in the world.

Finally, the Commonwealth Fund study also ignores massive problems with actual access to care in the countries it heralds. Every citizen of a country with socialised medicine may have insurance. But that doesn't mean they can get the care they need.

Treatment delays were so chronic in the United Kingdom, for example, the government had to issue a formal requirement that patients shouldn't have to wait more than four months for treatments authorised by their general practitioner.

The Royal College of Physicians found that poor care – including doctors trying to keep costs down – caused nearly two-thirds of asthma deaths in the United Kingdom in 2012.

In Canada, the average patient seeking an elective medical service has to wait four-and-a-half months between being recommended for treatment by their primary care physician and actually receiving it.

Waiting for care is the norm in Canada, even though Madam Chief Justice Beverley McLachlin of the Canadian Supreme Court declared nine years ago, in a ruling holding a ban on private health insurance in Quebec illegal, 'Access to a waiting list is not access to healthcare'.

The Commonwealth Fund is right about one thing – the U.S. healthcare system is too expensive. But rationing care – as Commonwealth's favoured systems do – is not the answer.

(Sally C. Pipes is President, CEO, and Taube Fellow in Health Care Studies at the Pacific Research Institute.)

World had never been in so much in imbalance.

Technology Deception by Elite Nations

On 14 June 2013, United States prosecutors charged Edward Snowden with espionage and theft of government property. In late July 2013, he was granted a one-year temporary asylum by the Russian government, contributing to a deterioration of Russia–United States relations. On 6 August 2013, U.S. President Barack Obama made a public appearance on national television where he reassured Americans that 'We don't have a domestic spying program' and 'There is no spying on Americans'. Towards the end of October 2013, the British Prime Minister David Cameron warned *The Guardian* not to publish any more leaks, or it will receive a DA notice. Currently, a criminal investigation of the disclosure is being undertaken by Britain's Metropolitan Police Service. In December 2013, *The Guardian* editor

Alan Rusbridger said: 'We have published I think twenty-six documents so far out of the 58,000 we've seen'.

The extent to which the media reports have responsibly informed the public is disputed. In January 2014, Obama said that 'the sensational way in which these disclosures have come out has often shed more heat than light' http://en.wikipedia.org/wiki/Global_surveillance_disclosures_(2013%E2%80%93present)_-_cite_note-npr.org-24 and critics such as Sean Wilentz have noted that many of the Snowden documents released do not concern domestic surveillance. In its first assessment of these disclosures, The Pentagon concluded that Snowden committed the biggest 'theft' of U.S. secrets in the history of the United States. Sir David Omand, a former director of the GCHQ, described Snowden's disclosure as the 'most catastrophic loss to British intelligence ever'.

Background

Barton Gellman, a Pulitzer Prize winning journalist who led *The Washington Post*'s coverage of Snowden's disclosures, summarised the leaks as follows:

'Taken together, the revelations have brought to light a global surveillance system that cast off many of its historical restraints after the attacks of 11 September 2001. Secret legal authorities empowered the NSA to sweep in the telephone, Internet and location records of whole populations'.

The Washington Post

The disclosure revealed specific details of the NSA's close cooperation with U.S. federal agencies such as the Federal Bureau of Investigation (FBI) and the Central Intelligence Agency (CIA) in addition to the agency's previously undisclosed financial payments to numerous commercial partners and telecommunications companies, as well as its previously undisclosed relationships with international partners such as Britain, France Germany and its secret treaties with foreign governments that were recently established for sharing intercepted data of each other's citizens. The disclosures were made public over the course of several months since June 2013 by the press in several nations from the trove leaked by the former NSA contractor Edward J. Snowden, who obtained the trove while working for Booz Allen Hamilton, one of the largest contractors for defense and intelligence in the United States.

George Brandis, the current Attorney General of Australia, asserted that Snowden's disclosure is the 'most serious setback for Western intelligence since the Second World War'.

Global surveillance

December 2013

Disclosures

Although the exact size of Snowden's disclosure remains unknown, the following estimates have been put up by various government officials:

- At least 15,000 Australian intelligence files, according to Australian officials
- At least 58,000 British intelligence files, according to British officials
- About 1.7 million U.S. intelligence files, according to U.S. officials

As a contractor of the NSA, Snowden was granted access to U.S. government documents along with top secret documents of several allied governments, via the exclusive Five-Eyes network. Snowden claims that he is currently not in physical possession of any of these documents, after having surrendered all copies to the journalists he met in Hong Kong.

Timeline

The Mira hotel in Hong Kong, where Edward Snowden hosted his first meeting with Glenn Greenwald, Laura Poitras, and journalist Ewen MacAskill of *The Guardian*

In April 2012, NSA contractor Edward Snowden began downloading documents. That year, Snowden had made his first contact with journalist Glenn Greenwald of *The Guardian* and he contacted documentary filmmaker Laura Poitras in January 2013.

2013

In May 2013, Snowden went on temporary leave from his position at the NSA, citing the pretext of receiving treatment for his epilepsy. Towards the end of May, he travelled to Hong Kong. After the U.S.-based editor of *The Guardian* held several meetings in New York City, it was decided that Greenwald, Poitras and the Guardian's defence and intelligence correspondent Ewen MacAskill would fly to Hong Kong to meet Snowden. On June 5, in the first media report based on the leaked material, *The Guardian* exposed a top secret court order showing that the NSA had collected phone records from over 120 million Verizon subscribers. Under the order, the numbers of both parties on a call, as well as the location data, unique identifiers, time of call, and duration of call were handed over to the FBI, which turned over the records to the NSA. According to *The Wall Street Journal*, the Verizon order is part of a controversial data programme, which seeks to stockpile records on all calls made in the United States but doesn't collect information directly from T-Mobile US and Verizon Wireless, in part because of their foreign ownership ties.

On 6 June 2013, the second media disclosure, the revelation of the PRISM surveillance programme (which collects the email, voice, text and video chats of foreigners and an unknown number of Americans from Microsoft, Google, Yahoo, Apple and other tech giants) was published simultaneously by *The Guardian* and *The Washington Post*.

Slide from a 2008 NSA presentation about XKeyscore, showing a worldmap with the locations of XKeyscore servers.

Der Spiegel revealed NSA spying on multiple diplomatic missions of the European Union (EU) and the United Nations Headquarters in New York. During specific episodes within a four-year period, the NSA hacked several Chinese mobile phone companies, the Chinese University of Hong Kong and Tsinghua University in Beijing, and the Asian fiber-optic network operator Pacnet. Only Australia, Canada, New Zealand and the United Kingdom are explicitly exempted from NSA attacks, whose main target in the EU is Germany. A method of bugging encrypted fax machines used at an EU embassy is codenamed Dropmire.

During the 2009 G-20 London summit, the British intelligence agency Government Communications Headquarters (GCHQ) intercepted the communications of foreign diplomats. In addition, the GCHQ has been intercepting and storing mass quantities of fiber-optic traffic via Tempora. Two principal components of Tempora are called 'Mastering the Internet' (MTI) and 'Global Telecoms Exploitation'. The data is preserved for three days while metadata is kept for thirty days. Data collected by the GCHQ under Tempora is shared with the National Security Agency (NSA) of the United States.

From 2001 to 2011, the NSA collected vast amounts of metadata records detailing the email and Internet usage of Americans via Stellar Wind, which was later terminated due to operational and resource constraints. It was subsequently replaced by newer surveillance programmes such as ShellTrumpet, which *processed its one trillionth metadata record* by the end of December 2012.

According to the Boundless Informant, over 97 billion pieces of intelligence were collected over a thirty-day period ending in March 2013. Out of all 97 billion sets of information, about 3 billion data sets originated from U.S. computer networks, and around 500 million metadata records were collected from German networks.

Several weeks later, it was revealed that the Bundesnachrichtendienst (BND) of Germany transfers massive amounts of metadata records to the NSA.

Stephen Vladeck, a professor at the American University's Washington College of Law, has argued that, without having to seek the approval of the court (which he has said merely reviews certifications to ensure that they – and not the surveillance itself – comply with the various statutory requirements), the U.S. Attorney General and the Director of National Intelligence can engage in sweeping programmatic surveillance for one year at a time. There are procedures used by the NSA to target non-U.S. persons and procedures used by the NSA to minimise data collection from U.S. persons. These court-approved policies allow the NSA to:

- keep data that could potentially contain details of U.S. persons for up to five years;
- retain and make use of 'inadvertently acquired' domestic communications if they contain usable intelligence, information on criminal activity, threat of harm to people or property, are encrypted, or are believed to contain any information relevant to cybersecurity;

In a document dated January 2013, the NSA acknowledged the efforts of the BND to undermine privacy laws:

The BND has been working to influence the German government to relax interpretation of the privacy laws to provide greater opportunities of intelligence sharing.

According to an NSA document dated April 2013, Germany has now become the NSA's 'most prolific partner'. Under a section of a separate document leaked by Snowden titled 'Success Stories', the NSA acknowledged the efforts of the German government to expand the BND's international data sharing with partners:

'The German government modifies its interpretation of the G-10 privacy law . . . to afford the BND more flexibility in sharing protected information with foreign partners'.

In addition, the German government was well aware of the PRISM surveillance programme long before Edward Snowden made details public. According to Angela Merkel's spokesman Steffen Seibert, there are two separate PRISM programmes – one is used by the NSA and the other is used by NATO forces in Afghanistan. The two programmes are 'not identical'.

Snowden also confirmed that Stuxnet was cooperatively developed by the United States and Israel. In a report unrelated to Edward Snowden, the French newspaper *Le Monde* revealed that France's DGSE was also undertaking mass surveillance, which it described as 'illegal and outside any serious control'.

Documents leaked by Edward Snowden that were seen by *Süddeutsche Zeitung* (SZ) and *Norddeutscher Rundfunk* revealed that several telecom operators have played a key role in helping the British intelligence agency Government Communications Headquarters (GCHQ) tap into worldwide fiber-optic communications. The telecom operators are:

- Verizon Business (codenamed 'Dacron')
- British Telecommunications (code named 'Remedy')
- Vodafone Cable (codenamed 'Gerontic')
- Global Crossing (codenamed 'Pinnage')
- Level 3 (codenamed 'Little')
- Viatel (codenamed 'Vitreous')
- Interoute (codenamed 'Streetcar')

Telecommunication companies who participated were 'forced' to do so and had 'no choice in the matter'. Some of the companies were subsequently paid by GCHQ for their participation in the infiltration of the cables. According to the SZ, the GCHQ has access to the majority of Internet and telephone communications flowing throughout Europe, can listen to phone calls, read emails and text messages, and see web sites that are accessed by Internet users all around the world. It can also retain and analyse nearly the entire European Internet traffic.

The United States runs a top-secret surveillance programme known as the Special Collection Service (SCS), which is based in over 80 U.S. consulates and embassies worldwide. The NSA hacked the United Nations' video conferencing system in Summer 2012 in violation of a UN agreement.

The NSA is not just intercepting the communications of Americans who are in direct contact with targeted foreigners overseas but is also searching the contents of vast amounts of email and text communications into and out of the country by Americans who mention information about foreigners under surveillance. It also spied on the Al Jazeera and gained access to its internal communications systems.

The NSA has built a surveillance network that has the capacity to reach roughly 75 per cent of all U.S. Internet traffic. The U.S. Law enforcement agencies use tools used by computer hackers to gather information on suspects. An internal NSA audit from May 2012 identified 2776 incidents, i.e. violations of the rules or court orders for surveillance of Americans and foreign targets in the United States in the period April 2011 through March 2012, while U.S. officials stressed that any mistakes are not intentional. The FISA court that is supposed to provide critical oversight of the U.S. government's vast spying programmes has limited ability to do so and it must trust the government to report when it unofficially spies on Americans. A legal opinion declassified on 21 August 2013 revealed that the NSA intercepted for three years as many as 56,000 electronic communications, a year of Americans who weren't suspected of having links to terrorism, before FISA court that oversees surveillance found the operation unconstitutional in 2011. Under the Corporate Partner Access project, major U.S. telecommunications providers receive hundreds of millions of dollars each year from the NSA. voluntary cooperation between the NSA, and the providers of global communications took off during the 1970s under the cover name BLARNEY.

The NSA has under a legal authority a secret backdoor into its databases gathered from large Internet companies enabling it to search for U.S. citizens' email and phone calls without a warrant.

The Privacy and Civil Liberties Oversight Board urged the U.S. intelligence chiefs to draft stronger U.S. surveillance guidelines on domestic spying after finding that several of those guidelines have not been updated up to thirty years. The U.S. intelligence analysts have deliberately violated rules designed to prevent them from spying on Americans by choosing to ignore the so-called 'minimisation procedures' aimed at protecting privacy and used the NSA's agency's enormous eavesdropping power to spy on love interests.

After the U.S. Foreign Secret Intelligence Court ruled in October 2011 that some of the NSA's activities were unconstitutional, the agency paid millions of dollars to major Internet companies to cover extra costs incurred in their involvement with the PRISM surveillance programme.

'Mastering the Internet' (MTI) is part of the Interception Modernisation Programme (IMP) of the British government that involves the insertion of thousands of DPI (deep packet inspection) 'black boxes' at various Internet service providers, as revealed by the British media in 2009.

In 2013, it was further revealed that the NSA had made a £17.2 million financial contribution to the project, which is capable of vacuuming signals from up to 200 fibre-optic cables at all physical points of entry into Great Britain.

The *Guardian* and the *New York Times* reported on secret documents leaked by Snowden showing that the NSA has been in 'collaboration with technology companies' as part of 'an aggressive, multipronged effort' to weaken the encryption used in commercial software, and the GCHQ has a team dedicated to cracking 'Hotmail, Google, Yahoo and Facebook' traffic. Israel, Sweden and Italy are also cooperating with American and British intelligence agencies. Under a secret treaty codenamed 'Lustre', French intelligence agencies transferred millions of metadata records to the NSA.

A special branch of the NSA called 'Follow the Money' (FTM) monitors international payments, banking and credit card transactions and later stores the collected data in the NSA's own financial databank 'Tracfin'. http:// en.wikipedia.org/wiki/Global_surveillance_disclosures_ (2013%E2%80%93present) - cite note-188 The NSA monitored the communications of Brazil's president Dilma Rousseff and her top aides. The agency also spied on Brazil's oil firm Petrobras as well as French diplomats and gained access to the private network of the Ministry of Foreign Affairs of France and the SWIFT network.

In the United States, the NSA uses the analysis of phone calls and email logs of American citizens to create sophisticated graphs of their social connections that can identify their associates, their locations at certain times, their traveling companions and other personal information. The NSA routinely shares raw intelligence data with Israel without first sifting it to remove information about U.S. citizens.

Under the heading 'iPhone capability', the document notes that there are smaller NSA programmes, known as 'scripts', that can perform surveillance on thirty-eight different features of the iOS 3 and iOS 4 operating systems. These include the mapping feature, voicemail and photos, as well as Google Earth, Facebook and Yahoo! Messenger.

On 9 September 2013, an internal NSA presentation on iPhone Location Services was leaked by *Der Spiegel*. One slide shows scenes from Apple's *1984*-themed television commercial alongside the words, Who knew in 1984 another shows Steve Jobs holding an iPhone, with the text '. . . that this would be big brother . . .' ; and a third shows happy consumers with their iPhones, completing the question with '. . . and the zombies would be paying customers?'

On 4 October 2013, *The Washington Post* and *The Guardian* jointly reported that the NSA and the GCHQ have made repeated attempts to spy on anonymous Internet users who have been communicating in secret via the anonymity network Tor. Several of these surveillance operations involve the implantation of malicious code into the computers of Tor users who visit particular web sites. The NSA and GCHQ have partly succeeded in blocking access to the anonymous network, diverting Tor users to insecure channels. The government agencies were also able to uncover the identity of some anonymous Internet users. The Communications Security Establishment Canada (CSEC) has been using a programme called Olympia to map the communications of Brazil's Mines and Energy Ministry by targeting the metadata of phone calls and emails to and from the ministry.

The Australian Federal Government knew about the PRISM surveillance programme months before Edward Snowden made details public.

The NSA gathered hundreds of millions of contact lists from personal email and instant messaging accounts around the world. The agency didn't target individuals. Instead it collected contact lists in large numbers that amount to a sizable fraction of the world's email and instant messaging accounts. Analysis of that data enables the agency to search for hidden connections and to map relationships within a much smaller universe of foreign intelligence targets.

The NSA monitored the public email account of former Mexican president Felipe Calderón (thus gaining access to the communications of high-ranking cabinet members), the emails of several high-ranking members of Mexico's security forces and text and the mobile phone communication of current Mexican president Enrique Peña Nieto. The NSA tries to gather cellular and landline phone numbers – often obtained from American diplomats – for as many foreign officials as possible. The contents of the phone calls are stored in computer databases that can regularly be searched using keywords.

The NSA has been monitoring telephone conversations of thirty-five world leaders. The U.S. government's first public acknowledgment that it tapped the phones of world leaders was reported on 28 October 2013 by *The Wall Street Journal* after an internal U.S. government review turned up NSA monitoring of some thirty-five world leaders. The GCHQ has tried to keep its mass surveillance programme a secret because it feared a 'damaging public debate' on the scale of its activities which could lead to legal challenges against them.

The Guardian revealed that the NSA had been monitoring telephone conversations of thirty-five world leaders after being given the numbers by an official in another U.S. government department. A confidential memo revealed that the NSA encouraged senior officials in such departments as the White House, State and The Pentagon, to share their 'Rolodexes' so the agency could add the telephone numbers of leading foreign politicians to their surveillance systems. Reacting to the news, German leader Angela Merkel, arriving in Brussels for an EU summit, accused the United States of a breach of trust, saying: 'We need to have trust in our allies and partners, and this must now be established once again. I repeat that spying among friends is not at all acceptable against anyone, and that goes for every citizen in Germany'. The NSA collected, in 2010 data, on ordinary Americans' cellphone locations but later discontinued it because it had no 'operational value'.

Under Britain's MUSCULAR programme, the NSA and the GCHQ have secretly encroached into the main communications links that connect Yahoo and Google data centres around the world and thereby gained the ability to collect metadata and content at will from hundreds of millions of user accounts.

The mobile phone of German Chancellor Angela Merkel might have been tapped by U.S. intelligence. According to the Spiegel, this monitoring goes back to 2002 and ended in the summer of 2013, while *The New York Times* reported that Germany has evidence that the NSA's surveillance of Merkel began during George W. Bush's tenure. After learning from *Der Spiegel* magazine that the NSA has been listening in to her personal mobile phone, Merkel compared the snooping practices of the NSA with those of the Stasi. It was reported in March 2014 by Der Spiegel that Merkel had also been placed on an NSA surveillance list alongside 122 other world leaders.

On 31 October 2013, Hans-Christian Ströbele, a member of the German Bundestag, met Snowden in Moscow and revealed the former intelligence contractor's readiness to brief the German government on NSA spying.

In France, the NSA targeted people belonging to the worlds of business, politics or French state administration. The NSA monitored and recorded the content of telephone communications and the history of the connections of each target, i.e. the metadata. The actual surveillance operation was performed by French intelligence agencies on behalf of the NSA. The cooperation between France and the NSA was confirmed by the Director of the NSA, Keith B. Alexander, who asserted that foreign intelligence services collected phone records in 'war zones' and 'other areas outside their borders' and provided them to the NSA.

The French newspaper *Le Monde* also disclosed new PRISM and Upstream slides coming from the 'PRISM/US-984XN Overview' presentation.

In Spain, the NSA intercepted the telephone conversations, text messages and emails of millions of Spaniards and spied on members of the Spanish government. Between 10 December 2012 and 8 January 2013, the NSA collected metadata on 60 million telephone calls in Spain.

The *New York Times* reported that the NSA carries out an eavesdropping effort, dubbed Operation Dreadnought, against the Iranian leader Ayatollah Ali Khamenei. During his 2009 visit to Iranian Kurdistan, the agency collaborated with the GCHQ and the U.S.'s National Geospatial-Intelligence Agency, collecting radio transmissions between aircraft and airports, examining Khamenei's convoy with satellite imagery and enumerating military radar stations. According to the story, an objective of the operation is 'communications fingerprinting': the ability to distinguish Khamenei's communications from those of other people in Iran.

The same story revealed an operation code named Ironavenger, in which the NSA intercepted emails sent between a country allied with the United States and the government of 'an adversary'. The ally was conducting a spear-phishing attack: its emails contained malware. The NSA gathered documents and login credentials belonging to the enemy country, along with knowledge of the ally's capabilities for attacking computers.

According to the British newspaper *The Independent*, the British intelligence agency GCHQ maintains a listening post on the roof of the British Embassy in Berlin that is capable of intercepting mobile phone calls, wi-fi data and long-distance communications all over the German capital, including adjacent government buildings such as the Reichstag (seat of the German parliament) and the Chancellery (seat of Germany's head of government) clustered around the Brandenburg Gate.

Operating under the code name 'Quantum Insert', the GCHQ set up a fake web site masquerading as LinkedIn, a social web site used for professional networking, as part of its efforts to install surveillance software on the computers of the telecommunications operator Belgacom. In addition, the headquarters of the oil cartel OPEC were infiltrated by the GCHQ as well as the NSA, which bugged the computers of nine OPEC employees and monitored the General Secretary of OPEC.

For more than three years, the GCHQ has been using an automated monitoring system code named 'Royal Concierge' to infiltrate the reservation systems of at least 350 upscale hotels in many different parts of the world in order to target, search and analyse reservations to detect diplomats and government officials. First tested in 2010, the aim of the 'Royal Concierge' is to track down the travel plans of diplomats, and it is often supplemented with surveillance methods related to human intelligence (HUMINT). Other covert operations include the wiretapping of room telephones and fax machines used in targeted hotels as well as the monitoring of computers hooked up to the hotel network.

In November 2013, the Australian Broadcasting Corporation and *The Guardian* revealed that the Australian Signals

Directorate (DSD) had attempted to listen to the private phone calls of the president of Indonesia and his wife. The Indonesian foreign minister, Marty Natalegawa, confirmed that he and the president had contacted the ambassador in Canberra. Natalegawa said any tapping of Indonesian politicians' personal phones 'violates every single decent and legal instrument I can think of – national in Indonesia, national in Australia, international as well'.

Other high-ranking Indonesian politicians targeted by the DSD include:

- Boediono (Vice President)
- Jusuf Kalla (Former Vice President)
- Dino Patti Djalal (Ambassador to the United States)
- Andi Mallarangeng (Government spokesperson)
- Hatta Rajasa (State Secretary)
- Sri Mulyani Indrawati (Former Finance Minister and current managing director of the World Bank)
- Widodo Adi Sutjipto (Former Commander-in-Chief of the Military)
- Sofyan Djalil (Senior government advisor)

Carrying the title '3G impact and update', a classified presentation leaked by Snowden revealed the attempts of the ASD/DSD to keep up to pace with the rollout of 3G technology in Indonesia and across Southeast Asia. The ASD/DSD motto placed at the bottom of each page reads: 'Reveal their secrets – protect our own'.

Under a secret deal approved by British intelligence officials, the NSA has been storing and analysing the Internet and email records of UK citizens since 2007. The NSA also proposed in 2005 a procedure for spying on the citizens of the United Kingdom and other Five Eyes nations alliance, even where the partner government has explicitly denied the U.S. permission to do so. Under the proposal, partner countries must neither be informed about this particular type of surveillance nor the procedure of doing so.

Towards the end of November, *The New York Times* released an internal NSA report outlining the agency's efforts to expand its surveillance abilities. The five-page document asserts that the law of the United States has not kept up with the needs of the NSA to conduct mass surveillance in the 'golden age' of signals intelligence, but there are grounds for optimism, because in the NSA's own words:

'The culture of compliance, which has allowed the American people to entrust NSA with extraordinary authorities, will not be compromised in the face of so many demands, even as we aggressively pursue legal authorities . . .'

The report, titled 'SIGINT Strategy 2012–2016', also said that the U.S. will try to influence the 'global commercial encryption market' through 'commercial relationships', and emphasised the need to 'revolutionize' the analysis of its vast data collection to 'radically increase operational impact'.

On 23 November 2013, the Dutch newspaper *NRC Handelsblad* reported that the Netherlands was targeted by U.S. intelligence agencies in the immediate aftermath of World War II. This period of surveillance lasted from 1946 to 1968, and also included the interception of the communications of other European countries including Belgium, France, West Germany and Norway. The Dutch Newspaper also reported that NSA infected more than 50,000 computer networks worldwide, often covertly, with malicious spy software, sometimes in cooperation with local authorities, designed to steal sensitive information.

On 23 November 2013, the Dutch newspaper *NRC Handelsblad* released a top secret NSA presentation leaked by Snowden, showing five 'Classes of Accesses' that the NSA uses in its worldwide signals intelligence operations. These five 'Classes of Accesses' are:

Third PARTY/LIAISON – refers to data provided by the international partners of the NSA. Within the framework of the UK–USA Agreement, these international partners are known as 'third parties'.

REGIONAL – refers to over eighty regional special collection services (SCS). The SCS is a black budget programme operated by the NSA and the CIA, with operations based in many cities such as Athens, Bangkok, Berlin, Brasília, Budapest, Frankfurt, Geneva, Lagos, Milan, New Delhi, Paris, Prague, Vienna, Zagreb and others, targeting Central America, the Arabian Peninsula, East Asia and Continental Europe.

CNE – an abbreviation for 'Computer Network Exploitation'. It is performed by a special cyber-warfare unit of the NSA known as tailored access operations (TAO), which infected over 50,000 computer networks worldwide with malicious software designed to steal sensitive information and is mostly aimed at Brazil, China, Egypt, India, Mexico, Saudi Arabia and parts of Eastern Europe. LARGE CABLE – twenty major points of accesses, many of them located within the United States

FORNSAT – an abbreviation for 'Foreign Satellite Collection'. It refers to intercepts from satellites that process data used by other countries such as Britain, Norway, Japan and the Philippines

According to the classified documents leaked by Snowden, the Australian Signals Directorate, formerly known as the Defence Signals Directorate, had offered to share information on Australian citizens with the other intelligence agencies of the UK–USA Agreement. Data shared with foreign countries include 'bulk, unselected, unminimised metadata' such as 'medical, legal or religious information'. *The Washington Post* revealed that the NSA has been tracking the locations of mobile phones from all over the world by tapping into the cables that connect mobile networks globally and that serve U.S. cellphones as well as foreign ones. In the process of doing so, the NSA collects more than five billion records of phone locations on a daily basis. This enables NSA analysts to map cellphone owners' relationships by correlating their patterns of movement over time with thousands or millions of other phone users who cross their paths. *The Washington Post* also reported that both the GCHQ and the NSA make use of location data and advertising tracking files generated through normal Internet browsing (with cookies operated by Google, known as 'Pref') to pinpoint targets for government hacking and to bolster surveillance.

The Norwegian Intelligence Service (NIS), which cooperates with the NSA, has gained access to Russian targets in the Kola Peninsula and other civilian targets. In general, the NIS provides information to the NSA about 'politicians', 'energy' and 'armament'. A top secret memo of the NSA lists the following years as milestones of the Norway–United States of America SIGINT agreement, or NORUS Agreement:

- 1952 – Informal starting year of cooperation between the NIS and the NSA
- 1954 – Formalisation of the agreement
- 1963 – Extension of the agreement for coverage of foreign instrumentation signals intelligence (FISINT)
- 1970 – Extension of the agreement for coverage of electronic intelligence (ELINT)
- 1994 – Extension of the agreement for coverage of communications intelligence (COMINT)

The NSA considers the NIS to be one of its most reliable partners. Both agencies also cooperate to crack the encryption systems of mutual targets. According to the NSA, Norway has made no objections to its requests from the NIS.

On December 5, Sveriges Television reported the National Defence Radio Establishment (FRA) has been conducting a clandestine surveillance operation in Sweden, targeting the internal politics of Russia. The operation was conducted on behalf of the NSA, receiving data handed over to it by the FRA. The Swedish–American surveillance operation also targeted Russian energy interests as well as the Baltic states. As part of the UK–USA Agreement, a secret treaty was signed in 1954 by Sweden with the United States, the United Kingdom, Canada, Australia and New Zealand, regarding collaboration and intelligence sharing.

As a result of Snowden's disclosures, the notion of Swedish neutrality in international politics was called into question. In an internal document dating from the year 2006, the NSA acknowledged that its 'relationship' with Sweden is 'protected at the TOP SECRET level because of that nation's political neutrality'. Specific details of Sweden's cooperation with members of the UK–USA Agreement include:

- The FRA has been granted access to XKeyscore, an analytical database of the NSA.
- Sweden updated the NSA on changes in Swedish legislation that provided the legal framework for information sharing between the FRA and the Swedish Security Service.
- Since January 2013, a counter-terrorism analyst of the NSA has been stationed in the Swedish capital of Stockholm.
- The NSA, the GCHQ and the FRA signed an agreement in 2004 that allows the FRA to directly collaborate with the NSA without having to consult the GCHQ. About five years later, the Riksdag passed a controversial legislative change, briefly allowing the FRA to monitor both wireless and cable bound signals passing the Swedish border without a court order, while also introducing several provisions designed to protect the privacy of individuals, according to the original proposal.

This legislation was amended eleven months later, in an effort to strengthen protection of privacy by making court orders a requirement and by imposing several limits on the intelligence gathering.

According to documents leaked by Snowden, the Special Source Operations of the NSA has been sharing information containing 'logins, cookies, and GooglePREFID' with the Tailored Access Operations division of the NSA, as well as Britain's GCHQ agency.

During the 2010 G-20 Toronto summit, the U.S. embassy in Ottawa was transformed into a security command post during a six-day spying operation that was conducted by the NSA and closely coordinated with the Communications Security Establishment Canada (CSEC). The goal of the spying operation was, among others, to obtain information on international development, banking reform and to counter trade protectionism to support 'U.S. policy goals'. On behalf of the NSA, the CSEC has set up covert spying posts in twenty countries around the world.

In Italy, the Special Collection Service of the NSA maintains two separate surveillance posts in Rome and Milan. According to a secret NSA memo dated September 2010, the Italian embassy in Washington, D.C., has been targeted by two spy operations of the NSA:

- Under the code name 'Bruneau', which refers to mission 'Lifesaver', the NSA sucks out all the information stored in the embassy's computers and creates electronic images of hard disk drives.

- Under the code name 'Hemlock', which refers to mission 'Highlands', the NSA gains access to the embassy's communications through physical 'implants'.

Due to concerns that terrorist or criminal networks may be secretly communicating via computer games, the NSA, the GCHQ, the CIA and the FBI have been conducting surveillance and scooping up data from the networks of many online games, including massively multiplayer online role-playing games (MMORPGs) such as World of Warcraft, as well as virtual worlds such as Second Life, and the Xbox gaming console.

The NSA has cracked the most commonly used cellphone encryption technology, A5/1. According to a classified document leaked by Snowden, the agency can 'process encrypted A5/1' even when it has not acquired an encryption key. In addition, the NSA uses various types of cellphone infrastructure, such as the links between carrier networks, to determine the location of a cellphone user tracked by Visitor Location Registers.

U.S. district court judge for the District of Columbia, Richard Leon, declared on 16 December 2013 that the mass collection of metadata of Americans' telephone records by the National Security Agency (NSA) probably violates the fourth amendment: prohibition of unreasonable searches and seizures. Leon granted the request for a preliminary injunction that blocks the collection of phone data for two private plaintiffs (Larry Klayman, a conservative lawyer, and Charles Strange, father of a cryptologist killed in Afghanistan when his helicopter was shot down in 2011) and ordered the government to destroy any of their records that have been gathered. But the judge stayed action on his ruling pending a government appeal, recognising in his sixty-eight-page opinion the 'significant national security interests at stake in this case and the novelty of the constitutional issues'.

However, federal judge William H. Pauley III in New York City ruled the U.S. government's global telephone data-gathering system is needed to thwart potential terrorist attacks, and that it can only work if everyone's calls are swept in. U.S. District Judge Pauley also ruled that Congress legally set up the programme and that it does not violate anyone's constitutional rights. The judge also concluded that the telephone data being swept up by NSA did not belong to telephone users but to the telephone companies. He further ruled that when NSA obtains such data from the telephone companies, and then probes into it to find links between callers and potential terrorists, this further use of the data was not even a search under the fourth amendment. He also concluded that the controlling precedent is Smith v. Maryland: 'Smith's bedrock holding is that an individual has no legitimate expectation of privacy in information provided to third parties', Judge Pauley wrote. The American Civil Liberties Union declared on 2 January 2012 that it will appeal Judge Pauley's ruling that NSA bulk the phone record collection is legal. 'The government has a legitimate interest in tracking the associations of suspected terrorists, but tracking those associations does not require the government to subject every citizen to permanent surveillance', deputy ACLU legal director Jameel Jaffer said in a statement.

In recent years, American and British intelligence agencies conducted surveillance on more than 1,100 targets, including the office of an Israeli prime minister, heads of international aid organisations, foreign energy companies and a European Union official involved in anti-trust battles with American technology businesses.

A catalog of high-tech gadgets and software developed by the NSA's Tailored Access Operations (TAO) was leaked by the German news magazine *Der Spiegel*. Dating from 2008, the catalogue revealed the existence of special gadgets modified to capture computer screenshots and USB flash drives secretly fitted with radio transmitters to broadcast stolen data over the airwaves and fake base stations intended to intercept mobile phone signals, as well as many other secret devices and software implants listed here:

Computer implants
Server implants and firewall implants
Covert listening devices
Mobile phone implants and related products

On 4 December 2013, *The Washington Post* released an internal NSA chart illustrating the extent of the agency's mass collection of mobile phone location records, which amounts to about five billion on a daily basis. The records are stored in a huge database known as FASCIA, which received over twenty-seven terabytes of location data within seven months.

2014

The NSA is working to build a powerful quantum computer capable of breaking all types of encryption. The effort is part of a US$ 79.7 million research programme known as 'Penetrating Hard Targets'. It involves extensive research carried out in large, shielded rooms known as Faraday cages, which are designed to prevent electromagnetic radiation from entering or leaving. Currently, the NSA is close to producing basic building blocks that will allow the agency to gain 'complete quantum control on two semiconductor qubits'. Once a quantum computer is successfully built, it would enable the NSA to unlock the encryption that protects data held by banks, credit card companies, retailers, brokerages, governments and healthcare providers.

According to *The New York Times*, the NSA is monitoring approximately 100,000 computers worldwide with a spy software named Quantum. Quantum enables the NSA to conduct surveillance on those computers, on the one hand, and can also create a digital highway for launching cyberattacks, on the other hand. Among the targets are the Chinese and Russian military and also trade institutions within the European Union. *The NYT* also reported that the NSA can access and alter computers which are not connected with the Internet by a secret technology in use by the NSA since 2008. The prerequisite is the physical insertion of the radio frequency hardware by a spy, a manufacturer or an unwitting user. The technology relies on a covert channel of radio waves that can be transmitted from tiny circuit boards and USB cards inserted surreptitiously into the computers.

CHAPTER 5

CENTRAL ENIGMA OF CONSCIOUSNESS BY CHRIS KING

The nature and physical basis of consciousness remains the central enigma of the scientific description of reality in the third millennium. This paper seeks to examine the phenomenal nature of consciousness and elucidate a possible biophysical basis for its existence, in terms of a form of quantum anticipation based on entangled states driven by chaotic sensitivity of global brain states during decision-making processes.

1. Introduction to the Enigma

The term 'consciousness' itself is enigmatic. Both 'mind and 'consciousness present a varied array of associated words and concepts, which we need to clarify, to even begin to close in on the central enigma, which the terms present to us. Mind conjures up a plethora of concepts from minding, i.e. emotional caring, or objecting, through the rational mind of thought and language-based reasoning, mindfulness or focused concentration, to absent-, clear- or small- mindedness to the mindless blunders many of us consciously make, despite ourselves. Consciousness can mean everything from the root capacity to have subjective experiences at all, through awake alertness, as opposed to the slumber, or coma, of unconsciousness, through the fuzzy boundary between subconscious or unconscious processing that accompanies conscious cognition, to the restrictive idea of self-consciousness, as knowing that you know – 'a conscious state is one which has a higher-order accompanying thought which is about the state in question'.

Wikipedia has the following introductory descriptions, chosen because they are a product of a social process of consensual agreement as to their meaning and content:

'Mind collectively refers to the aspects of intellect and consciousness manifested as combinations of thought, perception, memory, emotion, will and imagination; mind is the stream of consciousness. It includes all of the brain's conscious processes. This denotation sometimes includes, in certain contexts, the working of the human unconscious or the conscious thoughts of animals. 'Mind' is often used to refer especially to the thought processes of reason'.

'Consciousness has been defined loosely as a constellation of attributes of mind such as subjectivity, self-awareness, sentience and the ability to perceive a relationship between oneself and one's environment. It has been defined from a more biological and causal perspective as the act of autonomously modulating attentional and computational effort, usually with the goal of obtaining, retaining, or maximising specific parameters (food, a safe environment, family, mates). Consciousness may involve thoughts, sensations, perceptions, moods, emotions, dreams, and an awareness of self, although not necessarily any particular one or combination of these'.

Although these contain a constellation of meanings, in which mind is sometimes focused on the attributes of reasoned, or even language-based thought, and consciousness is sometimes given the more restrictive meaning of self-awareness, both contain a central arena of subjectivity and sentience, while conceding that the boundaries between consciousness and the sub- or unconscious may be fuzzy, both in varied brain states, from waking thought to sleep and coma, and in complex autonomous processes, which go on below the level of immediate awareness, during activities like driving a car.

The central enigma we are referring to is not self-consciousness, but subjective consciousness – the capacity of a conscious sentient being to have a subjective experience of the existential condition, both of the everyday world, and of dream, memory and reflection, hallucination, psychedelic reverie, and other forms of internal subjective experience, not necessarily correlated with the immediate events of the physical world.

In the face of the apparent causality of the Laplacian universe, many twentieth century philosophers assigned to consciousness the orphan status of an epiphenomenon, a mere reflection of physical reality which could have no influence upon it. Some, such as Gilbert Ryle, who coined the term 'the ghost in the machine', went further, attempting to deconstruct the dualistic notion of mind altogether, as a form of false reasoning, claiming 'that the idea of Mind as an independent entity, inhabiting and governing the body, should be rejected as a redundant piece of literalism carried over from the era before the biological sciences became established. The proper function of Mind–body language, he suggests, is to describe how higher organisms such as humans demonstrate resourcefulness, strategy, the ability to abstract and hypothesize and so on from the evidences of their behaviour'. Derived from the dualistic cosmology of Rene Descartes, this subjective arena is frequently referred to as the 'Cartesian theatre', sometimes constructively, as in Barrs, who describes the theatre of the conscious in terms of working memory and its associated backdrops, but other times in somewhat disparaging terms as in Dennett, who, rather than explaining consciousness, as he claims, replaces it with a 'multiple drafts model', more representative of the publishing industry, than either the conscious mind or the sentient brain.

Some of these criticisms arise from the practical difficulties of defining the borders of consciousness and the difficulty of finding the actual mechanisms for generating the 'internal model of subjective reality' in terms of brain centres and their electrochemical dynamics, in the absence of clear evidence characterising which brain states other than general focused global activity are responsible for consciousness, and as a result of the binding problem – how and where the disparate components of brain processing are all brought together in the hypothetical 'Cartesian theatre' of the mind. Some of these problems are misplaced because they are falsely identifying brain and mind states. For example, the 'binding problem' of brain dynamics may be resolved in practical terms through the phase coherence of excitations that are related, to form resonant neural circuits, differentiating them from the incoherent noise of the background, even though there is no specific brain centre as such where consciousness is generated.

At issue is a fundamental frame of subjective reference and a confusion on the part of brain researchers and philosophers alike, between the physical world, and our representation of it in the so-called 'internal model of reality', which tends to become finessed in the dialectics of discourse on the problem.

The veridical reality is that from birth to death each of us is a subjective, conscious observer of the existential condition. All our experiences of the physical universe are without exception subjective, conscious impressions, which only we as individual subjective observers have access to. Ultimately, all data and scientific observations of the universe likewise achieve validation through the subjective conscious experience of the researchers and those who read their papers and witness their results.

Far from being the fundamental components of veridical reality, the physical universe and all the constructs applied to it, from wave-particles through atoms and molecules, to complex biological systems such as the sentient brain and all our experiences of the everyday world around us are entirely, and without exception, purely and completely, abstract models of subjective conscious impressions, knitted together by a consensual agreement between subjective perceivers – that the table before us is solid and made of wood, plastic or metal, as the case may be, and that our impressions of the world, from the lemon, or coffee cup on the table, to the horizon upon which we gaze, from a lonely hill top, looking out to sea, or the stars and galaxies we perceive in the sky, and entertain the humbling specters of an eventual demise in the heat death or big crunch, according to cosmological theories of the time.

Subjective consciousness is thus the primary veridical conduit of existential reality and the phenomena of the objective world, for all the convincing lessons that we are biological organisms which bleed if we are cut and lose consciousness if we slumber or are concussed and are consensual stabilities of our subjective consciousness. This remains true, notwithstanding our obvious dependence on our brain states, and the fact that some of the most bizarre and interesting states of altered consciousness arise from psychoactive molecules, which mimic neurotransmitters or transport processes affecting synapses and thus radically altering brain states.

However, based on the consistency of the scientific description of the physical universe and our part in it, as biological organisms dependent on our functioning brains to survive, this veridical logic has tended to become reversed, on the basis of the inaccessibility of subjective experiences to objective experimental testing and replication, so that consciousness has either been relegated to an epiphenomenon, merely reflecting, but not influencing, physical processes, e.g., in the brain, or banished to the wilderness, as 'naïve or imaginary' concepts not well-founded in the domain of philosophical or scientific discourse.

Put in its completion, the relationship between consciousness and physical reality, rather than being either an epiphenomenon, or mere identity, or a fully divided Cartesian duality has characteristics more of the complementarity we see between the wave and particle aspects of the quantum world, in which a quantum can manifest wave, or particle natures, but not both at the same time, and in which the two aspects are also qualitatively symmetry broken, one being discrete and the other continuous. It is this type of complementarity that Lao Tsu called a Tao or 'way' of nature, and subjective consciousness and the objective physical universe clearly have just such a qualitative complementarity existentially.

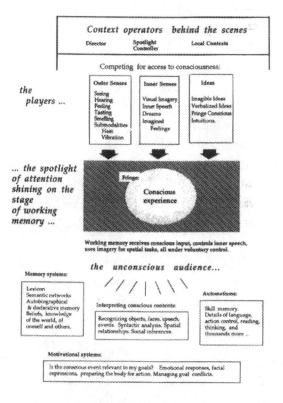

Fig 1: Baars's description of the Cartesian Theatre of consciousness and its 'players' in terms of functional working memory processes. The nature of this complementarity and its fundamentality in the light of attempts on the part of

functionalists to finesse consciousness to be merely and aspect of the attention process, or certain classes of excitation, such as those in the gamma range of the electroencephalogram or eeg (30–60 Hz) have been highlighted in David Chalmers's enunciation of the so-called 'Hard Problem' in consciousness research, – 'explaining why we have qualitative phenomenal experiences. It is contrasted with the 'easy problems' of explaining the ability to discriminate, integrate information, report mental states, focus attention, etc. Easy problems are easy because all that is required for their solution is to specify a mechanism that can perform the function'. For example, Crick and Koch identify conscious states accompanying attentive processes with higher frequency eeg signals in the gamma range. Defining consciousness as a functional process associated with attention and/or working memory is addressing an 'easy' problem in consciousness research. The dilemma of the 'hard' problem implies that no purely objective mechanism can suffice to explain subjective consciousness as a phenomenon in its own right.

Completing the enigma of consciousness is the thorny spectre of 'free-will', upon which all concepts of law and personal accountability hinge, as well as the assumptions of virtually every religious tradition.

Although it is possible to couch questions of personal accountability in purely behavioural terms of social conditioning, the problem of free will remains a shibboleth for the effectiveness of the scientific description. While many scientifically trained people consider that they may in principle be a chemical machine driven by their brain states, the notion that subjective consciousness decision-making has no capacity whatever to influence the physical circumstances around leads to catatonic stasis. Everyone who gets up in the morning and does something so predictable as pouring a cup of coffee is making a direct investment in the notion that they are in some sense in control of their personal decisions and that their feeling of subjective autonomy is a valid expression of their condition. We act in the world on this assumption and upon this investment.

Like subjective consciousness, free will has become an orphan of the scientific description, seemingly inconsistent with the hypothesis that the behaviour of the organism is purely a function of its brain reacting as an electrochemical machine, albeit a very complex one to the physical conditions of the organism's environment. However, from the outset of the quantum era, scientific researchers have noted that since the quantum description of reality is not deterministic, the apparently stochastic nature of quantum uncertainty could provide a loophole for free will, since the universe is no longer in principle a Laplacian mechanism. Arthur Eddington, for example, noted that the uncertainty of position of a synaptic vesicle was large enough to correspond to the thickness of the cell membrane, giving a possible basis for a change in neurodynamics arising from quantum uncertainty. Concluding that intentional volition might then be inconsistent with the chance probability-based calculations of particle statistic, Eddington then effectively suggested a form of hidden correlation in sub-quantum dynamics: a correlated behaviour of the individual particles of matter, which he assumed to occur for matter in liaison with mind.

This 'loophole' has led to a continuing tradition of physicists, mathematicians and brain researchers, speculating on various models by which the quantum world might interpenetrate with the sort of brain dynamics associated with conscious decision-making. We will look at these in detail, once we have examined the brain dynamics associated with conscious states.

2. A Dynamic View of the Conscious Brain

Unlike the digital computer which is a serial digital device based on a discrete logic of 0s and 1s, the brain is a massively parallel dynamic organ. Although the action potential of long neuronal axons is a pulse coded firing rate proportional to membrane depolarisation, many neurons and indeed those forming the organising centre of many processes have continuously graded potentials. Thus, although some individual neuron outputs may be pulsed action potentials, the electrical activity of the human brain, as expressed in the eeg consists of broad spectrum excitations indicative of chaos, rather than the discrete resonances of ordered states. While some aspects of the eeg, such as the alpha rhythms of visual relaxation, may be housekeeping activities, as noted, oscillations in the gamma band have been associated with specific conscious thought processes. The basis of the eeg appears to lie in dynamic feedback between excitatory and coupled inhibitory neurons which set up mutual oscillations through a phase-delayed feedback loop, which implicates it as a major dynamical feature of cerebral processing.

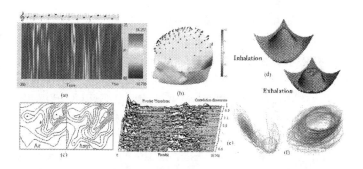

Fig 2: Evidence for both dynamical chaos and phase wave front 'holographic' processing. (a) Wavelet (morlet) transform, showing time evolution of amplitudes with a peak in the gamma band accompanying recognition of an anomalous note is consistent with phase-front processing. Broad-spectrum excitation (extended vertical distribution of frequencies) is also consistent with chaotic dynamics in the time domain. (b) Coherent distribution of electroencephalogram over the cortex is consistent with globally coupled excitation. (c) Extended spatial distribution of cortical activation accompanying recognition of an odour. (d) Freeman's model of olfactory recognition involves a transition from high-energy chaos on inhalation to enter a new or existing strange attractor basin as the energy is lowered on exhalation. Although this is a transition from chaos to an ordered outcome, the attractor may be a strange attractor, still supporting chaos locally within the basin. (e) Fourier transforms of electroencephalogram, showing broad-spectrum excitation and correlations dimensions consistent with global chaotic dynamics. (f) Putative strange attractors in the electroencephalogram.

While it might seem a contradiction that a brain state leading to any form of strategic decision could be chaotic, this is not actually the case. Ordered-dynamical systems are inexorably drawn towards existing equilibria or resonant attractors making them insensitive to their surroundings. A key characteristic of chaotic dynamics is the 'butterfly effect' – their arbitrary sensitivity on their initial, or boundary conditions – which in the words of Lorenz – enable fluctuations as small as those of a butterfly's wings to become amplified onto a tropical cyclone.

The dynamical brain needs to be arbitrarily sensitive to its external conditions to respond effectively to the sometimes very subtle clues from the world around us that are absolutely essential for survival. A second key characteristic particularly of high-energy chaos is that it tends to explore the entire space of available states, sometimes called the 'phase space', pseudo-randomly, so that it can appear anywhere, without prejudicing the outcome or missing an angle. Thus a fundamental theme, which has proved very useful in exploring brain dynamics, is a transition from chaos to order, in which an unstable high-energy chaotic exploration falls into an ordered attracting state, corresponding to recognition of a smell, or the 'aha' of eureka that replaces the confusion of a problem with the flash of inspiration of an insight that appears to pop out of nowhere. While these excitations may be chaotic in the time domain, the dynamics accompanying perceptual recognition shows spatially correlated excitations similar to a hologram, in which the recognition process arises from populations of neurons firing together in a resonant phase-coherent manner, which distinguishes the recognised stimulus from the random ground swell of unrelated excitations. In this respect, Karl Pribram has noted that such processes are analogous, if not identical to, quantum measurement based on constructive phase-dependent wave interference.

Phase coherence is consistent with chaotic dynamics in the time domain because mode-locked resonances between oscillators are a feature of non-linear systems. For example, the heartbeat, although approximately periodic, has dynamics comparable to a chaotic sinusoidally kicked rotator, which enables it to maintain mode-locked non-linear resonance with heart pacemaker cells which in turn are under central nervous system influence.

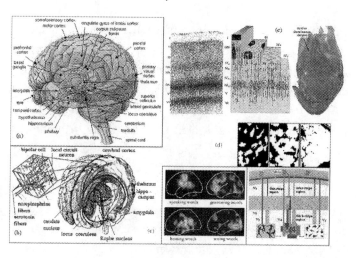

Fig 3: Structural outlines of the brain as a dynamical organ. (a) Major anatomical features including the cerebral cortex, its underlying driving centres in the thalamus, and surrounding limbic regions involving emotion and memory,

including the cingulate cortex, hippocampus and amygdala. (b) Conscious activity of the cortex is maintained through the activity of ascending pathways from the thalamus and brain stem, including the reticular activating system and serotonin and noradrenaline pathways involved in light and dreaming sleep. (c) Processing in the cortex consists of up to six layers of neurons, forming modular processing columns around 1 mm in size, illustrated in cortex stained for ocular dominance (right). (d) Such modularity is dynamic as shown by changes on ocular dominance as a result of covering one eye during development. (e) Modular cortical processing illustrated in pet scans of cortical activity during language processing and the parallel processing of movement and colour in the visual cortex.

By contrast with a digital computer, which relies on gigahertz speed to perform discrete serial computations, the brain is a massively parallel organ, using wave front processing, containing between 10^{10} and 10^{11} neurons each of which can have up to 10^4 excitatory and inhibitory synapses using a variety of chemical neurotransmitters to modulate electrochemical transfer. The extreme parallel distributed basis of this processing is emphasised by the fact that there may only be around ten serial synaptic junctions between sensory input and motor output. By contrast, a digital computer needs to make as many serial iterations as the computation requires before coming up with an answer, and the latest PCs allow for only up to four parallel units and even the largest super computers have no more than a few thousand, principally used in a restricted form of matrix calculation, such as weather prediction, where each unit is essentially carrying out a similar computation on differing initial conditions.

As shown in Figure 3, the cerebral cortex of the mammalian (and thus human) brain consists of a large convoluted sheet about 1 mm^2 consisting of up to six layers of neurons, organised into functional columns on a scale of around 1 mm2 and minicolumns of 28–40 μm performing unique processing in a modular manner on aspects of sensory and cognitive processing, from lines of a given orientation, through sounds of a given pitch to more abstract features, such as recognition of specific faces or facial expressions, to associating the sound of a word with its semantic meaning. The cortex is broadly divided between frontal areas responsible for action and its abstraction in terms of plans and goals and perception and its abstractions in terms of spatial orientation (parietal), semantic meaning (temporal) and other creative, expressive and classificatory skills.

The organisation of these modular columns is dynamic to the extent that covering one eye will dynamically alter the balance of binocular dominance. A blind person even uses visual areas for spatial orientation based on sound rather than vision. Many aspects of sensory processing occur in a parallel modular manner, for example, separate local regions process colour and movement, so that pathological conditions can result in loss of colour, or motion perception, independently of the other.

The electrical activity of the cortex is driven by centres in the underlying nuclei in the thalamus, which have reciprocal connections with corresponding areas of the cortex. In isolation, cortical tissues tend to be electrochemically quiescent, which emphasises that to a certain extent the cortex represents complex boundary conditions, modulating underlying thalamic excitations. Moreover, the entire span of cortical activity accompanying waking consciousness is dependent on a general level of excitatory activity welling up from the brain stem centres of the reticular activating system and major modes of dynamical brain activity modulation, such as light and dreaming sleep are likewise modulated through ascending norepinephrine, dopamine and serotonin pathways passing from the brain stem upwards to permeate specific layers of the whole cortex.

Active cognition is believed to involve an interplay of the so-called 'working memory' in which frontal regions modulating the goals and direction of the thought process are interacting with parietal and temporal areas providing the spatial and semantic information involved. There are actually two cortices, left and right, connected by large parallel tracts of nerve fibres, the corpus callosum. The left and right cortices are lateralised to varying degrees, particularly in men, so that language articulacy and other more structured forms of cognitive processing are predominantly in the left cortex, and more generalised diffuse types of processing occurs in the right cortex.

Consistent with edge of chaos processing involving a transition to order from chaos, studies of the kind of insight process that leads to phenomena such as Archimedes' 'Eureka!' appear to stem from the right anterior superior temporal gyrus, when distracting structured 'thinking' activities of the left hemisphere have been replaced by the relatively 'contemplative' relaxation of alpha activity.

In addition, feedback systems involving emotional recognition, flight and fight reactions and the establishment of long-term sequential memory surround the periphery of the cortex in the so-called limbic system, comprising the cingulate cortex, fornix, hippocampus, amygdala and associated structures. The semantic significance of the temporal cortex appears also to be able to combine with the intense emotional significance of the closely associated amygdala to create mystical and other symphonic experiences in temporal lobe epilepsy, a region coined by Ramachandran as 'the God Spot' for this mix of emotional significance and ultimate meaning. This association may have a genetic basis in religiosity as an evolutionary adaptation enabling larger, more dominant societies.

3. Chaos and Fractal Sensitivity

Between the global, the cellular and the molecular levels are a fractal cascade of central nervous processes, which in combination, make it theoretically possible for a quantum fluctuation to become amplified into a change of global brain state. The neuron is itself a fractal with multiply branching dendrites and axonal terminals, which are essential to provide the many-to-many synaptic connections between neurons, which make adaptation possible. Furthermore, like all tissues, biological organisation is achieved through non-linear interactions which begin at the molecular level and pass upward in a series of scale transformations through supra-molecular complexes such as ion channels and the membrane, through organelles such as synaptic junctions, to neurons and then to neuronal complexes such as cortical minicolumns and finally to global processes.

At the molecular level, the ion channel is activated by one, or two, neurotransmitter molecules.

Because neurons tend to tune to their threshold with a sigmoidal activation function, which has maximum slope at threshold, they are capable of becoming critically poised at their activation threshold. It is thus possible in principle for a single ion channel, suitably situated on the receptor neuron, e.g., at the cell body where an activation potential begins to act as the trigger for activation.

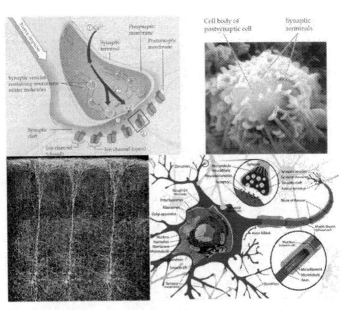

Fig 4: Quantum fractality differs from classical fractality, in that it becomes discrete at the quantum level. Fractal scale transformations emerge from quantum non-linearities forming the chemical bond, in emergent stages through tertiary and quaternary molecular structures, to cellular organelles, cells, tissues and finally the whole organism, with its successive bifurcations of development to form the tissue layers and later, interactive migrations of specific cell types.

Nervous system organisation is thus fractal, running from the molecular level of ion-channels, to neurotransmitter vesicles and synaptic junctions (upper), then to neurons (lower right), then to neuronal complexes such as minicolumns (lower left) and finally to whole brain activation.

The lessons of the butterfly catastrophe combined with evidence for transitions from chaos in perceptual recognition therefore suggest that if a brain state is in a transition at the edge of chaos or is in a state of self-organised criticality, in which the system tunes to a critical state such as a sand pile where there are fractal 'avalanches' of activity global instabilities, which are encoding for the unresolved perceptual or conceptual context may be 'resolved' through amplification of a local fluctuation at the neuronal, synaptic or ion-channel level.

Although neuroscientists have tended to discount the idea that micro-instabilities could lead to global changes in brain dynamics, on the basis that mass action will overwhelm such small effects, a variety of lines of evidence have demonstrated that fluctuations in single cells can lead to a change of brain state.

In addition to the issue of sensitive dependence in chaotic systems, two further lines of evidence suggest changes in ion channels and/or single cells can influence global brain states.

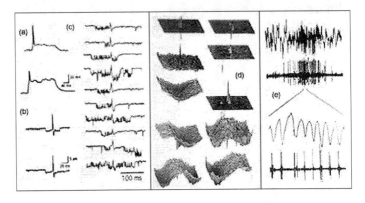

Fig 5: Evidence for complex system coupling between the molecular and global levels. Stochastic activation of single ion channels in hippocampal cells (a) leads to activation of the cells (b). Activation of such individual cells can in turn lead to formation of global excitations as a result of stochastic resonance (b). Individual cells are also capable of issuing action potentials in synchronisation with peaks in the eeg (d).

The first of these phenomena is stochastic resonance, in which the occurrence of noise, somewhat paradoxically, leads to the capacity of ion channels to sensitively excite hippocampal cells and in turn to cause a change in global brain state. In this sense, noise is playing a similar role to the ergodic properties of dynamical chaos, which likewise distribute the dynamic pseudo-randomly and so as to prevent the dynamic getting stuck into the rut of a given ordered attractor and it is thus able to fully explore its 'phase' or dynamical space. Thermodynamic 'annealing' is likewise used in classical artificial neural nets to avoid them becoming locked in sub-optimal local minima.

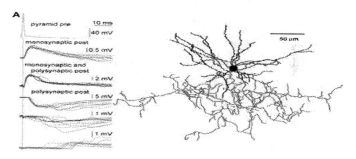

Fig 6: Left: Single pre-synaptic pyramidal action potential leads to multiple post-synaptic excitations. Right: Structure of chandelier or axon-axonal cells with dendrites (blue) and axons (red).

More recently it has been discovered that a specific class of cortical neuron, the chandelier cell is capable of changing the patterns of excitation between the pyramidal neurons that drive active output to other cortical regions and to the peripheral nervous system, in such a way that single action potentials of human neurons are sufficient to recruit Hebbian-like neuronal assemblies that are proposed to participate in cognitive processes. Chandelier cells, which were only discovered in the 1970s, and are more common in humans than other mammals such as the mouse and were originally thought to be purely inhibitory, are axon-axonal cells, which can result in specific poly-synaptic activation of pyramidal cells.

The research paper and review note:

> The increased signal-to-noise ratio in the network provided by hyperpolarising GABAergic synapses is further amplified by the coincident action of chandelier cells, resulting in a sparse and potentially task-selective activation of pyramidal neurons. Thus, the human microcircuit appears to be tuned for unitary EPSP-activated Hebbian-like functional cell assemblies that were proposed as building blocks of higher-order cortical operations and could contribute to single cortical cell-initiated movements and behavioural responses.

This reveals an extremely efficacious means of activity propagation in the cortical network. Although earlier work had shown polysynaptic activations following a single chandelier spike, the current study demonstrates much longer responses. Moreover, one of the most interesting results relates to the temporal structure of the activity patterns elicited after stimulation of a single neuron. While most of them appear to propagate through the circuit with increasing disorganisation, occasionally the authors were able to trigger an amazingly precise temporal pattern. This implies that the microcircuit is capable under some circumstances of generating patterns of activation with low jitter and high temporal precision.

Given the potential for fluctuations at the molecular, ion channel, synaptic or neuronal level to become the organising centre resolving instabilities in global brain dynamic, it becomes possible to form an edge-of-chaos model for resolving situations of cognition involving intuition, insight and the 'eureka' attributed to Archimedes' sudden discovery of his principle. In this model, the dynamic of the 'problem' remains unresolved and thus contains instabilities, which in turn become sensitive to perturbation on descending fractal scales leading to the molecular and quantum level.

Such an unstable dynamic is tending to a transition from higher-energy chaos to order by developing a new attractor, out of the fractal diversity of repelling attractors in the chaotic dynamic. In terms of an active brain state, this would be likely to correspond to a global excitation, say in the gamma range containing several uncorrelated phase components representing features of the problem that cannot be put into coherent relationship. Hence the essential instability at the fractal level would consist of a transition from multiple uncorrelated phases to the emergence of a correlated 'organising centre' resolving the global instability.

4. Computational Intractability, Classical Chaos and Quantum Uncertainty

The apparent contradiction between the idea of precise classical computation (which abhors disrupting noise) and the apparent unruliness of chaotic excitation (which, although being in principle deterministic, becomes unpredictable, through amplification of small discrepancies due to sensitive dependence, resulting in an 'ergodic' trajectory, filling phase space in a similar to a random walk) can be resolved immediately when we look more closely at the sort of computational problems a living nervous system actually needs to solve in minimal time to survive.

The traveling salesman problem – how to find the shortest path around in cities – is classed as incomplete. Characteristically, to classically compute a given solution requires checking each of the $(n$-1$)$! / 2 possible cyclic paths and finding the smallest. However, because this is super-exponential, even for a small number of cities, like twenty-five, the computation time required stretches out to the age of the universe. The same consideration applies to virtually every environmental decision-making process a living organism faces, such as which path to take to the water hole, since these involve an exponentially increasing number of combinations of contingent factors in the open environment. An animal cannot afford to wait more than a split second making a real survival decision, or it may be leapt upon by a tiger and consumed, so nervous systems have to find an immediate real-time way of solving any such potentially intractable decision-making problem.

The solution used by artificial neural nets, which model a problem like the traveling salesman problem as an energy minimisation on a landscape representing the distances between the cities, is to apply thermodynamic annealing, starting with a high temperature which prevents the dynamic becoming stuck in a high local minimum, gradually reducing the temperature of random fluctuations, arriving at a reasonable sub-optimal local minimum. Statistical computational methods of solution work similarly.

The Freeman Model of Perception in Fig 2(d) uses a transition from high-energy chaos to a lower energy strange-attractor in much the same way, using the high-energy chaos to avoid the system becoming trapped in a far-from-optimality attractor until the 'phase' space of the system has been fully explored. Such a system provides for a smooth transition between a situation in which the boundary conditions lead to a clear computational outcome and hence a decision based on one choice having a manifestly higher probability of survival, and other situations, in which, like the problem of Archimedes' possibly crown, there is no predisposing resolution of the system because the problem has not yet been solved and the contextual factors remain ambiguous or inconsistent.

Unlike the discrete Von Neumann or Turing machine, biological nervous systems appear to work on dynamical principles which provide the capacity to induce a transition from chaos to order, where the classical computer would run into the Turing halting problem – unable to determine whether, or when, the computational process will end. Clearly such a transition will involve sensitive dependence on initial and other boundary conditions and will be in a classical sense unpredictable (just as the butterfly effect is), and since it involves molecular processes at the quantum level, may invoke quantum uncertainty as well. We thus need to investigate how these two effects might come together and explore whether and how they might play upon the processes of perceptual recognition and conceptual insight.

The first point of reference is a brief review of the wave–particle relationship and how the uncertainty relationship comes about. By Einstein's law $E = h\nu$, the energy of a particle is equivalent to the frequency of the wave as the momentum is likewise to the wavelength. If we then want to measure the energy, this will be equivalent to measuring the frequency, but as we cannot sample parts of a quantum wave, the only way we can know the frequency is effectively to count the beats against a reference frequency. The time delay $V t = 1/V v$ between successive fronts where the two waves are in phase, giving constructive interference, then gives us the uncertainty relation $V E \times V t = h/2Pi$

Constructive interference from corresponding phase fronts passing through two slits also gives us the basis in wave–particle complementarity of the two-slit interference experiment (Fig 7). Complementarity is demonstrated in the release of a photon from an excited atom in the bulb, as a discrete localised 'particle', corresponding to an orbital transition from an excited atomic orbit. The photon then travels through both slits as a wave, which overlaps itself to form bright bands of constructive interference and is again absorbed as a particle by a silver atom on the photographic film. Although these discrete particles arrive one at a time and could appear anywhere, the wave function is not precisely zero. As numbers of particles arrive, their statistical probability of occurrence is distributed according to the complex square of the amplitude of the wave $P = {}^{\varphi * \varphi}$

The particle incidence gives rise to one of the fundamental unresolved questions of quantum theory. As the wave function does not determine where the particle should end up, it is deemed that the wave function has 'collapsed' at the point the particle is detected, and unlike the linear evolution of the wave function, this collapse process is stochastically unpredictable, leading to the idea that there may be a deeper 'hidden variable' theory explaining how each photon actually 'decides' where it ends.

The contrast between quantum theory, which leads only to parallel probabilities that the photon could be anywhere in its wave function, and the real world in which unique histories always occur led to Schrödinger coining the 'cat paradox', in which a cat is predicted to be both alive and dead by quantum theory with differing probabilities, if a Geiger counter is set to break a vial of cyanide – but when we open the box, the cat is either alive or dead but not both. Various approaches, including hidden variable theories and quantum decoherence caused by interaction with 'third-party' quanta have been invoked to explain this process but none eliminates the essential complementarity.

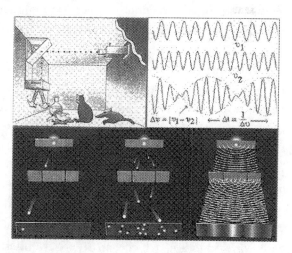

Fig 7: Top right: Beats of constructive wave interference determine the uncertainty principle. Bottom: Two-slit interference experiment illustrates wave–particle complementarity. Top left: Cat paradox experiment.

When we come to consider how systems, which would classically display features of chaos behave in the quantum world, we find a series of apparent contradictions in the so-called quantum suppression of chaos. In Figure 8, the quantum stadium is used to illustrate several features of this phenomenon. The classical stadium billiard is chaotic because the periodic orbits, some of which are shown in (d), are unstable, so that a ball with a trajectory differing by an arbitrarily small amount is deflected by increasing amounts by the curved boundary of the region, so that the periodic orbits are all repelling and almost every orbit is a chaotic trajectory which eventually fills the region 'ergodically' in an unpredictable, pseudo-random manner, as in (a), due to sensitive dependence on initial conditions.

The quantum wave function solutions (b) work differently, displaying peaks of the probability function around the periodic orbits, defying their repelling nature. The reasons can be easily understood if we use a semi-classical approximation, by releasing a small wave packet and watching the way it bounces back and forth as in (c). Whenever the wavelength of the packet forms a rational relationship with the length around a transit any of the reflecting periodic orbits, we get an eigenfunction of the quantum wave function, which constructively interferes with itself, as a standing wave, just as do the orbitals of an atom, to form a probability peak around the periodic orbit. Even when a trajectory is a little off the periodic orbit, the spreading wave packet still overlaps itself contributing to the probability peak.

The end result is that for a variety of closed quantum systems, wave spreading eventually represses classical chaos by scarring, causing the periodic eigenfunctions to become eventual solutions of any time-dependent problem, although the initial trajectory behaves erratically, just as does an orbit in the classical situation. For example, a periodically kicked quantum rotator will stochastically gain energy, just as in the classical situation, until a quantum break time, after which it will become trapped in one of the quantum solutions. A highly excited atom in a magnetic field will have its absorbance peaks at the periodic solutions, and quantum tunneling will likewise use scarred eigenvalues as its principle modes of tunneling.

These constraints do not apply to open systems, such as molecular kinetics where diffusion can carry molecules relatively vast distances. As a rough example, a glycine molecule at biological temperatures has a self-diffraction angle of wave-spreading of about 6.5°, showing this effect is significant.

Moreover, the larger the system, the longer the delay until quantum break time sets in.

The implication is that sensitive dependence on initial conditions eventually gives way, at the quantum level, to quantum uncertainty of the scarred orbit, globally traversing

the space concerned, and it does so by performing a transition
from chaos to order dependent on the initial conditions
initially following a chaotic trajectory and eventually
entering into a periodic orbit. Since a chaotic system,
whether quantum or classical has a dense set of periodic
orbits there, is potentially an infinite number of these,
although quantum separation of chaotic eigenfunctions,
another feature of quantum repression of chaos, will lead
to only a finite number being available at the energies
concerned.

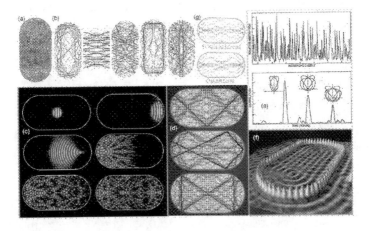

Fig 8: Quantum chaos: The classical stadium billiards is
chaotic. A given trajectory has sensitive dependence on
initial conditions. As well as space-filling chaotic orbits (a)
the stadium is densely filled with repelling periodic orbits,
three of which are shown in black in (d). Because they
are repelling, neighbouring orbits are thrown further away,
rather than being attracted into a stable periodic orbit, so
arbitrary small deviations lead to a chaotic orbit, causing
almost all orbits to be chaotic. The quantum solution of the

stadium potential well (b) and (d) shows 'scarring' of the wave function along these repelling orbits, thus repressing the classical chaos, through probabilities clumping on the repelling orbits. A semi-classical simulation (c) shows why this is so. A small wavelet bounces back and forth, forming a periodic wave pattern, because even when slightly off the repelling orbit, the wave still overlaps itself and can form standing wave constructive interference when its energy and frequency corresponds to one of the eigenvalues of a periodic orbit, even though the orbit is classically repelling. The quantum solution is scarred on precisely these orbits (d). This causes resonances such as absorption peaks of a highly magnetically excited atom (e) to coincide with the eigenfunctions of the repelling periodic orbits, just as the orbital waves of an atom constructively interferes with themselves, in completing an orbit to form a standing wave, like that of a plucked string. The result is that, over time, in the quantum system, although the behaviour may be transiently chaotic, it eventually settles into a periodic solution. Experimental realisations such as the scanning tunneling view of an electron on a copper sheet bounded by a stadium of carefully placed iron atoms (f) confirm the general picture, although in this experiment, tunneling leaked the wave function outside too much to demonstrate proper scarring. The semi-classical approach matches closely to the full quantum calculation (g).

The implications are threefold:

1. Quantum suppression of chaos leads to a situation where:

   (a) Quantum chaotic systems model a transition from chaos to order, just as insight processes involve a transition from chaos to order (b) Quantum suppression of chaos by phase coherence parallels the way brain processes may use coherence to distinguish critical processes in conscious attention from the background.

2. The eigenfunctions of chaotic quantum processes are globally distributed over the phase space and thus, in so far as the outcomes depend on stochastic properties of wave-particle reduction, enable uncertainty to affect outcomes on the scale of the phase space orbit.

3. In processes that involve open systems, or large phase spaces whose quantum break time is much longer than the real-time window, chaos and quantum uncertainty may combine to amplify uncertainty, so that it can affect global outcomes.

4. The Evolution of Chaotic Sensitivity and the Emergence of Consciousness

We now return to the biological arena, to consider how nervous systems might have evolved the dynamics we associate with consciousness. Is the sort of dynamics we associate with the conscious brain a product of the complex interconnectivity of circuitry of relatively trivial neurons, as work with artificial neural nets and computational approaches, such as artificial intelligence might suggest? Or is it a fundamental aspect of living cells, which evolved with the earliest eukaryotes? Is it in the senses of a single-celled organism that we will naturally find the origin of chaotic excitability as a source for the quantum sensitivity that ultimately shaped the evolution of the conscious brain in higher organisms?

A realistic assessment of pyramidal neurons confirms that they are very complex dynamical systems in their own right, far from the trivial additive units which McCulloch-Pitts 'neurons' present in theoretical artificial networks, containing up to 10^2 synaptic junctions, having a variety of excitatory and inhibitory synaptic inputs involving up to four or five different types of neurotransmitter, with differing effects depending on their location on dendrites, the cell body or axon–axonal connections.

Furthermore, many of the critical features we associate with neurons and their associated neuroglia, in the conscious brain, including excitability and the use of neurotransmitter molecules are not only shared by other cells in the human body but extend down to the earliest single-celled eukaryotes.

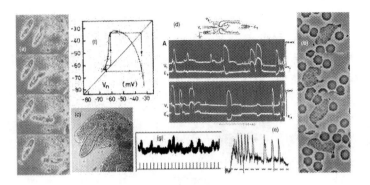

Fig 9: Real-time purposive behaviour in single cells (a) Paramecium reverses, turns right and explores a cul-de-sac. (b) Human neutrophil chases an escaping bacterium (black), before engulfing it. (c) Chaos chaos engulfs a paramecium. Action potentials in Chaos chaos (d) and paramecium (e). Period 3 perturbed excitations in Nitella confirm chaos. (g) Frog retinal rod cells are sensitive to single quanta in an ultra-low intensity beam, with an average rate of one photon per click, but sometimes zero, or two, due to uncertainty in the beam.

The connection between bursting and beating in excitable cells was established by the Chay–Rinzel model and ensuing experiments, which established chaotic dynamics in neurons, pancreatic B-cell exocytosis and inter-nodal cells in the alga Nitella. The association between excitability and exocytosis spanning the eukaryotes is doubly significant, in that, in addition to graded electrochemical and action potentials in the neuron, synaptic vesicles are also produced by exocytosis.

Earlier work had already demonstrated membrane potentials in Amoeba proteus associated with pseudopod formation, and action potentials in the amoeba Chaos chaos, aptly so-named by Linnaeus. In ciliated protozoa, such as Paramecium and Tetrahymena action potentials are associated with the motile actions of cilia in cellular locomotion.

The aggregation of slime moulds such as Dictyostellium is mediated by cyclic-AMP. The ciliated protozoan Tetrahymena pyriformis and flagellated Crithidia jasciculata utilise serotonin; the former also metabolises dopamine and epinephrine. Tetrahymena pyriformis also has circadian light-related melatonin expression.

Both amoebae and ciliates show purposive coordinated behaviour over real-time, as do individual human cells such as macrophages. The multi-nucleate slime mould Physarum polycephalum can solve shortest path mazes and demonstrate a memory of a rhythmic series of stimuli, apparently using a biological clock to predict the next pulse. Chaotic excitation provides an excitable single cell with a generalised quantum sense organ. Sensitive dependence would enable such a cell to gain feedback about its external environment, perturbed by a variety of quantum modes – chemically through molecular orbital interaction, electromagnetically through photon absorption, electrochemically through the perturbations of the fluctuating fields generated by the excitations themselves and through acoustic and mechanical interaction. Amoebae, for example, although they lack specific sense organelles, are highly sensitive to chemical and electrical signals, as well as to bright light.

Such excitability in the single cell would predate the computational function of neural nets, making dynamical chaos fundamental to the evolution of neuronal computing rather than vice-versa. A single cell has no capacity to solve decision-making problems through a neural net consisting of many cells, so has to rely on membrane excitation and internal regulatory systems, such as biological clocks and genetic switches to provide memory and a strategy for survival.

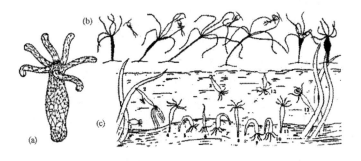

Fig 10: Hydra has only an undifferentiated nerve net (a), yet catches prey by coordinated action of its tentacles (b) and has no less than twelve different forms of motion, from stages of somersaulting to snail-like gliding.

When we move to the earlier metazoa such as Hydra, which supports only a primitive diffuse neural net and whose tissues can dynamically reorganise themselves, for example if it is turned inside out, we find the organism has a rich repertoire of up to twelve forms of 'intuitive' locomotion and is able to coordinate tentacle movements and tumbling and other forms of movement using similar global dynamics to those in amoebae and Paramecium or a more advanced organism, such as a snail. We can thus see that nervous systems have arisen from the adaptive dynamics of individual eukaryote cells, rather than being composed of a logical network made out of essentially trivial formal neurons.

As we move up the evolutionary tree to complex nervous systems, such as in vertebrates, we still see the same dynamical features, now expressed in whole system excitations such as the eeg, in which excitatory and inhibitory neurons still provide a basis for broad-spectrum oscillation, phase coherence and chaos in the global dynamics, with the synaptic organisation enabling the dynamics to resolve complex context-sensitive decision-making problems, involving memories of past situations and specific adaptations to current ones. However, the immediate decision-making situations around which life or death results, in the theatre of conscious attention in real-time, are qualitatively similar in nature to those made by single-celled organisms, such as Paramecium, based strongly on immediate sensory input, combined with a short-term anticipation of immediate threats, in a context of remembered situations from the past that bear upon the current existential strategy.

Looking back more deeply in time, chaotic excitability and electrochemistry generally may be one of the founding features of eucaryote cells, dating from the RNA era, before coded protein translation. Nucleotide coenzymes, believed to be molecular fossils from the RNA era, pervade electron transport pathways. Key chemical modifiers may have been precursors of the amine-based neurotransmitters, spanning acetyl-choline, serotonin, catecholamines and amino acids such as glutamate and GABA, several of which have potential pre-biotic or trans-biotic status. Positive amines, for example, may have chemically complemented negatively charged phosphate-based lipids in modulating membrane excitability in primitive cells without requiring complex-coded proteins.

The sense modes we experience are not simply biological as such but more fundamentally are the qualitative modes of quantum interaction between molecular matter and the physical universe. They thus have potential cosmological status. Vision deals with interaction between photons and orbitals, hearing with the harmonic excitations of molecules and membrane solitons, as evidenced in the action potentials arising from cochlear cells. Smell is the consequence of orbital–orbital interaction, as is taste.

Touch is a hybrid sense involving a mixture of these.

The limits to the sensitivity of nervous systems are likewise constrained by the physics of quanta, rather than biological limits. This is exemplified by the capacity of retinal rod cells to record single quanta, as in Fig 9(g), and by the fact that membranes of cochlear cells oscillate by only about one H atom radius at the threshold of hearing, well below the scale of individual thermodynamic fluctuations and vastly below the bilayer membrane thickness. Moth pheromones are similarly effective at concentrations consistent with one molecule being active, as are the sensitivities of some olfactory mammals.

The very distinct qualitative differences between vision, hearing, touch and smell do not appear to have a physiological support in the very similar patterns of electrical excitation evoked in their cortical areas. However, if all these excitations can occur simultaneously in the single cell, chaotic excitation could effectively become a form of cellular multi-sensory synaesthesia, which is later specialised in the brain in representing each individual sense mode. Thus in the evolution of the cortical senses from the most diffuse, olfaction, the mammalian brain may be using an ultimate universality, returning to the original quantum modes of physics in a way which can readily be expressed in differential organisation of the visual, auditory and somato-sensory cortices according to a single common theme of quantum excitability. This is consistent with cortical plasticity which, for example, enables a blind person to use his/her visual areas for other sensory modes.

It is thus natural to postulate that cellular 'consciousness', as a focused global dynamical electrochemical response to a cell's environment, is a pivotal feature which as been elaborated and conserved by nervous systems because it has had unique survival value for the organism. It is a logical conclusion that the conscious brain has been selected by evolution because its biophysical properties provide access to an additional principle of predictivity not possessed by formal computational systems. One of the key strategies of survival implicated in brain dynamics is anticipation and prediction of events. Computational systems achieve this by a combination of deductive logic and heuristic calculation of contingent probabilities. However, quantum non-locality may also provide another avenue for anticipation, which might be effective even across the membrane of a single cell, if wave reductions are correlated in a non-local manner in space-time. We shall examine this possibility next.

5. Quantum Entanglement and the Transactional Interpretation

All forms of quantum field theory stem from the special relativistic form of the energy $E = \pm \sqrt{P^2 + m^2}$. This gives two solutions, one a positive energy solution traveling in the usual (retarded) direction in time and the other a negative energy (advanced) solution, traveling backwards in time.

All quantum mechanical calculations are based on these dual solutions of special relativity, including those of quantum electrodynamics, the most accurate physical theory ever devised. Wheeler and Feynman noted that 'absorber' theory, in which the advanced solutions were included, gave the same predictions as descriptions in which the advanced solutions were omitted as unphysical. Indeed, all Feynman space–time diagrams implicitly contain both the advanced and retarded solutions. For a photon, which is its own anti-particle, the advanced and retarded solutions of electron–electron repulsion by exchanging virtual particles, as in Fig 11(3a–c) are identical, as a negative energy advanced photon IS a positive energy retarded photon. Likewise electron scattering becomes positron creation annihilation when time is reversed (d). The delayed choice experiment and quantum erasure, as in Fig 11 (1, 2), confirm that changes after emission, or even at absorption, can influence the path taken by a photon or other exchanged particles.

In John Cramer's transactional interpretation, such an advanced 'backward traveling' wave in time gives a neat explanation, not only for the above effect but also for the probability aspect of the quantum in every quantum experiment. Instead of one photon traveling between the emitter and absorber, there are two shadow waves, which superimposed make up the complete photon. The emitter transmits an offer wave both forwards and backwards in time, declaring its capacity to emit a photon. The potential absorbers of this photon transmit a corresponding confirmation wave. These, traveling backwards in time, send a hand-shaking signal back to the emitter, as shown in Fig 11(4a). The offer and confirmation waves superimpose constructively to form a real photon only on the space–time path connecting the emitter to the absorber.

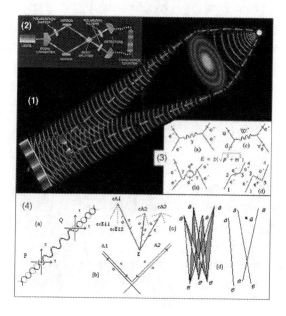

Fig 11: Wheeler delayed choice experiment (1) shows that a decision can be made after a photon from a distant quasar has traversed a gravitationally lensing galaxy by deciding whether to detect which way the photon travelled or to demonstrate it went both ways by sampling interference. The final state at the absorber thus appears to be able to determine past history of the photon. Quantum erasure (2) likewise enables a distinction already made, which would prevent interference, to be undone after the photon is released. Feynman diagrams (3) show similar time-reversible behaviour. In particular time, reversed electron scattering (d) is identical to positron creation-annihilation. (4a) In the transactional interpretation, a single photon exchanged between emitter and absorber is formed by constructive interference between a retarded offer wave (solid) and an advanced confirmation wave (dotted). (b) EPR experiments of quantum entanglement involving pair-splitting are resolved by combined offer and confirmation waves, because confirmation waves intersect at the emission point. Contingent absorbers of an emitter in a single passage of a photon (c). Collapse of contingent emitters and absorbers in a transactional match-making (d).

The transactional interpretation offers the only viable explanation for the apparently instantaneous connections between detectors in pair-splitting EPR experiments in which a pair of correlated photons are emitted by a single atom, in which neither of the photons has a defined polarisation until one of them is measured, upon which the other immediately has complementary polarisation.

In Fig 11(4b), rather than a super-luminal connection between detectors A1 and A2, the two photons' advanced waves meet at the source emission point in a way which enables the retarded waves to be instantaneously correlated at the detectors. One can also explain the arrow of time, if the cosmic origin is a reflecting boundary that causes all the positive energy real particles in our universe to move in the retarded direction we all experience in the arrow of time and increasing entropy. The hand-shaking space–time relation implied by the transactional interpretation makes it possible that the apparent randomness of quantum events masks a vast interconnectivity at the sub-quantum level, reflecting Bohm's implicate order, although in a different manner from Bohm's pilot wave theory.

Because transactions connect past and future in a time-symmetric way, they cannot be reduced to predictive determinism, because the initial conditions are insufficient to describe the transaction, which also includes quantum boundary conditions coming from the future absorbers. However, this future is also unformed in real terms at the early point in time when emission takes place. My eye didn't even exist, when the quasar I look out at emitted its photon, except as a profoundly unlikely branch of the combined probability 'waves' of all the events generating parallel 'probability universes' throughout the history of the universe between the time, long ago, that the quasar released its photon, and me being in the right place, at the right time to see it distant epochs later.

In the extension of the transactional approach to super causality, a non-linearity collapses the set of contingent possibilities to one offer and confirmation wave, Fig 11 (4c, d). Thus at the beginning, we have two sets of contingent emitters and absorbers, and at the end each emitter is now exchanging with a specific absorber. Before collapse of the wave function, we have many potential emitters interacting with many potential absorbers. After all the collapses have taken place, each emitter is paired with an absorber. One emitter cannot connect with two absorbers without violating the quantum rules, so there is a frustration between the possibilities, which can only be fully resolved if emitters and absorbers are linked in pairs. The number of contingent emitters and absorbers are not necessarily equal, but the number of matched pairs is equal to the number of real particles exchanged.

This transactional time symmetry is paralleled in the implicit time reversibility of quantum computation, which also depends on a superposition of states. The transactional interpretation may thus combine with effective forms of biological quantum computation to produce a space–time anticipating quantum entangled system, which may be pivotal in how the conscious brain does its processing.

6. Consciousness Revealed

It is at this point that the influence of the conscious observer and the hard problem become an intriguing challenge to the scientific description. The brain is not a marvellous computer in any classical sense – we can barely manage a seven-digit span, but it is a phenomenally sensitive anticipator of environmental and behavioural change. Subjective consciousness has its survival value in enabling us to jump out of the way when a tiger is about to strike, not so much in computing which path the tiger might be on (because this is an intractable problem, and the tiger can also take it into account in avoiding the places we would expect it to most likely be) but by intuitive conscious anticipation.

Fig 12: Evidence of immediate anticipatory subjective consciousness. A seagull just manages to escape a shark strike, before flying off. The brain, using phase correlation in its own wave dynamics, as a basis for decision-making, parallels the way in which the wave function and its constructive interference determines the probabilities in the reduction of the wave packet. We thus may need to consider the possibility that global brain excitations form an 'inflated' quantum system and that the brain uses a form of quantum anticipation involving emission and absorption of its own excitations in a way which enables it to have an 'intuitive' non-computable representation of future states

which complement computational processing and which would be unavailable to a classical computer. Quantum coherence is already a technique in imaging, demonstrating an example of quantum coherence in biological tissues at the molecular level.

In this sense, the enigma of subjective consciousness may exist partly because such excitations cannot be reduced to classical prediction, or quantum transactions would introduce a causal 'back-to-the-future' feedback loop. Thus the brain, in developing the internal model of reality represented by the 'Cartesian theatre', may have opted for a complementarity between subjective consciousness and objective brain function, to maintain 'entangled' anticipation, which is an evolutionary adaptation to the transactional relationship underlying wave–particle complementarity, bringing the two complementarities into conjunction.

In this respect, subjective consciousness may present an existential cosmological situation, as noted in Indian philosophy, in which consciousness is described as 'finer' than matter, thus gaining a complementary existential status to the physical universe, in the manner of the Tantric dance of Shiva as the undivided field of subjective consciousness and Shakti as maya – the multiplicity of material manifestations, again reflecting the continuous-discrete wave–particle relationship, and do this by manifesting in subjective consciousness aspects of the space–time traversing sub-quantum dynamics that underlies the wave–particle complementarity at the foundation of the quantum description of the cosmological universe.

To conclude, we narrate the following descriptive evolutionary account:

> A hunter is at a fork in the path to the water hole, seeking to get an antelope for meat, but is wary of himself getting taken by a big cat in the process. As the man stands pondering and studying the tracks on the path and the sounds and smells blowing across the savannah and through the jungle, his brain develops a resonant coherent excitation – the hunter's 'stealth' – a state of awareness empty of structured thought, anticipating the slightest movement around him.

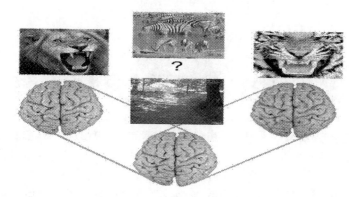

Fig 13: Transactional view of a hunter trying to find a safe path to the waterhole. Both the open hilly path and the jungle path (right) have lions or tigers, which might attack the hunter. Paranoia suggests the hunter who takes the hilly path, as his quantum anticipation makes him feel uneasy about the forested path, since in the probability universe

where he takes this path he gets a severe fright. Usually, these anticipations will be almost immediate, as in Fig 12.

There are two histories of varying duration, from immediate awareness to the imminent future, that the vagaries of fate on the day could bring about. The man could walk down the shady path or the one over the rocks.

As things transpire, there is a hungry tiger on the shady path, which is poised to leap on anything coming its way. However, the man's brainwave is resonating in an entanglement with his future brain states, and there are two parallel universes of future states: one down the shady path and the other down the rocky one.

Now the brain state going down the shady path has a catastrophe – one hell of a scare or outright death, painfully mauled by the big cat. The hunter's stalking brain state gets absorbed down there and the absorber's advanced wave runs back through space–time in his brain state along the path he just traversed, to the point where the man is still standing at the fork trying to decide what to do.

On the other path, he simply walks to the water hole, because the lions are elsewhere today, and shoots a small antelope with his poisoned arrow and takes it back to a woman in the village, so she might consent to have sex with him. This outcome also absorbs the resonating brain wave and sends its advanced wave back to the hunter at the crossroads, but it doesn't excite his paranoia.

At the crossroads, the man is feeling disquiet. His amygdala is giving him conniptions of foreboding. He feels bad about the shade under the trees. He doesn't like the rocky path either, because lions spend a lot of time slouching in the little gullies in the rocky hills, but having already pondered for long enough to contemplate, and being desirous of having sex before the moon sets, he decides, on a sheer hunch, which he can't fully describe, to go ahead on the hunt, by walking carefully along the stony path.

He ends up having children, and his children have too and each have often since felt pretty paranoid about a lot of things, but sometimes they just feel its a sunny day and the shade under the trees looks cool, and although a few have been picked off by big cats, most of them have taken some good hunks of meat back to the village and had some sex for themselves too. And so the story carries on long enough for the hunter's great-grandson to sit down and get ready to share a good roast leg of antelope, while the women throw some sweet potatoes into the fire, to pick up his flute and cock his bowstring against a cooking pot to pluck for a tune, and tell a few jokes, and scary stories too, to get the woman he admires to draw in close and put her arms around him, and do that funny thing of wiggling her middle finger in the palm of his hand that means she wants to take him off for the night for a 'walking marriage', once the fire has died down low.

So it is that the anticipatory quantum chaos of the living cell has become the contemplative mind of the lonely hunter, in the generations of conscious beings traversing the sentient wave–particle universe.

Brains generate microtubular consciousness through change of tubulin protein gel/sol form. Disparate areas of the brain integrate through parallel processing, global synchrony as one integrated experience of consciousness. In this experience, senses see all the physical space around physical body, a holistic map is constructed in the brain of its immediate environment and memory through R process of quantum mechanics. Now this experience involves future vision in the form of prescient (Present to future). This is the non-reversible, asymmetrical R part of quantum mechanics different from U reversible process of quantum mechanics and anticipatory consciousness where subject and object is on equal footing. Inflated system through chaos an order is maintained, collapse of two pole objects and subject take places in the presence of subject, a personal experience of long duration. This is the physical brain consciousness which experience and a memory of event is created in the physical brain state and astral subtle mental state also. Not only this, an astral objective reality is transferred to astral universe without the transfer of matter from physical universe of matter to astral universe. A purely non-local effect through the intermediary of consciousness Consciousness transfers non-local effects or non-signal transfer of information between two different worlds; other astral is more conscious than this physical one. This storage of physical memories of earth events creates a morphogenic field in the astral phase space, this phase space increases with the increase of entropy and world appears safe from construction of realities in the future direction with free will of sentient being like us, but astral phase space creates a morphogenic field in the form of quantum states, this space can collapse because of its own energy breakpoint and it depends on the development of astral subtle mental mind receptivity. When we sleeps we sometimes touch this space non-locally and memories of past are repeated, but astral universe stored the history of our earth events in the morphogenic fields (Rupert Sheldrake). Earth events history is repeated once this morphogenic fields start collapsing in the direction of past quantum states which have already have taken place on earth in past, therefore our past on earth is their (astral world) present. This delay in time is important and tells us about our universe is conscious and connected through non-local interactions.

But here there are certain difference in this collapse, here entropy decreases not increases, this is astonishing as all the physical process entropy always increases, this is the only process in nature where entropy gets lower and lower and clock is reset again, This is subjective–objective collapse of past quantum states in the presence of subjective quale. Subject is orphan in this state as no free will and sees objective collapse of past quantum states. Subject helplessly sees collapse of this state as an monistic collapse, subject has no will of its own sees whole consciousness collapse as observer only for the self-reference, This self-reference system of consciousness is the unique advantage of consciousness to replay what has happened in the past. It shades light on the past history of observer when it was involved in creating future quantum states and collapse of subjective–objective complementarities at the level of brain consciousness collapse in the physical world.

Therefore, we can broadly divide quantum–consciousness hierarchy into two level: First is the physical level which includes the brain, physical world surrounded by physical objects, trees, houses, air, space, other living objects and all the minute level objects which creates our surroundings called environment.

Another world which is not physical and not visible to naked eyes and the five senses of sensation and five senses of actions called astral universe but without it, this physical world has no existence, these two worlds are co-dependent on each other, they do not exchange matter between the two, but they can exchange consciousness and thus pass information without signal called non-local effects, on local interaction with the intermediary of consciousness.

Consciousness is a active force which is not separate from matter but interacts non-locally and makes the existence of this universe possible. Consciousness can co-create this universe and govern the future development of matter and living beings by two basic mechanisms, which are unique to consciousness only. It can create the future as per its desires and aspirations in the form of possibilities waves into actualities with two poles: subject and object complementarity. This is the monistic theory with no echoes of dualism, but this primary consciousness affects the non-local space time in the morphogenic astral universe and astral mental body of subject, this is called 'bottom to top approach of consciousness' in the form of creating hierarchical objective-consciousness structure from physical world to astral world and from physical brain to astral mental mind structure:

Top to bottom approach of consciousness: Subject helplessly experience non-local collapse of past quantum memory states of astral quantum states, replay of memory and self-reference of consciousness with the decrease of entropy and disentanglement of quantum states. This is the unique process of nature in the form of reactionary counter-consciousness where subjective pole is all attractive but lacks free will when collapse occurs. It can only observe its past quantum state but cannot changes it. This is one of the *real processes of consciousness.*

Consciousness is transcendental in nature; it not only crosses the brain and physical cosmos but also the astral mental. Mind in the realm of astral and casual world of cosmos.

CHAPTER 6

AMERICAN MODEL OF UNSUSTAINABILITY BY CHRIS CLUSTON

Introduction

In his article "On American Sustainability: Summary," Chris Clugston argues that Americans are living with "historically unprecedented living standards" which have caused an increase in "dysfunctional ecological and economic behavior" (Clugston, 2008). Clugston believes that America is facing an imminent social collapse because the culture of more is better and is unsustainable. Clugston presents evidence of the unprecedented growth American has experienced in the last 200 years where the growth of the economy increased over 1,600 times and the population increased over 50 times.

> Once the population and economy have overshot the physical limits of the Earth, there are only two ways back: Involuntary collapse caused by escalating shortages and crises, or controlled reduction of throughput by deliberate social choice.– Dennis Meadows et al

Original sin had nothing to do with a garden and an apple; it occurred the first time when one of our hominid ancestors used a non-renewable natural resource.

I initiated my research on American sustainability during the Spring of 2006, before I had ever heard the term "sustainability" or knew that my research would culminate in an "opus" on the subject. At the time, the U.S. housing market was booming, the U.S. economy was booming, and Americans were spending money like there was no tomorrow.

I had been concerned for some time about our ability to continue our seemingly endless binge of economic growth and prosperity, but, like most Americans, I had been too busy with my day-to-day activities to look into the details. That Spring, however, I decided to investigate our economic situation.

My initial research was haphazard; I was not sure where to look, nor was I sure exactly what I was looking for. Various government and mainstream web sites informed me that while we were depleting our economic asset reserves, incurring debt and underfunding our future financial obligations at historically high levels, the U.S. economy was fundamentally sound and its perpetual growth would enable us to address any conceivable future financial challenge.

I was beginning to think that my concerns were unfounded when, quite by accident, I encountered a group of economic analysts who argued that we were living far beyond our means economically, and that both our current economic behavior and our current economic prosperity were unsustainable – and they presented compelling evidence to support their arguments. So I dug deeper.

During the Summer of 2006, again quite by accident, I encountered several entirely different groups of analysts who claimed that we were also living far beyond our means ecologically – we were using natural resources at levels exceeding those at which they were being replenished, and we were degrading natural habitats at levels exceeding those at which they were being regenerated. These analysts presented compelling evidence that both our current ecological behavior and our American way of life were unsustainable as well.

Since that time, my goals have been to quantify the extent to which we in America are living beyond our means, both ecologically and economically, and to articulate the cause, implications, and resolution associated with our situation. After three years of research, feedback, soul searching and countless iterations, I believe that I have accomplished my goals.

My findings on American sustainability, which are presented in the following pages, will shock most Americans.

As America enters the new millennium, we find ourselves in a "predicament." We are living hopelessly beyond our means, ecologically and economically, at a time when available supplies associated with many of the critical ecological resources and economic resources upon which we depend will soon be insufficient to enable our American way of life.

Global demand for these resources is enormous and is ever-increasing, while supplies available to the United States are becoming increasingly scarce – due to both market factors and geological factors.

As a result, our American way of life – 330+ million people enjoying historically unprecedented material living standards – is unsustainable; it must and will come to an end, soon.

The inescapable conclusion is that we are about to experience the inevitable consequence associated with our predicament – societal collapse.

The primary purpose of this is to substantiate America's predicament – to present conclusive evidence of its existence, its significance, its magnitude, and its imminent and inevitable consequence. The secondary purpose of the book is to put forth the only rational solution to our predicament – an American Cultural Revolution – a solution that we will never adopt.

This presents a message of reality but not of hope – for America, there can be no happy ending. Perhaps however, with the benefit of advanced warning, we will collapse gracefully.

America's Predicament – Societal Overextension

> In nature, the over-extension of a population upon
> a resource which diminishes is well known, and the
> results tend to be disastrous. – Walter Youngquist.

Our American society is irreparably overextended – we are living hopelessly beyond our means ecologically and economically, at a time when many of the critical resources upon which we depend are rapidly approaching limits – available resource supplies will no longer be sufficient to enable our American way of life.

As a result, our American way of life – 330+ million people enjoying historically unprecedented material living standards – is unsustainable.

The only rational solution to our "predicament" – transitioning voluntarily to a sustainable lifestyle paradigm – is obvious and straightforward. However, because we lack the collective will to adopt this solution, our society and our American way of life will collapse – quite probably within the next twenty-five years.

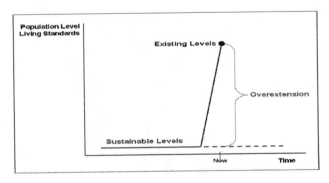

Societal Overextension

Societal Overextension

"Societal overextension" (overextension) is a condition in which a society is living beyond its means ecologically and economically. The significant consequence associated with societal overextension is that the society's population level and material living standards are unsustainable.

Overextension occurs when a society's lifestyle paradigm, its "way of life," is enabled by the persistent overexploitation of ecological resources and economic resources.

Ecological Resources – Enablers of Economic Activity

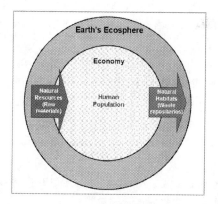

In industrialized societies, ecological resources are the raw materials (natural resources) and waste repositories (natural habitats) that enable economic activity – the production, provisioning and utilization of man-made goods and services.

Ecological resource overexploitation occurs when a society:

Persistently utilizes renewable natural resources that are critical to its existence – such as water, croplands, grazing lands, wildlife, and forests – at levels exceeding those at which nature can replenish them;

Persistently utilizes nonrenewable natural resources that are critical to its existence – such as oil, natural gas, coal, minerals and metals – which nature does not replenish; and/or persistently degrades atmospheric, aquatic, and terrestrial natural habitats that are critical to its existence, at levels exceeding those at which nature can regenerate them.

Economic resources such as income, savings, and debt provide the "purchasing power" that enable people to procure natural resources and the man-made goods and services derived from those natural resources. Economic resource overexploitation occurs when a society:

Persistently depletes its previously accumulated economic asset (wealth) reserves,

Persistently incurs intergenerational debt, which it has neither the capacity nor the intention to Repay, and/or

Persistently underfunds investments critical to its future well-being.

An overextended society is unsustainable and will inevitably collapse.

1.2 American Societal Overextension

Our American way of life is enabled by a culture of persistent resource overexploitation in which we live ever-increasingly beyond our means – ecologically and economically.

Our American Way of Life

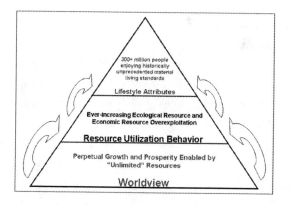

At the foundation of our American way of life are a worldview that promises perpetual growth and prosperity enabled by "unlimited" resources and resource utilization behavior that encourages our persistent overexploitation of both ecological and economic resources.

Our "predicament" – irreparable societal overextension – is the unintended but inevitable consequence associated with our distorted worldview and our dysfunctional resource utilization behavior.

America's Distorted Worldview

Most Americans believe that we can and will achieve perpetual population growth, living standard improvement and economic growth through our ever-increasing utilization of the earth's "unlimited" natural resources.

Those who hold this belief fail to realize that we live within an enclosed planetary ecosystem in which resource supplies are finite. Except for sunlight and an occasional meteor, no additional resources enter earth's ecosphere – unlimited natural resource supplies are, therefore, physically impossible. And, because perpetual economic growth and prosperity are contingent upon unlimited natural resource supplies, perpetual economic growth and prosperity are physically impossible as well.

America's Dysfunctional Resource Utilization Behavior

Our prodigious use of ecological resources and economic resources has enabled spectacular increases in our production level, consumption level, population level and material living standards over the past 200 years – to levels far exceeding those attainable had we lived sustainably within our means. Unfortunately, the inescapable consequence associated with this resource utilization behavior is the systematic elimination of the resources upon which our way of life and our very existence depend. Such behavior has obvious limits.

1.3 American Overextension Quantified

The extent to which we are currently living unsustainably beyond our means is appalling.

2007 American Societal Overextension ($).

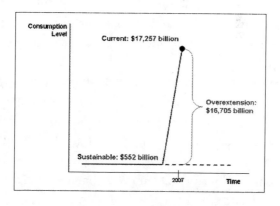

In 2007, nearly 97 per cent of our total consumption level was enabled by ecological resources and economic resources, the supplies of which are unsustainable.

The Inevitable Consequence of Societal Overextension

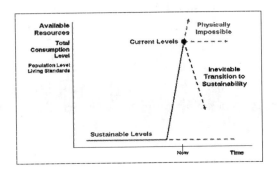

Our American way of life is absolutely dependent upon ecological resources and economic resources, the supplies of which will be utterly insufficient in the not-too-distant future to support our existing population level and living standards, let alone continued increases in either or both. As a result, our American way of life – 300+ million people enjoying historically unprecedented material living standards – is not sustainable; it must come to an end.

As the historically abundant and cheap resources upon which our American way of life depends become increasingly scarce and expensive, a scenario that is already in process, the total level of natural resources and derived goods and services available for our consumption will decline dramatically, as must some combination of our population level and material living standards.

Even under the most optimistic scenario, whereby we transition voluntarily to a sustainable lifestyle paradigm, our population level and living standard combinations attainable 'at sustainability' will be substantially lower than those that we currently enjoy.

Absent immediate fundamental changes to both our distorted worldview and our dysfunctional resource utilization behavior, American society will collapse – not in 1,000 years, or 500 years, or even fifty years but almost certainly within twenty-five years. America, as we know it, will cease to exist well before the year 2050. And while it may not be too late to avert societal collapse, thereby mitigating the horrific lifestyle disruptions associated with an apocalyptic transition to sustainability, it is, unfortunately, too late to avoid a painful transition – there can be no soft landing.

The Origin of America's Predicament

Industrial Civilization doesn't evolve. Rather, it rapidly consumes 'the necessary physical prerequisites' for its own existence. It's short-term, unsustainable. 2-1 – Richard Duncan

A society's worldview determines its resource utilization behavior, which determines its total consumption level, which determines its population level and material living standards. Our cornucopian worldview and detritovoric resource utilization behavior 2-3 have enabled our extraordinary American way of life – 330+ million people enjoying historically unprecedented material living standards.

The first human beings migrated to America over 40,000 years ago from Berengia, the "landbridge" that spanned the Bering Sea between today's Northeast Siberia and Alaska at the time of the Wisconsin glaciation. During the ensuing millennia, ancestors of these original Americans migrated to every habitable region in North, Central, and South America.

As was the case with human inhabitants in other regions of the world, Americans evolved through three lifestyle paradigms: hunter-gatherer, agrarian, and industrial. Each of the three paradigms has distinct attributes, which differentiate it from the other two in terms of the worldview, resource utilization behavior, and resulting lifestyle attributes associated with its human societies.

The Hunter-Gatherer Lifestyle Paradigm

The American hunter-gatherer (HG) lifestyle paradigm spanned more than 1,200 human generations, from the time of the first Native American settlers in approximately 40,000 BC to approximately 10,000 BC. HG societies consisted of small nomadic clans, typically numbering between 50 and 100, that subsisted primarily on naturally occurring vegetation and wildlife. While the HG lifestyle was extremely uncomplicated and "free," it was also harsh by today's standards – daily existence was often precarious, and HG life expectancy barely exceeded thirty years. The HG lifestyle was essentially subsistence living, as comparatively little human knowledge and technologies were employed to improve upon "the natural state of things." Hunter-gatherers produced few man-made goods and accumulated no appreciable wealth surplus beyond the necessities required for their immediate survival.

The HG worldview revered Nature as the provider of life and subsistence; this view fostered a passive lifestyle orientation through which hunter-gatherers sought to live harmoniously within the context defined by Nature.

Hunter-Gatherer Resource Overexploitation

The HG resource mix consisted almost entirely of renewable natural resources such as water and naturally occurring edible plant life and wildlife. A clan would typically overexploit one or more of these resources within a local area, then migrate to another area, while Nature replenished the depleted resource or resources.

2.2 The Agrarian Lifestyle Paradigm

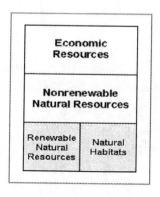

The American agrarian lifestyle paradigm commenced in approximately 10,000 BC and lasted until approximately AD 1800, spanning nearly 500 human generations. American agrarian societies existed primarily by raising cultivated crops and domesticated livestock. As crop and livestock yields increased, agrarian societies became increasingly larger and more complex, often clustering around permanent settlements such as villages, towns, and small cities.

Agrarian societies also became increasingly stratified, with the emergence of religious, political and military elites. Too, human technology and labor specialization and diversification became increasingly prevalent, as man-made goods, both essential and non-essential, were demanded by those who could afford them.

While small to moderate wealth surpluses were sometimes produced, agrarian existence typically offered little more in the way of material living standards for most of the population than did the HG paradigm. Day-to-day life remained harsh by today's standards, and agrarian life expectances were only marginally greater than those of the hunter-gatherers.

The agrarian worldview perceived Nature as something to be augmented through human effort, by domesticating crops and livestock. The agrarian lifestyle orientation was proactive, in the sense that it sought to improve upon what Nature had provided.

Agrarian Resource Overexploitation

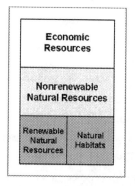

The agrarian resource mix consisted primarily of renewable natural resources – water, land, forests, and wildlife – which were increasingly overexploited by ever-expanding permanently settled agrarian populations. As America's human population continued to increase – to over 5 million by AD 1800 – and as agrarian cultivation and grazing practices became increasingly intensive, renewable natural resource reserves were increasingly depleted and natural habitats were increasingly degraded as well.

America's agrarian lifestyle paradigm was essentially self-sufficient, in the sense that most population clusters could exist in the absence of outside subsidization; but because our predecessors persistently and increasingly overexploited the renewable natural resources and natural habitats that enabled their existence; the agrarian way of life was not sustainable.

The Industrial Lifestyle Paradigm

The inception of the industrial lifestyle paradigm occurred with England's industrial revolution in the early eighteenth century, less than 300 years ago. Today, approximately 18 per cent of the world's population is considered to be "industrialized." Industrialized societies are characterized by highly complex mosaics of interdependent yet independently operating human and nonhuman elements that mass produce a broad array of goods and services in centralized production facilities. The populations associated with industrialized societies are typically clustered in towns, cities, and mega-cities.

Industrialized societies are highly stratified, typically consisting of lower, middle, and upper classes – typically with multiple sub-classes comprising each of the three primary levels.

Industrialized societies are also characterized by technical sophistication and by labor specialization and diversification, which enable such societies to produce and provision the myriad goods and services upon which they depend.

Tremendous wealth surpluses are generally produced by industrialized societies, enabling living standards well beyond the subsistence level for large segments of the population. The copious array of essential and nonessential goods and services in conjunction with sophisticated and pervasive support systems – i.e., food production, energy production, transportation, communication, law enforcement, healthcare, and waste management – enable human life expectancies well in excess of seventy years.

The industrialized worldview perceives Nature as something to be harnessed, through industrial processes and facilities, in order to improve the human condition. It is an exploitive worldview that seeks to use natural resources and habitats as the means to promote human ends, namely, ever-increasing population levels and material living standards.

Industrial Resource Overexploitation

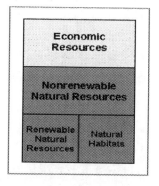

The resource mix associated with industrialized societies now consists almost exclusively of non-renewable natural resources, which, in addition to renewable natural resources and natural habitats, have been increasingly overexploited since the dawn of the industrial revolution. It is precisely this persistent overexploitation of natural resources and natural habitats that have enabled the "success" associated with the industrialized lifestyle paradigm – success being defined here as continuous increases in both population levels and material living standards.

However, because industrialized societies have come to depend almost exclusively upon global sources of finite and dwindling nonrenewable natural resources and upon the man-made goods and services derived from these resources, such societies are neither self-sufficient nor sustainable.

America: A Unique Industrialized Society

Our industrial lifestyle paradigm, which commenced in the early nineteenth century, has existed for less than 200 years – less than eight of the nearly 2,000 generations during which humans have occupied what is now the United States of America. America is a unique industrialized society – an extreme case with regard to our worldview, resource utilization behavior, and resulting lifestyle attributes.

America's Cornucopian Worldview

Most Americans believe that through their heroic efforts, determination and resolve . American pioneers settled our vast, essentially uninhabited country and took control of its virtually unlimited natural resources. During the 500 years since Columbus "discovered" America, successive generations of Americans dramatically improved our level of well-being through hard work, innovation, perseverance, and courage – we "earned it."

Most further believe that in the process of settling this bountiful land, we rightfully exploited Native Americans and Nature for our benefit, both through divine justification and self-endowed justification. We perceive ourselves to be "exceptional" people – in fact, we are the Christian God's chosen people. We see America as the greatest nation the world has ever known and believe that it will remain so forever.

The American worldview perceives Nature as something to be conquered, as we seek to achieve perpetual population growth, living standard improvement, and economic growth through our ever-increasing utilization of the earth's "unlimited" natural resources. This distorted cornucopian worldview is the logical outgrowth of our misinformed historical perspective and our adversarial relationship with Nature.

America's Detritovoric Resource Utilization Behavior

U.S. Resource Utilization Shift

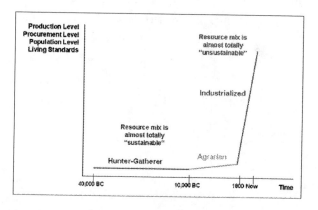

Our evolution from hunter-gatherer to agrarian to industrial has been enabled not by divine ordination or by American exceptionalism but by fundamental "shifts" in our resource utilization behavior over time.

U.S. Natural Resource Mix

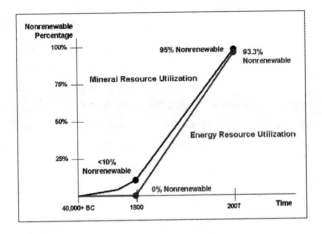

During the past 8,000 to 10,000 years, but especially since the inception of our American industrial revolution, our natural resource mix has shifted from "almost exclusively renewable" to "almost exclusively nonrenewable."

U.S. Economic Resource Mix

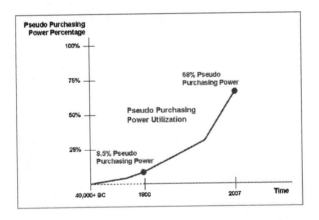

Since the early/mid twentieth century, as historically abundant-and-cheap natural resources have become increasingly scarce-and-expensive, our economic resource mix has shifted from "almost exclusively real purchasing power" to "almost exclusively pseudo purchasing power."

Pseudo purchasing power enables us to increase our "current" procurement level of natural resources and of the man-made goods and services derived from those resources, through fiscal imprudence – that is, by liquidating our previously accumulated economic asset reserves, by incurring ever-increasing levels of intergenerational debt, and by underfunding investments critical to our future well-being.

America's Production and Procurement Levels

U.S. Production and Procurement Levels

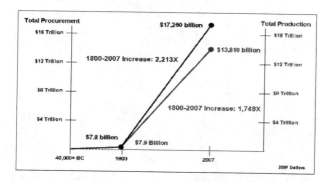

Between the years 1800 and 2007, the total value of goods and services produced in the United States (GDP) increased nearly 1,750 times – from US$ 7.9 billion/year to US$ 13,810 billion/year.

During the same period, the total value of goods and services procured in the United States increased over 2,150 times – from US$ 7.8 billion/year to US$ 17,260 billion/year.

The phenomenal increases in our production level and procurement level over the past 200 years are without historical precedent. However, because this meteoric growth was enabled by the fundamental shift in our resource mix from renewable natural resources and real purchasing power to non-renewable natural resources and pseudo purchasing power, our current production level and procurement level are unsustainable.

America's Population Level and Material Living Standards

U.S. Population Level and Material Living Standards

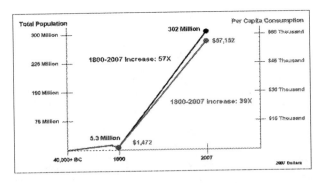

Between the years 1800 and 2007, the total U.S. population level increased 57 times from 5.3 million to 302 million. During the same period, the average U.S. material living standard (average annual per capita consumption level) increased 39 times from US$ 1,472/year to US$ 57,152/year.

A society's level of well-being – the average material living standard enjoyed by its population – is determined by the society's total consumption level at any point in time. Because our current total consumption level – which is almost completely enabled by unsustainable ecological and economic resources – is unsustainable, our current level of societal well-being – 300+ million people enjoying historically unprecedented material living standards – is unsustainable as well.

The Magnitude of America's Predicament

The 'developed' nations have been widely regarded as previews of the future condition of the 'underdeveloped' countries. It would have been more accurate to reverse the picture . . . – William Catton, Jr.

The extent to which American society is currently overextended – living unsustainably beyond our means ecologically and economically – is appalling.

Quantifying Societal Overextension

Only by quantifying societal overextension – that is, by measuring the extent to which we are currently living beyond our means ecologically and economically – can we appreciate the magnitude associated with our predicament and estimate the extent to which our existing population level and material living standards exceed sustainable levels.

Quantifying overextension involves measuring the extent to which our current levels of resource utilization have diverged from sustainable levels. Two methods for quantifying overextension are considered below, the Ecological Footprint Analysis (EFA), and the Societal Overextension Analysis (SOA).

Ecological Footprint Analysis Metrics

The EFA measures societal resource utilization in terms of biologically productive global surface area; i.e., acres of land area and water area that produce the resources and absorb the wastes required to support human populations. In the EFA lexicon, a society's current total resource utilization level is referred to as its "ecological footprint"; its sustainable resource utilization level is referred to as "biocapacity, and the difference between the two is referred to as its "ecological deficit" (in the case of America) or "ecological surplus."

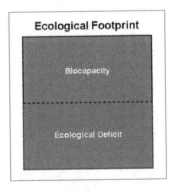

Societal Overextension Analysis Metrics

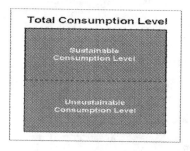

The SOA measures resource utilization in terms of the total monetary value associated with the natural resources and derived goods and services consumed – i.e., produced and procured – by a society's population. Using SOA terminology, a society's total resource utilization level is referred to as its "total consumption level"; its sustainable resource utilization level is referred to as its "sustainable consumption level"; and the difference (in the case of America) is referred to as its "unsustainable consumption level."

Ecological Footprint Analysis

The EFA quantifies the extent to which America's annual ecological footprint – our total utilization of global natural resources and natural habitats – exceeds our annual biocapacity – Nature's capacity to replenish our domestic natural resource reserves and to regenerate our domestic natural habitats.

According to the Global Footprint Network (GFN), an ecological footprint "measures how much land and water area a human population requires to produce the resource it consumes and to absorb its wastes, using prevailing technology." For example, in the year 2005, Iraq had a per capita ecological footprint of 3.3 acres, China 5.2 acres, India 2.2 acres, the United Kingdom 13.2 acres, and America 23.3 acres – the world average per capita ecological footprint was 6.7 acres.

On average, 23.3 acres of planet earth's surface area were utilized to produce the resources consumed and to assimilate the waste products generated by every American during 2005.

However, America's biocapacity, the domestic U.S. surface area available to produce resources for consumption and to assimilate resulting waste products, was only 12.4 acres per capita – leaving a per capita ecological deficit of 10.9 acres.

EFA Assessment of American Societal Overextension

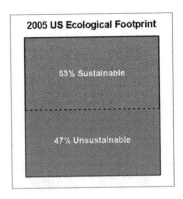

According to GFN data, 47 per cent of America's 2005 total resource utilization level, as defined by our ecological footprint, was unsustainable; that is, enabled by "importing biocapacity, liquidating existing stocks of ecological capital, or allowing wastes to accumulate and ecosystems to degrade." Only 53 per cent of our 2005 total resource utilization level was sustainable.

Based upon the GFN analysis, America is overextended by a factor of 1.9 (23.3 acres of ecological footprint/12.4 acres of domestic biocapacity); that is, we are currently utilizing ecological resources at nearly twice the level at which they are available domestically on a sustainable basis.

EFA Limitations

The EFA methodology was the pioneering attempt to quantify the extent to which human populations are living beyond their means; it offers a "bottom-up" assessment of the extent to which current human utilization of specific renewable natural resources and natural habitats – cropland, pastureland, forests, fisheries and carbon dioxide assimilation capacity – exceeds Nature's capacity to replenish these resources and regenerate these habitats on a sustainable basis.

However, by considering only renewable natural resources and by failing to consider explicitly the economic aspects of overextension, the EFA methodology tends to significantly understate societal overextension, especially in the case of industrialized societies such as America.

America's natural resource mix and our consequent overexploitation of natural resources are heavily skewed toward nonrenewable energy resources and mineral resources, which are not considered by the EFA method. Too, Americans have been able to augment the extent to which we live beyond our means ecologically, through our unsustainable economic resource utilization behavior, which is not explicitly considered by the EFA method.

Chapter 7

Metaphysical Concept of Pi by Patrick Mulcahy

Pi or π is a mathematical constant which represents the ratio of any circle's circumference to its diameter. Pi is also the ratio of a circle's area to the square of its radius. It is approximately equal to 3.14159. Pi is one of the most important mathematical constants – many formulae from mathematics, science and engineering involve π (Pi).

[Wikipedia]

It can be said the circumference of a circle represents a full cycle – like the 360° rotation of a wheel. Let's give the circle a diameter of 1 unit. (We can assume that this derives the simplest form of a circle.)

This means that the length of the circumference of the circle is equivalent to the Pi constant (π). 1 Therefore, the length of the cycle that the circle represents is also symbolised by Pi (π). π = 3.14159265358979323846426433832795 . . . (*ad infinitum*)

That is because an 'irrational number cannot be precisely represented by a fraction comprised of whole integers'.

The Intersection of Linear and Non-linear Reality

A non-linear [problem] is any problem where the variable(s) to be solved for cannot be written as a linear sum of independent components. Generally, non-linear problems are difficult (if not impossible) to solve and are much less understandable than linear problems. Even if not exactly solvable, the outcome of a linear problem is rather predictable, while the outcome of a non-linear is inherently not. Non-linear equations are difficult to solve and give rise to interesting phenomena such as chaos. The weather is famously non-linear, where simple changes in one part of the system produce complex effects throughout. (Wikipedia)

'Mundane' human consciousness is essentially 'linear' in nature and we tend to interpret the events of human life from a purely linear perspective – i.e., our understanding is that event 'a' causes event 'b' which then causes event 'c', etc.

A Linear Relationship between Events

Mundane human consciousness naturally flows in this linear direction through time and space, and life tends to remain comfortable while our personal world conforms to this principle. Thus, we wake up in the morning, we go to work, we come home in the afternoon, we go to bed, and then we repeat that secure rhythmic cycle indefinitely, but as long as that pattern repeats, there is little evolution occurring in our lives. A personal evolutionary shift occurs when we encounter an experience that is represented by the following diagram.

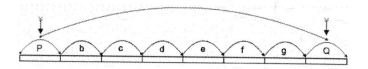

A Non-linear Relationship between Events

It is not easy for us to understand *rationally* the appearance of personally significant events that arise out of nowhere – that emerge out of the apparent chaos of the world around us, but that powerfully impact upon our lives. The 'chaos' of these kinds of events can disrupt our mundane lives by challenging and altering the well-established comfortable linear flow of things.

In the figure above, the event (or experience) 'P' is directly and causally linked to event 'Q', but they appear separate, distinct and unrelated from the vantage point of normal linear consciousness. For example, event 'P' might represent you losing your job, and event 'Q' might represent you finding a new job. These two events are, of course, linked together within your own *subjective* consciousness, but it is the surrounding *objective* circumstances that compose each event (and that are beyond your control) that we often assume are not directly causally linked with each other. The circumstances surrounding these two events *would* be obviously causally connected with each other if, for example, your boss dismissed you from one position in the firm and then rehired you in another position in the same firm. In this case, the will and intent of your boss represents the obvious causal connection. But consider this alternative example: During event 'P' you might have lost your sales job as a result of your employer going out of business. In this case, event 'P' appears to be the result of impinging 'chaotic' forces that are beyond your control, and that impose new challenging conditions on your life (and upon your boss's life). Let's say that in the lead up to event 'P' you felt extremely dissatisfied with your job as a salesperson, and that you always wanted to instead work as a designer in the fashion industry. But you stayed in your sales position for the financial security it provided, and your interest in fashion design remained merely a hobby. But during event 'P', *fate* seemed to strike and you were forced out of your dreary job.

Then, two weeks later during event 'Q', you receive a lucky 'break' a work offer via an acquaintance who has recommended you to their friend who you don't know, but who works for a fashion label and suddenly urgently needs an assistant designer. This is a life-changing opportunity, and one that eventually leads to you becoming a very successful fashion designer (some years down the track). In this example, it is evident that the chaotic circumstances of event 'P' occurred somehow in anticipation of the equally 'chaotic' occurrence of event 'Q'. But, the intervening events in the linear flow of consciousness between 'P' and 'Q' do not rationally explain the occurrence of the final outcome. Obviously, the application of your conscious will have not played a part in the emergence of event 'Q'. In other words, it seems that a lucky coincidence based on random chance has taken place. In this example, there is a gap in linear consciousness that would need to be filled (with some kind of 'lateral' understanding) in order to explain the apparent causal relationship (or 'synchronicity') between experience 'P' and experience 'Q'.

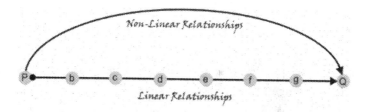

Linear and Non-linear

To the normal linear flow of consciousness, this correlation of personally significant objective events (or experiences), widely separated in space and time, does not make sense it is not rational. What is not easily apparent to the linear mind is that there is, in fact, a higher order of rationality to which these two seemingly chaotic events are adhering. Linear consciousness defines what it doesn't understand as 'irrationality' (or, chaos) because from its limited perspective it cannot see the larger pattern that is unfolding. A good analogy is a farmer standing in a field of corn on a patch of his crop that has been flattened to the ground. From his perspective at ground level, he cannot see the wonderful symmetry of the immense crop circle pattern that surrounds him.

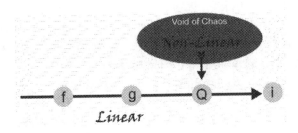

A Non-linear Event 'Q' Disrupts the Linear Flow

Here's another (perhaps more trivial) example of the intersection between linear and non-linear reality . . . Suppose that, during the normal course of your day, you lost your wedding ring (event 'g') and searched everywhere for it, but couldn't find it. Then, after you had given up the search, an apparently unrelated event occurs – your home phone stops working (event 'Q'). You decide to test your phone line connector to see if that is the problem. So you go to where the phone lead is plugged into the wall and move the couch away from the wall so you can get to the phone line connector. In the process, you find your wedding ring (event 'i'). In this example, the loss of the wedding ring and the malfunctioning phone line appear to linear consciousness as two unrelated events. That is because they belong to two different streams of influence, linear and non-linear. One way to explain these kinds of non-linear (or 'lateral') experiences is to posit the existence of a higher form of creative intelligence whose vision comprehends widely separated (i.e. in time and space) events in the same manner as we comprehend the immediate events that are linked together in the continuous stream of our normal awareness.

In other words, the higher intelligence is somehow able to see what we would consider to be the past and future as its present. And from that far-reaching perspective is able to pull 'strings' and organise the occurrence of significant events before we, from our more limited perspective, are able to perceive them.

What we regard as past and 'future' is only considered so from the perspective of our lower level of consciousness. At the higher level it would appear as the 'present' in the same way is the normal linear flow of events appears as the 'present' to us. To put it another way, the higher intelligence is able to see larger chunks of reality in each moment of consciousness than we are able to at our lower level of awareness. Indeed, it sometimes appears to our normal linear perception that these kinds of events (i.e. synchronicities) have been preternaturally coordinated by a higher order of intelligence to synchronise and to 'magically' manifest as they do, and that we are *consciously* out of that causal loop. It also seems sometimes as if the proposed higher intelligence is intimately connected to us (i.e. that it somehow knows our mind and heart even better than we do). These kinds of non-linear causally related events seem to arise by chance (or 'coincidence') from out of the objective chaos of the world around us. But as you will see, there is in fact an underlying logical (or 'meta-logical') principle that governs their appearance. This essentially 'metaphysical' (or 'irrational') principle is hidden in the basic structure of the mathematical constant Pi.

It is interesting to note that modern science is also realising that the appearance of 'randomness' (or 'chance') is part of the great illusion of the material world and is also presently seeking to find an answer to the enigma. **The Sacred Fraction: 22/7**

As mentioned previously, the Pi constant (π) is approximately equal to the fraction 22/7.

The fraction 22/7 can also be expressed as 3 1/7. Also from this, we can deduce that:

$22 = 7 \times \pi$. And also that:

$22 \times 17 = \pi$. The diagram we are creating needs to incorporate and visually portray all these various characteristics of the Pi constant.

Our diagram needs to clearly express the fractional part of Pi (i.e. 17 or 0.142857) and also its three diameter units (i.e. $1 + 1 + 1 = 3$).

The easiest way to adhere to these guidelines is if we divide the Pi constant into 22 equal parts; in which case, each part will amount to 1/7 (i.e. because $22 \times 1/7 = \pi$).

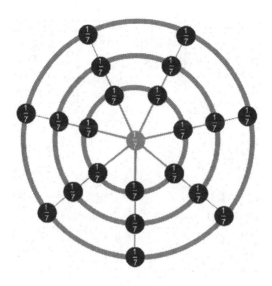

Twenty-two Divisions of Pi

The above diagram conforms precisely to our established guidelines for representing the Pi constant.

The three concentric circles (green) each contain seven seventeen fractions meaning that each concentric circle is equal to '1' (i.e. 7 × 17 = 1), and that therefore together the three concentric circles symbolise the '3' diameter units of Pi (i.e. the '3' portion of 3 1/7). As you may recall, one of our main purposes during the course of this treatise is to derive some basic principles of cycles using the Pi constant as our basis. We started by establishing that:

1. *A circle with a diameter of 1 will have a circumference equal to Pi.*

2. *The circumference of a circle symbolises a complete cycle, like the rotation of a wheel.*

3. *Therefore, Pi will symbolise somehow in its structure the basic essence of a complete cycle.*

These are our initial premises.

We then proposed that a cycle at its essence will be divided into three equal portions – representing three diameter units of the circle – the three units of the integer '3' of 3 1/7.

We also proposed a fourth aspect of the cycle that is represented by the fractional part of Pi – that is, 17 or 0.142857 (approx.).

The three concentric circles in the diagram above represent the three equal (and easily defined) portions of the cycle. Together they symbolise the integer '3' portion of 3 1/7.

The fractional component of Pi (i.e. 17) is symbolised by the central circle (i.e. coloured red) in the diagram. Thus, in the diagram, the four basic components of the Pi constant are clearly identifiable . . . The $1 + 1 + 1 + \mathbf{1/7}$ = Pi $1 + 1 + 1 + 1/7 = \pi$

Our diagram, however, still does not fully conform to our initial requirements because its three circles (or rings) do not represent a continuous (or perpetual) cycle like the circumference of the original circle does. But that is easily remedied by joining the three circles together so as to form three loops of a spiral and then closing the ends of the spiral so that it becomes continuous.

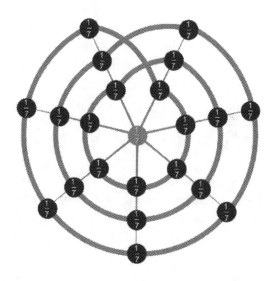

The Pi Spiral

You will notice that the fractional portion of Pi (i.e. 1/7 at the centre of the diagram) is separated from, and bears a unique relationship to, the three concentric rings that make up the figure.

The reason is because it exists in another dimension – i.e. the *fractional* dimension to the right of the decimal point in the number 3.142857 (i.e. in Pi). The seven components of each ring are unified so that together they achieve the value '1', and then by further addition, the value '3'. The number 0.142857 is the decimal equivalent of the fraction (i.e. 1/7 and is in a different dimension of scale to the integer '3' – which latter is on the left side of the decimal point.

So to recap: The three concentric circles (or loops of the spiral) represent the integer '3'. The central 17 represents the decimal portion of Pi. The philosophical implications of this configuration will become clearer later in this treatise.

Abstraction to Manifestation

Metaphysically speaking, our diagram (as it now stands) is actually in a state of *unmanifest potential* because all of its twenty-two individual components are fractions (i.e. 1/7). In other words, even though together the individual components of the three rings total a whole rational number (i.e. '3') it still exists in the 'fractional' dimension (because its individual parts are fractions). In esoteric lore, a thing does not become *manifest* until unity (or singularity) is achieved. This is the case, for example, with regard to the manifestation of the ten sefirot of the kabbalistic Tree of Life. In order to bring our diagram into manifestation (or into the next dimension), we must multiply each of its twenty-two components by seven thereby allowing them to achieve unity.

Thus, $7 \times 1/7 = 1$.

This process of multiplication by seven to effect a transition from one state (or dimension) into another is a fundamental metaphysical principle. At the moment, our universal Pi diagram represents the original circle with a diameter of '1' and a circumference of Pi. Of course, the circle *is* manifest, but it is manifest at a very simple and ethereal (i.e. 'fractional') level. If we say that our original circle with a diameter of '1' symbolises unity, as well as the closed system/cycle of a universe (or dimension), then in order to progress to the next dimension, we must multiply that circle by seven. Remember that the circumference of the circle (representing the bounds of the universe) is equal to Pi.

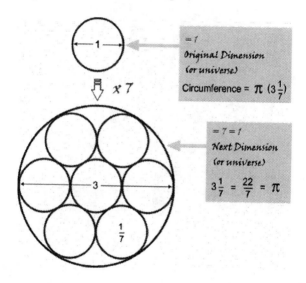

Multiplication by Seven

Notice in the newly formed dimension (i.e. or universe symbolised by the green circle) that the original singularity (i.e. the red circle) is maintained, but that it is now seventeen of the new singularity (i.e. the green circle). Simplicity has transformed into complexity, but the original simplicity is retained within the essence of the new form.

As you know, the fraction 1/7 (or 0.142857) represents the fractional part of the Pi constant. The diagram above illustrates that this fractional number permeates the new universe at a fundamental and 'subterranean' level (symbolically speaking).

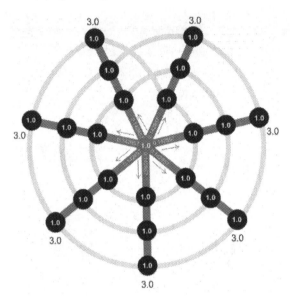

The Pi Spiral Manifests in a New Dimension

In this new version of our Pi diagram, I have emphasised the seven spoke-like arms of the figure because they now exhibit an interesting characteristic. On each of the seven spokes is positioned as three components valued '1' each. This, of course brings the total component value of each spoke to '3'.

We saw in the simple 'pre-manifestation' version of the diagram that the three concentric circles (or rings) together totalled '3'. (That is, as 21 × 1/7 = 3.)

Now we see, in this new 'manifest' version, that each of the seven spokes are valued '3' (i.e. when their three component units are tallied). (That is, 3 × 1 = 3.) The central component (valued '1' and coloured red) of the diagram is the originating source of the seven radiating spokes. Its value is '1', but this must be divided equally among the seven spokes in order to maintain mathematical equilibrium in the figure. Therefore, each of the radiating spokes obtains a value equal to '1' divided by '7'.

Thus, 1/7 = 0.142857

This value represents the fractional component of Pi, and when added to the sum of the three components positioned on a spoke (i.e. '3' because 1 + 1 + 1 = 3) we derive the full value of Pi (i.e. 3.142857).

Thus, in this manifest version of our Pi diagram, each of the seven spokes is representative of the Pi constant, that is, 3.142857.

Rational and Irrational

An important distinction now needs to be made. We need to remember to differentiate between the twenty-one components that constitute the Pi *spiral*, and the central singular component that is the source of the seven radiating *spokes*. On each of the seven spokes is positioned three components, but these three components are not *integral* to the existence of the spoke upon which they are placed. They are integral to the composition of the triple spiral but not the spokes. This is an important distinction. The triple spiral (i.e. as defined by the twenty-one components that constitute it) exists in a different dimension to the seven spokes that radiate laterally through it.

This becomes apparent when we realise that the 'manifest' value of each of the twenty-one spiral components is '1', but the value of each of the seven radiating spokes is 0.142857, which is a decimal fraction and therefore is considered to be in another dimension (i.e. the 'fractional' dimension). This suggests that the radiating force of the seven spokes (or 'rays') is directly linked to the pre-manifest version of our universal Pi diagram – that is, before our new diagram underwent the manifestation process of multiplication by seven. In other words, the seven rays represent an harmonic influence that subtly links together the 'pre-manifest' and 'manifest' dimensions.

Some wonderful paradoxes are presented to us by this new Pi diagram. Notice also that the diameter of the new universe (i.e. the green circle) is equal to 3 diameter units (i.e. three adjacent red circles – the red circle having a diameter of 1).

Thus, the inner structure of the new universe (i.e. the green circle) reflects precisely our esoteric version of the Pi constant: 31/7, or 22/7. 13. In fact, the diagram above demonstrates all the characteristics (but in a different form) of the universal Pi diagram we are in the process of constructing during the course of this treatise.

Reincarnation

Because the emanations of the Monad radiate out from the centre and cut laterally through the arcs of the spiral, it means that each ray of influence intersects the spiral in several places. But these important junctures are widely separated in terms of the rate of flow of linear consciousness around the spiral. Because the central Monadic influence unifies with Its divine Purpose, the evolutionary intent of all of its emanations, this means for example, that the evolutionary event that occurs at point 'a' of the spiral has a meaningful causal relationship with events 'h' and 'o'. And because these kinds of laterally linked events are caused by an influence that moves through the void between the arcs of the linear space–time spiral, it means that the monadic influence can extend between human incarnations (i.e. even though there usually occurs then a break in linear consciousness). It is because there is no break in the extension of the monadic rays as they emanate laterally through the spiral of linear consciousness, that they are able to impress their unifying influence into the consecutive incarnations of the human ego as it sojourns within the dimension of linear space and time (i.e. on the spiral). Thus, is the Monad able to impress its unfolding evolutionary intent into the lives of its physical human embodiments across the normal boundaries of time, space, and consciousness? In other words, the Monad is able, through its emanating lateral rays, to establish evolutionary continuity and progress across human incarnations, even while the human ego's linear consciousness is periodically broken (i.e. between incarnations) and therefore unaware of its own progressive development.

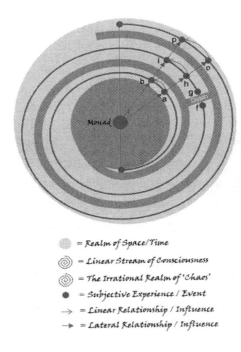

    = *Realm of Space/Time*

    = *Linear Stream of Consciousness*

    = *The Irrational Realm of 'Chaos'*

    = *Subjective Experience / Event*

    = *Linear Relationship / Influence*

    = *Lateral Relationship / Influence*

Death – : A Break in Linear Consciousness

In the figure above, event 'f' represents a moment in the flow of linear consciousness before the onset of death and event 'g' represents the resumption of the flow of linear consciousness after re-birth upon the spiral. As you can see, the break occurs only from the perspective of the human ego as it proceeds on its linear path through time and space. During the break, the essence of the ego returns to the Monad's realm of chaos (i.e. it returns to its source) before reincarnating back into the space–time continuum to continue upon its spiral path of evolution (i.e. beginning at event 'g' in the diagram).

—*The twenty-one vibrations of the Law of Attraction or Motion* are listed as:

I. *Ray of Power*

1. Destruction of forms through group interplay
2. Stimulation of the self or egoic principle
3. Spiritual impulse or energy

II. *Ray of Love Wisdom*

4. Construction of forms through group intercourse
5. Stimulation of desire, the love principle
6. Soul impulse or energy

III. *Ray of Activity or Adaptability*

7. Vitalising of forms through group work
8. Stimulation of forms, the etheric or pranic principle
9. Material impulse or energy

IV. *Ray of Harmony, Union*

10. Perfecting of forms through group interplay
11. Stimulation of the solar angels or the manasic principle
12. Buddhic energy

V. *Ray of Concrete Knowledge*

13. Correspondence of forms to type, through group influence
14. Stimulation of logoic dense physical body, the three worlds
15. Manasic energy or impulse

VI. *Ray of Abstract Idealism or Devotion*

16. Reflection of reality through group work
17. Stimulation of the man through desire
18. Desire energy, instinct and aspiration

VII. *Ray of Ceremonial Order*

19. Union of energy and substance through group activity
20. Stimulation of all etheric forms
21. Vital energy

And we must remember that the text also mentions the *basic vibration* that is, *the synthesis of the twenty-one*. This latter, of course, corresponds to the unifying influence of the Monad that is positioned at the centre of our universal Pi diagram.

Printed in the United States
By Bookmasters